LIFE AND RELIGION
OF
THE HINDOOS

LIFE AND RELIGION
OF
THE HINDOOS
WITH
A SKETCH
OF
MY LIFE AND EXPERIENCE

JOGUTH CHUNDER GANGOOLY

GYAN

Published by

GYAN

Gyan Publishing House
5, Ansari Road
Daryaganj, New Delhi-110002
Phone: 011-47034999, 9811692060
E-mail: books@gyanbooks.com

Distribution Network
gyanbooks.com
India, USA, Canada, UK, Australia, France

ISBN: 978-81-212-8614-5 (PB)
First Published, 1860

2nd Impression 2023

Printed at: Gyan Press, Delhi.

LIFE AND RELIGION OF THE HINDOOS
Author: Joguth Chunder Gangooly

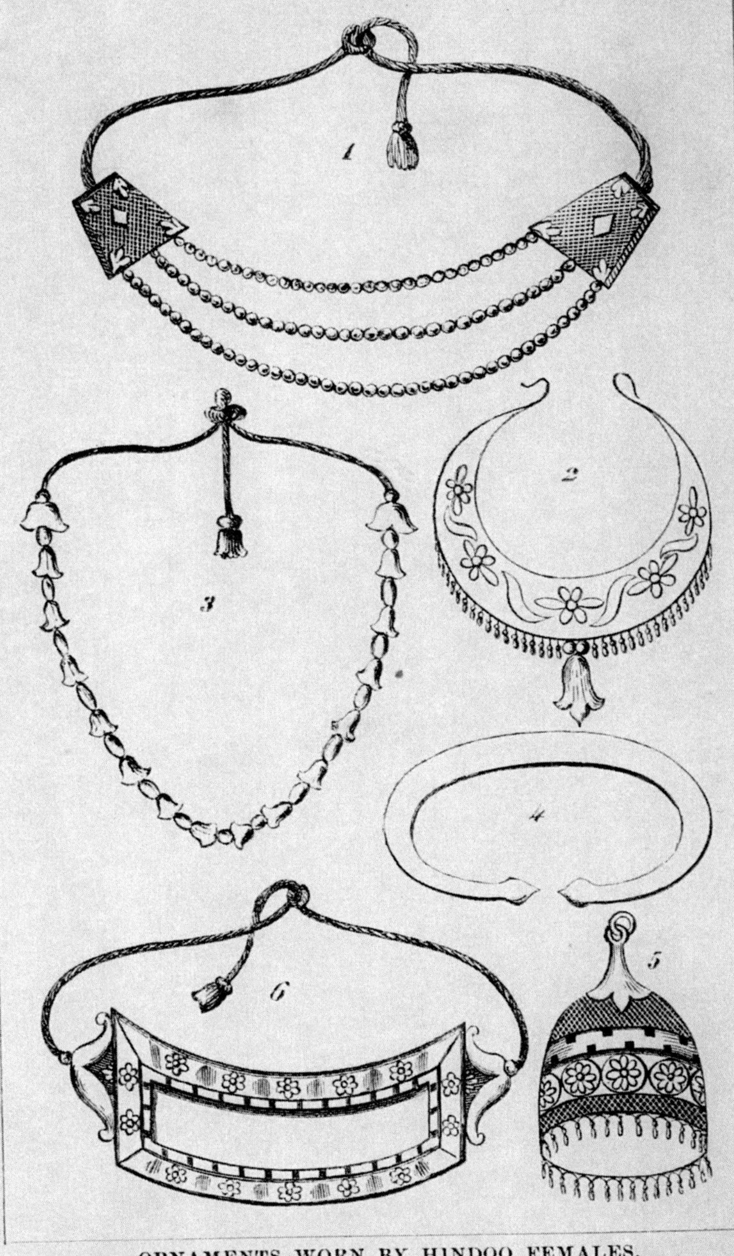

ORNAMENTS WORN BY HINDOO FEMALES.

1. *Tre no lē*, } Necklaces.
3. *Conth măla*, }
4. *Bála*, worn round the Wrist.
2. *Cambălā*, } Worn in the Ear.
5. *J'hoomka*, }
6. *Bajoo*, worn over the Arm.

DRAWN BY MR. GANGOOLY.

LIFE AND RELIGION

OF

THE HINDOOS.

WITH

A SKETCH

OF

MY LIFE AND EXPERIENCE.

BY

JOGUTH CHUNDER GANGOOLY

(BAPTIZED PHILIP .

BOSTON:

CROSBY, NICHOLS, LEE AND COMPANY,

117 Washington Street.

1860.

EDITOR'S PREFACE.

HAVING suggested to the writer of the following pages that he should do what some who are more competent, and a great many who are far less competent than himself are doing daily, viz. write a book, I brought upon myself the office of revising his manuscript, and supervising its publication. It was a particular sort of a book which I proposed to him, and as he has come so near to the ideal which I had of what he might write, I have taken care to leave it as he wrote it, with no betterments and no injuries received while the manuscript was in my hands. Something of the interest of Mr. Gangooly's composition might have been expected to lie in its style and in his peculiar modes of expression. So scrupulous have I been to allow the whole work to stand as his own, that I have seldom ventured to correct even his occasional slips of grammar, and have in no case altered his idiom. The reader will hardly fail to notice how charming and attractive the contents of these pages are made by the natural eloquence, the hearty frankness, and the wonderful power of discernment of this very young and marvellously endowed Hindoo convert to Christ. The perusal of his little book will deepen the impression made upon the minds of a large number of most intelligent persons who had any intercourse with him, that his experience has been profoundly interesting, that he possesses genius and many signal qualities of character, and that he is fitted to accomplish a most serious and useful work in life, if the circumstances hereafter appointed for him shall be propitious, and if he shall remain steadfast in his Christian purposes and zeal.

I have leave to print here the following letter containing information, which I asked for my own personal satisfaction, from a most faithful friend of Mr. Gangooly, to whom, as will appear in the closing pages (as well as from the Preface) of this volume, the latter expresses so much gratitude for kindness in his home, and for service in the training of his mind.

Rev. George E. Ellis, D. D.: —

My dear Sir, —

I cheerfully comply with your request to give you some facts relating to the education of Mr. Gangooly while in this country, and also a brief notice of his opinions, together with a few impressions of his mind and character. I do this the more readily, because Mr. Gangooly was so much engaged with preparations for his return home as to be unable to write as fully, in the "Narrative of his Religious Experience," of his studies here and his opinions, as he had intended.

Mr. Gangooly came to this country expressly to prepare himself as a Christian missionary. The plan or extent of his future labors were not distinctly apprehended at the time of his arrival, and the few words he uttered in the Bedford Street Church, in which he said he had come to learn more of the Christian religion, so that on his return he might be better enabled to instruct his countrymen, express his general purpose. This has been gaining in strength and breadth, as his mind has enlarged its knowledge, and as his character has unfolded under positive Christian influences. On his arrival, though it was evident that he was a young man of quick powers of perception, and unusual aptness for learning a new language, yet he was, as it were, only a child thrown upon wholly untried experiences. Indeed, after he had been in this country eight months, — which was the time when he became a resident of my family, and was put under my instruction, — he was even then as ignorant of many of our conventional customs as a child. Everything was so new and strange to him. The details of social life, modes of thought, forms of speech, — in fact, the whole structure of society, — and our political and religious institutions were so unlike those of Bengal, that he seemed to live in another world. Notwithstanding this, he conformed to his new social conditions with remarkable adaptation, and fell into the routine of custom with quickness and ease. He rarely made the same mistake a second time.

It was this entire difference between his previous training, his race, mental habitudes, and social surroundings and our own, which made the question of his education a difficult one. What should we do with this young Hindoo? He had not come to be Americanized. He did not propose to occupy our pulpits as a permanent minister, or to address those who had grown up with our habits of thought, traditional convictions, or peculiarities of race and nation. He came to prepare himself to teach and preach Christianity to the people in India, and to translate the fresh and vigorous ideas of a rational Christian faith into his native tongue. As yet he had to learn more fully the English language. A recent convert, he had all the fresh enthusiasm of a neophyte. Thus far he had learned chiefly from Christ, and had caught glimpses of the moral elevation and spiritual beauty of his religion as seen in the Gospels, or idealized by his own vivid Oriental imagination. He had not fully seen the wide gulf which separates the pure religion of Christ and that which is so often taught and lived by imperfect disciples. He was wholly unfitted to enter intelligently, all at once, into those intellectual discussions which arise from the conflict between established belief and prevailing doubt. In the first stages of his Christian experience, it might permanently injure him to be exposed to that destructive and critical tone of thought which is a result of the principles of free inquiry, and which is so rife in our colleges and theological schools. These various considerations made the case of this young man an exceptional one. The Executive Committee of the Unitarian Association, who had the direction of his education, could not be guided by the wisdom of experience. His coming was itself an experiment, and the case had no precedent. What then was to be done? In view of all the facts, it was decided, that the early period of Mr. Gangooly's studies should be under the direction and care of persons who should act in the twofold capacity of parent and instructor. That he might have the benefit of the rich result of different minds, he recited to various clergymen, and was thus brought under the influence of their scholarship and piety. It also, I believe, formed a part of the original plan of his education that he should finish his preparatory studies at one of our theological schools. But the brief period of his stay in this country, and the absorption of his time in the practical work connected with his mission, prevented the execution of this part of the original design beyond the attendance of a few lectures at the Divinity School in Cambridge. To a great degree he was his own instructor, and he gained more by the independent action of his own mind than by the direct efforts of his teachers.

Throughout the two years of his sojourn he kept constantly in view the great object of his life. To gain efficiency for this, he gave more attention to the working of Christianity among men and in institutions, than to the study of books. His mind has been directed more to religion as expressed in practical life, than as speculative thought embodied in theology. He came to study man under a civilization, institutions, race, literature, and religion, wholly unlike those where he had lived, and the course he pursued was better fitted to make him a missionary than a scholar. The chief of his studies was the New Testament. To the Gospels he gave a more systematic reading than to anything else. But even here he manifested the same intellectual features which universally characterized him. He was more careful to get at the thought of the writer than to dwell on the minute distinctions of textual philology. His Oriental mind aided him in his Scripture studies, and he vividly apprehended the local allusions and the general costume of the thought in the New Testament. To this study of the New Testament he added that of the evidences of Christianity. His time did not permit him to enter upon this subject as fully as was desirable. Beside these he took a rapid survey of portions of ecclesiastical history, enough perhaps to give him an idea of the relation which the history of the Church holds to the vital truths of the Gospel. These, together with writing, were the chief subjects of study. As one of the most important parts of his future labors would be that of a translator, much of his study had reference to this. He never wrote what are called compositions, — never had assigned him set themes. His mind was so enriched with new impressions, and his feelings were so aroused by ever-varying scenes, that he never was at loss for a subject. His mind was full, and in his writing he gave utterance to some existing thought or emotion. To have adopted any other method would have endangered the quaintness, vigor, and natural freshness of his style. When we remember that he has spoken English but a little more than two years, the mastery he has gained over our language, and his power of expressing his thoughts will be evident to every reader of his book.

It is more difficult to speak with accuracy of a young man's opinions, especially if he be a foreigner. The faculty of expressing these with clearness and distinctness is the result of high mental training, or original power of intellectual discrimination. Still, Mr. Gangooly's general religious views existed in his mind as clear and definite ideas. In his reception of Christianity he has been influenced chiefly by the internal evidences. The superiority and the sanctity of the Saviour's life and instructions have taken the deepest hold of his convictions. The miracles recorded in the Gospels never had much weight with him as grounds of evidence. Often he said that it would be useless to urge them — as a proof of the Christian religion — on the attention of the intelligent Hindoo. This state of mind did not arise so much from a philosophical difficulty, as from the fact that wonderful narratives were wrought into the superstitions of his own people, and that he associated the two together. His general theory on this subject was the well-known axiom, that the miracle must be tested by the Truth connected with it, and not the truth by the Miracle.

We can also trace the same influence on his mind in his estimate of the Jewish Scriptures. He became a Christian directly through Christ. He passed at once from Brahminism into the Christian Church, and had listened to the voice of Jesus before he knew of Moses. He was thus led, I think, to undervalue the positive side of Judaism as a religious faith. With a caste of mind strongly rationalistic, he accepted the truths of Christ as those in harmony with the conclusions of the rational faculties. He believed that Christianity was a rational religion. But it was more to him than a philosophy, — it was a Divine life. Coexisting with his rational bent was a deep religiousness. The spirituality of the Gospel and the moral beauty of Christ's character made a deep impression on his heart. His piety had its roots in trust and love. The affectionateness which he exhibited in his constant and always abiding love for his mother, he carried into his religion. In his sadness, sorrow, and temptations, he lived as a child in the presence of a Father, and in his New Testament readings or in conversations on his future plans he would give utterance to the loftiest sentiments of piety. Indeed, piety with him is stronger as a sentiment than as a principle. This I apprehend is true of all Christian converts among the Hindoos. In the darkest hour of disappointment or of lonely homesickness, his face would light up with a smile as he gave utterance to the words of trust. He reposed with unfaltering confidence in the Divine Providence. Called, as we all are, to struggle against weakness, error, and sin, as he grew into a diviner knowledge of Christ, he increased in strength. He often spoke of his need of Christ. It was the Saviour who satisfied the deepest yearnings of his nature. He expressed this after reading the "Experience of Theodore Parker." Although on many points he was in intellectual sympathy with Mr. Parker, he differed from him in his estimate of Christ. He often spoke of the Saviour as his absolute teacher, and often spoke with deep feeling of the value of Christ's invitation to sinners, "Come unto me all ye that labor and are heavy laden, and I will give you rest. Take my yoke upon you and learn of me, for I am meek and lowly in heart, and ye shall find rest unto your souls; for my yoke is easy and my burden is light."

He laid great stress on the doctrine of the simple Unity of God. As the Hindoo Trinity was associated in his mind with the superstitions of his old faith, he always had the same feeling with respect to the Christian Trinity. As he emancipated himself from idolatry by a natural law of thought, he seized hold of the truth of the simple unity of God, and clung to it with great tenacity of conviction. In his mind Unitarianism, that is, the idea of the Oneness of God, was synonymous with that of Christianity. He left the idols of men's creating, and clung to the doctrine of the one living and true God.

But the most interesting feature of his life here was to see the power of the Gospel, as a spiritual force, working out moral results in his character. He came among us the creature of impulse. This in the early period of his sojourn here led him into hastiness of action. His impulsiveness was the weak side of his character. But through the influence of prayer, and the spirit of Christ strengthening him, he was enabled to overcome this defect to a great degree. At first, like a child, the desire and the effort to gratify the desire followed each other without reflection intervening. But he learned through experience the important lesson of self-control. He had great truthfulness. This is the more remarkable, because lying is a universal sin among the Bengali. With the knowledge of this national vice, and with a scrutiny which sometimes ran into an unwarranted and ungenerous suspicion, and in the most confidential intercourse for a year, I cannot recall a single instance of wilful prevarication. He also blended great simplicity with a sagacity which bordered on cunning. This was so evident that often he would say he had the cunning of the serpent with the gentleness of the dove. It was the union of these opposites, in connection with his impulsiveness and ignorance of our conventional prudence, which gave his friends solicitude. While they had confidence in his character, they feared he might be misunderstood from his apparent indiscretions. How few of our own youth are enabled to go through the various exposures of life and come out with Christian victory! It is therefore no disparagement of our young Hindoo brother to confess to a feeling of deep solicitude lest in the moral dangers of our society he might have been lured from the Christian path. But the longer he remained the stronger he became, until armed with the spirit of a Christian faith and devotion he was consecrated for his life-work.

Sir John Bowring, in a speech at the Unitarian Collation in London, last May, in reply to a sentiment, — that Christianity may gain new triumphs in heathen lands, — gave some very valuable suggestions as to the best methods of Christianizing the heathen. The report of his speech as given in the London Inquirer is well worth the consideration of every missionary. Any one who will read the remarks of the British statesman, and the Farewell Address of Mr. Gangooly, on Sunday, June 10, in Boston, will see in many respects the striking similarity of the views of both speakers in their idea of the best method of approach to the Hindoo mind. Mr. Bowring says: "The result of my observation was that there was everywhere a vast deal of truth to respect, and everywhere a vast deal of truth to love, and if we went forth with a desire to discover that with which we could sympathize, and a disposition to recognize that there was much that was excellent in the religion of others, we should the more easily prepare the way for the advancement of our religion." As an illustration he cites Brahminism, and uses thoughts very like those of Mr. Gangooly's Address. Again, in the same speech, Sir John adds: "If the missionaries, however, recognized that there was much in their books — (i. e. those of the Brahmins and the Buddhists) — that was attractive and lovable, they would win the affections of those people, who would easily be led into argument. If the Unitarians sent forth missionaries, as he hoped they would at some future period, he was convinced they would not meet with so many difficulties as the Orthodox missionaries met at every step. There were many absurdities, and a recognition of a vast deal that was abominable in the religious systems of heathenism; but at the same time there were great truths, and if we sympathized with these we should obtain greater success than had hitherto been achieved. It was certainly our duty, as far as we are able, to enter as harbingers of civilization, and as teachers of wisdom and virtue, into regions which had hitherto been but imperfectly explored." This is the language of an intelligent observer, who has spent many years among the Oriental nations. He testifies to the transitions of society which are going on in India, and expresses the rational ground for belief that the times are propitious for carrying there the light of Christianity. I allude to this here so fully because his views of the state of India, and his opinion of the best methods of missionary effort, coincide with those entertained by Mr. Gangooly, and confirm the justness of the latter's conclusions. Indeed, if there is any striking peculiarity in Mr. Gangooly, it is a remarkable tact in adapting himself to the state of mind of the persons whom he addresses. His perception of character is rapid and unusually correct, and he has the eclectic power of drawing from a system its excellences. In his revolt from his old faith he still discriminates between original Brahminism and the present effete religion and superstitious idolatry of India. Here again his conversations on this point were in striking agreement with the opinions of Sir John Bowring.

But I have already taken up too much of your time. I have not exaggerated my estimate of the mind and character of Mr. Gangooly. From the time he first came to my house to the present hour, his mind has ripened and his character gathered up strength. He returns to his home to begin the fiery struggle. His moral courage is greater than his physical, but he goes with the conviction that he is in the hands of Divine Providence. If his life is spared, I can see no reasonable ground to doubt that he will be an instrument of good to his darkened and superstitious people. But the future belongs to God. He has found a host of sympathizing friends. To carry out his plans he will need the aid of our prayers and active co-operation. That he deserves these I have not the shadow of a doubt; that he ought to have them is my firm and deep conviction.

Truly yours,

S. W. BUSH.

Medfield, July 20, 1860.

Mr. Gangooly's manuscript was put into my hands just as he was about leaving the country for England, on his way home to India. Had he been near me I should have been glad to have consulted him about some points of his composition, especially about the spelling of some words. It will be observed that his orthography in the spelling of words of his own language familiar to us is peculiar.

It was his wish and expectation that his Sketch of Religion and Life in India, and his account of his own Religious Experience should appear separately, each as a distinct publication. Perhaps, in view of the sectarian position which he will be understood as assuming in the latter piece, it might have been better that his intentions should have been carried out. But his friends and the publishers have concluded to pursue a different course, chiefly because each composition helps to illustrate the other, while the two together barely reach to the dimensions of a book.

I have been requested by friends of Mr. Gangooly to make proper reference here to some most unworthy and disgraceful remarks in three or more of the Calvinistic and Baptist newspapers — "religious journals," so called — about the conversion, the mission, and the objects of this Hindoo disciple. I have had these papers before me, and have noted the gibes and sneers which they have cast, in the interest of a poor and discomfited bigotry, upon the personal character and history and the aims of an unoffending and thoroughly earnest believer of the Gospel of Christ, who has come to it through a process unlike that which for methods and results they approve. But I have not thought that it would help the cause of Christian charity, or be in harmony with the beautiful spirit exhibited in the pages following, for me to name those "religious papers," or to extract their offensive matter. The harm they can do is steadily, year by year, becoming more circumscribed, as the readers for whose poor entertainment or "edification" they are edited form a proportionately smaller and smaller portion of our intelligent communities, and have an equally diminished importance or influence in giving a tone to the religion of the time. If this book should fall into the hands of any of those readers whose sectarian journals have lavished their abuse or ridicule upon its author, while it will be sure to engage their interest for him, it may also soften some of their own prejudices.

G. E. E.

CONTENTS.

LIFE AND RELIGION OF THE HINDOOS.

BOOK I.

CHAPTER I.

CHAPTER II.

CHAPTER III.

CHAPTER IV.

CHAPTER V.

CHAPTER VI.

CHAPTER VII.

BOOK II.

CHAPTER I.

BOIS-AK, APRIL.

CHAPTER II.

JO-ISTO, MAY.

CHAPTER III.

AUSH-ER, JUNE.

CHAPTER IV.

SHRA-BUN, JULY.

CHAPTER V.

VAUTHRO, AUGUST.

CHAPTER VI.

AUSHEEN, SEPTEMBER.

CHAPTER VII.

KARTIC, OCTOBER.

CHAPTER VIII.

OG-GROW-HAW-UN, NOVEMBER.

CHAPTER IX.

CHAPTER X.

MAGH, JANUARY.

CHAPTER XI.

FAL-GOON, FEBRUARY.

CHAPTER XII.

CHOITHRO, MARCH.

A SKETCH OF MY LIFE AND EXPERIENCE.

THE
LIFE AND RELIGION
OF
THE HINDOOS.

TO THE REVEREND C. H. A. DALL.

MY DEAR FRIEND AND PASTOR:—

Desirous of acknowledging the precious religious instructions you have imparted to me, and the blessings you are still bestowing on my beloved country, I, in your name, respectfully present this small volume to your countrymen, that they may know the manners, customs, and religious institutions of that distant nation for whose regeneration you are cheerfully spending the best part of your life, away from home and family. That your Christian labors may be ever attended with success, and your life be crowned with the smile of Heaven, is the heartfelt prayer of

Your disciple,

JOGUTH CHUNDER GANGOOLY.

MEDFIELD, MASS., 27 October, 1859.

PREFACE.

THE true knowledge of a thing is always desirable, whatever be its nature, — soft or hard, sweet or bitter.

Arriving in this part of the world, I saw several works on India in which their learned authors have attempted to treat of the manners, customs, and religion of the Hindoos. It is no wonder that so inquisitive, learned, and civilized a people as the American should want to know all about Hindostan, the "Golden Orient," which was the dream of the enterprising Europeans of the thirteenth and fourteenth centuries. But how far these books give the true account of the thing, a Brahmun can well judge. A story is prevalent in this country, on the authority of missionaries, to the effect that the Hindoo devotees throw themselves under the heavy car of Juggernauth as sacrifices. Again, wherever I go my friends ask me, "Do the Hindoo mothers throw their babies into the Ganges now?"* and other questions of similar purport. I am quite amused to see the little

* See Appendix.

school-boys and girls in America, who seem to know more of India than I do. I never heard such stories even from the lips of my grandmother. I admit, however, other facts, — as the burning the Shotees, and Hook-swinging, etc.

It is very difficult for a foreigner to understand the life and religion of the Hindoos, a people who, owing to their caste system, have no social intercourse with the Jobuns (the people who are not Hindoos). A foreigner spending a quarter of a century in a Hindoo village, would understand little of their peculiarities. His attempt to describe the Hindoo life is similar to that of sketching the buildings within the walls of China. But the walls of superstition which guard the Hindoo are impregnable, and stronger than those of China. Hence the imperfect, and for the most part untrue accounts which European and American travellers bring home to their friends. They tell merely according as they see, but not what they know. Seeing the cabinets of my friends here full of imperfect, broken, meaningless curiosities from India, I thought of helping them with something true and substantial; not what I picked up on " India's coral strand," but what I lived and moved among from my infancy. And again, being a Brahmun of the highest caste in the community, all the religious and social institutions were open for my inspection, hence my information is genuine. Though I desired very much on my arrival to write a book on Indian life and religion, yet my imperfect knowledge of the English language prevented me.

At the kind invitation of my valued friend, Rev. George E. Ellis, D. D., of Charlestown, Mass., I gave two lectures on India, before his people. Hearing what I had to say, and finding it novel and of interest, he desired me to give it to the public in the form of a book, and promised his precious help in the enterprise. Thus the old desire, burning unseen in my heart, grew stronger, and I started in the enterprise at once.

I owe much to the kind aid of my friend and teacher, Rev. Solon W. Bush, of Medfield, Mass., whose incessant help was my guide all the way through. To enumerate the ways in which kindness was shown to me by him, I would say, besides unfolding the peculiar idioms and arbitrary rules of the English language, he put words to my lips, gave motion to my pen, and offered to correct my manuscript.

My main object in writing this is to do India justice, and give to my Christian friends some correct information respecting her manners, customs, and religious institutions. Having a full knowledge of the subjects, I have attempted to treat of them in full, explaining their meaning and showing the occasion which gave their rise. I have divided the book into two parts, the first giving a sketch of Hindoo life just as it is, with all its peculiarities; and the second, of the Hindoo Religion as observed by the friends at home in these days. To add a part more, and devote it to the description of striking similarities that exist between the traditional, historical, mythological, and scriptural accounts of the Hindoos and of other nations, had been my earnest desire, but various circumstances, especially the want of time, sadly interfered with my plan. Not knowing when the summons would come for my return to India, I have guided my pen with railroad speed, so as to get the book finished in season.

In conclusion, I would say once more, that the reader will not find a richly decorated style, but the bare, true statement of facts as known by one who is a Hindoo by birth, and knows what he says from personal experience. Hoping that the kind reader will overlook the inevitable deficiencies in my style, and accept the genuine information I faithfully give, I remain,

J. C. G.

LIFE AND RELIGION

OF

THE HINDOOS.

CHAPTER I.

HINDOO CASTE.—ITS ORIGIN, ELEMENTS, DIVISION, SUBDIVISION, STRENGTH, AND INFLUENCE ON THE PEOPLE.

ALMOST every school-boy or girl in America or England knows that in India the people are divided into castes. Foreigners interpret the caste system of the Hindoos in various ways. Some say that it is something like the religious sects in Christendom, while others affirm that it is to show and preserve the distinction between men of intelligence, worth, renown, and riches; such as Whigs, Tories, Democrats, Aristocrats, &c. But it is not so. It is a very different system, and foreigners understand it very imperfectly.

Among the primitive Hindoos there were only four castes:—1. the Brah-mun; 2. the Kais-th; 3. the Khetry-as; 4. the Soodras. They emanated from Broh-mò; hence the name Brah-mun, from the root Broh-mò. The Kais-th took its rise from the body of the Broh-mò, and is composed of two Sanscrith words, *Kay*, which means body, and *isth*, placed. The Khetry-as are from the arms, and the Soodras from the feet of the Broh-mò. These are the four primary "jathēē" or castes. In order to discharge all the social duties, and perform whatever is absolutely necessary for the growth and comfort of society, these four castes took upon themselves to execute faithfully the functions prescribed for them.

The manner in which these occupations have been assigned, is rather philosophical and systematic. The Brahmun, rising from the mouth of Broh-mò, assumed the precedence, directed the other three as they fitly deserved, and put all the sacerdotal functions in their own hands. To the Kaisths was assigned the business of writers, clerks, accountants, &c. Hence the Hindoos believe the record-keeper of Pluto (Jom) is a Kais-th, named Chith-ro-Goopto. The Soodras are to perform all the menial services, because they originated from the feet of Broh-mò. The Hindoos make great distinctions between the different parts of the body. The sanctity rests on the highest parts; there is nothing good at the feet. As the custom in India is to wear silver, gold, and other jewelry on the body, the females wear no gold ornaments round the ankles, for gold is the most sacred metal, being valuable and scarce.

To touch a man by the foot is regarded as an insufferable insult; a kick, "nathēē," is worse than a heavy stroke of a cudgel. But the Brahmuns have a right to touch other castes by the foot, as their scripture declares them the Master of all, "*Bornanang Brah-monogooroo.*"

The four primary castes, notwithstanding they had one and the same religion to profess and the same language to speak, had no intimate dealings with each other, such as the intercourse which binds family to family and relative to relative. From the beginning, we do not see the institution of intermarriage among them, and what is surprising, after all, the one caste does not eat any food boiled with salt at another caste's house. Only Brahmuns are excepted. Their houses and everything therein are sacred to the Hindoos.

In course of time, as the descendants of these castes grew numerous, the injustice and disorder grew also. Though there were no intermarriages among them, yet some children were born from what they emphatically call "unnatural connection." These children were termed "Burno sunker," corrupted blood. Measures were readily taken to remodel the society, as well as to put a stop to the promiscuous connections, which were so common then that distinction of castes seemed to groan under its pressure, by lengthening the structure of the caste system, and bringing the "corrupted blood" within its jurisdiction. And, agreeably to the original method, some fixed profession was enjoined upon them. Hence, at the present day there are thirty-four castes; each stands on a separate and distinct ground from its neighbor.. Let us trace them in their respective professions. We often see two or three low subcastes do the same business, while others have some subdivision in them. 1. Brahmun, priest; 2. Aucherjeă, astrologers; 3. Boid-tho, physicians; 4. Kaisth, clerks; 5. Suth-goap, farmers; 6. Goap, dairymen; 7. Napith, barber; 8. Nundy, dealer in salt; 9. Talēē, common store-keeper; 10. Kormo-kar, blacksmith; 11. Sorno-kar, goldsmith; 12. Tonth-boy, weaver; 13. Koy-borth; 14. Moduck, confectioner; 15. Rojoçk, washer; 16. Sooth-rodar, carpenter; 17. Coomar, idol-maker, potter, &c.; 18. Poto, painter; 19. Mălā, fisher on the river; 20. Jālā, fisher in artificial ponds, as well as in the river; 21. Doolā, bearer; 22. Bagthēē, fish-seller; 23. Joogy, weaver and priest of common-place idols, whom the Brahmuns are forbidden to attend to; 24. Barooē, pan-leaf cultivator; 25. Chundal, publican, always mason; 26. Moochēē, shoemaker; 27. Kaŏra, hog-keeper; 28. Bathea, fowler; 29. Moortho-roras, funeral-place cleaner; 30. Harie, women who do the business of nurses to the infants till twenty-one days from their birth; 31. Dome, basket-maker; 32. Nag, snake-charmer; 33. Bānā, banker; 34. Shooree, wine-seller.

Perhaps some may question whether the member of one caste is able to change his caste or not. I say, no. In other countries, a man from an obscure origin can possibly exalt himself to a conspicuous footing in society, by means of his opulence, learning, experience, &c.; but in India there are impregnable walls between the castes, so that nobody can exalt himself to a caste higher than his own. When we come to examine well the caste system of the Hindoos, we are led to think that it is something like the dispensation of nature in one respect. It is impossible to transform a dog into an ox, a deer into a camel, or a horse into an elephant; indeed, there is the same difficulty in attempting to make a weaver out of a barber, a physician out of a shoemaker, and a Brahmun out of a physician. To confirm the remarks just made, I will bring an instance from the Hindoo antiquity, and present it to the reader to show the impracticability of changing one's caste for a higher one.

There was a pious Kaisth king, named Bisha-mithra, who wanted to be a Brahmun. As it is only in the power of Krish-no to make him a priest, he determines to please him in spending his time in "toposhia," prayer. Leaving his kingdom, riches, friends, and sundering the ties of relationship, he entered into a forest, and there, among the wild beasts, spent centuries in unceasing prayer. As self-torture is regarded very essential to propitiate some gods, this king used to kindle fires round his seat in the summer, and in winter immerse his body up to the neck in water, offering prayer to Krish-no. His meal was, at the early part of his retired life, once a day, afterwards once a week, and even that consisted only of wild fruit. Year after year passed away, witnessing the mistaken piety of this king. At last pity awoke in the breast of Krish-no, and he descended from his *goluck*, heaven, to bless the pious devotee. "Borung boorno," — "Ask a boon, child," — the god said. "Thy devotion, faith, and prayer have reached me. Now I have come to bless thee; tell me, what dost thou want?" The king, thus addressed, replied, "Object of universal adoration! If my tears, fasting, and prayers are so successful as to find a place in thy consideration, will not my heart's desires, also, meet thy approbation? Yes, Lord, it is in thy power to cause a lame man to climb to the summit of mountains, a pigmy to reach the moon, and a babe to cross the unbounded 'seven oceans,' by swimming. What is unknown to thee? Art thou not the Inspector of all hearts? If thy servant has been commanded to reveal to thee his wants, he would then say that neither the aim for absolute lordship over the world, nor the desirable combination of long life and health, has made him to devote these tedious years in prayer and abstinence. What he earnestly wished for, is the life, the caste, the privilege of a Brahmun." "Be still, child," the Krish-no replied; "ask for a home in my *goluck*, and it will be granted thee. But to make thee a Brahmun, in this thy present life, is impracticable. But I would meet thy demands partially. Henceforth thou shalt be a Rhēē-sēē, not Monēē (a title of a Brahmun saint), write sacred books for the edification of thy castes, and have the discipline, not the caste, of Brahmun." I hope this instance will clearly show to the reader the strength of the castes as it is in India. A man after losing his caste, for small offences, can regain it by undergoing some penances; but he cannot by any means whatever purchase a higher caste, or regain his own if he is guilty of some heavy crime. By heavy crime I do not mean anything more than the violation of ordinances and the restrictions pertaining to the caste system.

If a man commits adultery, deceives the people, indulges in intoxication, and practises all sorts of vices which degrade humanity, he is regarded as a sinner, an odious, vile creature. The good people do not keep any intimate correspondence with him; but, nevertheless, he stands in his caste. When a Brahmun marries a low-caste woman, who is endowed with a seraph's charms and purity, or eats the forbidden meat, such as beef, veal, ham, or pork, he loses his caste forever.

The astrologers, Aucherjeă, are of the same creed with the Brahmuns. They have equal rights in the study of sacred books, but have no dealing with them. They are regarded as a very low caste, so much so that even a barber, blacksmith, or goldsmith would not drink water in their houses.

All the Brahmuns do not belong to one and the same class, although they are members of the same caste. There are a great many orders among them, high or low, according to the nature of the castes to which they preside over. Thus the priest of the Brahmuns stands higher than the priest of the physicians, clerks, barbers, and blacksmiths; and the last is higher than the Brahmun who presides over the goldsmith. It is to be observed here that one Brahmun can exercise his priestly sway over the physicians, clerks, farmers, barbers, &c., and retain his position firmly; although the above-mentioned castes have high and low among them, and have no intercourse between them. The reason is, nine castes immediately below the Brahmuns are known by a common name, "Nŏbō Shawk," and this justifies the priest in looking at them in the same light. But the castes below the "Nŏbō Shawk" being distinctly lower castes, one quite separate from the other, each has a priest of its own respectively. The priest Brahmun of a goldsmith would not attend to the marriage or funeral service of a fisher, shoemaker, or hog-keeper. I hope the Christian reader will not feel sensitive when I speak of the lowest castes, such as shoemaker, hog-keeper, &c.; he must remember that I am speaking of the Hindoos, and not of the Christians. Each country has its own peculiarity: what is regarded high, respectable in one, is considered sometimes the very reverse in another. In the present case we see the banker is a respectable gentleman in this country, and a high caste, too; but in India he is low in caste, so much so that his priest Brahmun cannot officiate in temples built by other castes.

The following are the leading, high orders of the Brahmuns:—The Banerjea, Chatterjea, Mookerjea, and Gangooly, &c.

When a Brahmun gives you his address with either of these, it will be known as a sure fact what Brahminical stock he is from. These also stand for the family name of the man. There are, however, low order Brahmuns bearing the above-mentioned titles, which do not amount to anything; they neither can eat with a Brahmun of high order, nor marry his children to the same, and what is more absurd, after all, is the fact that they are not admitted to the temples, nor to worship the gods who pretend to be of all, in all, and for all. In the public feasts of the Brahmuns, when thousands sit at the meal at the same time, some brisk priests are commissioned to examine the order, name, and place of the strangers. If it be known that there is a Brahmun of low order, that is, a priest of the bankers, goldsmiths, or wine-sellers, the whole assembly would not eat anything until the despised one had been hunted out and set apart. Hence the well-known Brahmuns from different places stand near the door, admit their fellow-citizens, and sharply, with a lawgiver's cunning, examine the strangers who happen to be there. Thus carefully they guard their orders and maintain them distinct and pure from others.

The Brahmuns of all orders wear a few stitches of cotton — the Pobitho — round the neck, which other castes do not dare to touch even. Astrologers, formerly being of the same caste with the Brahmuns, wear the sacred thread, the Pobitho; but the other castes pay little regard to him. The Boitho, the physician, wears a thread also, but they are required to keep it under their clothes lest anybody should notice it and pay it the homage due to the Brahmun only. If, unfortunately, a physician be found in the streets with his pobitho on, the Brahmuns would insult him by tearing it off or taking it away from him. In our village some physicians — young men — used to wear their thread visible to all, in spite of the jokes and reproaches of others. On a holiday they were going to Calcutta with a party of young men from four or five castes, and the weather being very hot, were compelled to sit on the piazza of the temple raised by a Brahmun. It happened that the son of the gentleman was at the window, who, seeing the group of aristocratic young men on his premises, came out, received them kindly, and entertained them with a good supply of cocoa-nuts, sugar, &c. Now, as the Brahmun boy would not eat with the others or the physicians, they all had to take their seats according to their castes. The poor physician-boys sat apart from the Brahmun, exposing their thread to the public gaze, and felt very badly for it. The host, good and kind as he was, asked their address, and finding they were not Brahmuns, rebuked them very harshly. Ashamed and insulted they came home, and were never after seen with their thread on an exposed place of the body. The peculiar ceremony which offers the pobitho or the sacred badge to the Brahmun, will be described in its proper place by and by. I will consider the circumstance which gave rise to the astrologers, and made them a distinct caste from the Brahmuns. This caste is, as we have observed before, called Aucherjeă. They write almanacs, tell fortunes, appease the grohos — evil spirits — for and at the solicitation of the people.

I have said before that the use of forbidden meat deprives a man of his caste, and the following are two instances to this point. It has been customary with the Brahmuns, of late, to offer burnt sacrifices on some grand festivals. A cow or a horse, being cut into several pieces, was thrown into the sacred fire, "*home ugnee*," and at the close of the ceremony, it is said, the priests could tell the animal from its ashes. Once on a time a venerable priest offered for sacrifice a cow, and when all the quartered parts of her were found, at the end, only a small piece was missing. Others bore witness to what had been done, held an ecclesiastical council, examined the cow, and outcasted the worshipper, charging him with using a portion of the sacrifice for his own benefit. His descendants are Aucherjeă, and form a low caste, though they are Brahmuns in some respects.

Another class of Brahmuns is called Perēēlēē, having had its rise from a curious fact. A Brahmun, who used to serve a Mohammedan Nabob in the capacity of prime minister, happened once to be in a room adjoining the kitchen. The Nabob suddenly came in, and in the course of conversation asked him what he thought of the smell which then filled the room. He unfortunately, drawing in his breath, answered his master, saying, "The smell is sweet and pleasant." Upon this, the Nabob asked him again whether he knew whence the smell came, and, receiving a negative answer, he said it was from a dish of beef. The minister was struck as if by lightning, fell down and fainted. Being restored to his senses, he summoned a meeting of the Brahmuns, who heard his dismal case, and as, according to the statute, "ghrăna ortho vogono," smelling is equivalent to partially tasting, deprived him of his privileges in the society. As he could not marry his children to other low caste, not even to astrologers, he had to prevail on some poor Brahmuns to intermarry with his family, and in time numerous families sprung up in this way.

This dividing of the people into castes has covered the Hindoo community with a thick mantle of darkness, ignorance, poverty, and vice. Whatever be the pretended happy results of such classification to a Hindoo, as conducive to the interest and prosperity of his community, it would obviously appear absurd to those who feel equally for every member of a society.

This system, as if by a thousand hands, confers upon the Brahmuns numerous blessings, and, on the other hand, administers poison to the prosperity, happiness, and true interests of the low castes. They have no chance of getting religious or secular instruction, and consequently there is no hope of even arriving at a point where they could reach the interests and privileges which every man would ordinarily require. To enumerate the defects of the caste system, as it is in India, it is necessary to trace it in its full length, commencing from the head to the feet,—from the Brahmun to the Kaoră, hog-keeper. The Brahmuns have monopolized all the advantages of religious instruction. Their words are law, in the Old Testament sense; their will is divine; their bodies are sacred; to worship and serve them is just the same as to worship the gods. "Thābār theer bŏ theejā thothath," offer the things of god to a "second born."

Seven or eight castes below the Brahmuns enjoy a scanty allowance of secular knowledge, while the rest have nothing to do with that even. These poor people, doomed to be under this perilous system, generation after generation, are the true wrecks of degeneracy. It pains me to say, that a Kaoră would very likely resemble, in his manner, customs, and ignorance, the animal he keeps.

To speak the truth, the caste, with all its distinctions and orders, is the only mighty obstacle to the regeneration of the Hindoos. Under its domination the Hindoo community presents a strong, brilliant crown on its head, studded with diamonds of rare value, a necklace of gold, a breastplate of silver, a belt of brass round its waist, copper garters on its knees, and dark, hard iron shoes for its feet. The arrangement is in perfect harmony with the prevailing fashion respecting dress. As the crown, the garland, the belt, the shoes, have their proper place in personal adornment, so the Hindoo community has set the different castes into different places. But there is no justice in it. It has transformed the gold into iron, denying it its necessary care. There is no respect for sanctity, intelligence, and accomplishments, if these be found among the low. In a conversation, I remarked that if a washerwoman could help me with good advice, I would not walk a mile to the priest's for the same. My friends, who were then present, were all astonished at this, gazed upon me with indignant eyes, and lamented my remark as the dictate of infidelity.

There are other defective peculiarities in the castes, which cut the tie of love and brotherhood at the bottom. Observing from the stand-point of the high castes, we see that one caste does neither eat with another caste, nor marry, nor even sit on the same carpet. At the feasts the Brahmuns have the best seats in the hall or parlor, and the Kaisths, physicians, and barbers have separate seats for each, or sometimes one for all; but for the shoemakers, fishermen, and bearers there is no decent mat even. If a goldsmith should accidentally touch a Brahmun with some confectioneries or a pitcher of water in his hand, the Brahmun would immediately throw the former before a dog or any animal, and empty the latter of its contents.

God hasten the day when the very roots of the poisonous tree of caste shall be pulled up, and the balmy shrub of equality, of love, of universal brotherhood, be planted in its place. Let the spirit of true religion, O God, shine upon India. Let her know thou art her Father; that thou carest equally for all. Let her recognize thy image in all thy children. Chase, Eternal One, the darkness with thy salutary light, — the darkness which like a canopy has covered the heathen world; and thine shall be the glory for ever!

CHAPTER II.

THE BIRTH. — DISTRIBUTION OF PRESENTS. — WRITING ON THE FOREHEAD. — THE FEAST OF EIGHT PEAS. — THE DAY OF PURIFICATION, ETC.

THE Hindoos hold their male and female children in different degrees of estimation. They prefer one son to ten daughters, whom they represent as the worthless slaves of others, and the objects of pity, constant watchfulness, and particular anxiety. The preference arises from various sources. After the death of a Hindoo parent his oldest male child, or in his absence the younger one, is required to attend the funeral, perform the leading parts of the service, and on a fixed day redeem the spirit of the departed parent by some particular ceremony, which I will treat of in its proper place. But a female, being early separated from the family connection by marriage, is not privileged to do the same. If there be ten daughters present, and not one son, in that case the wife, or brother, or a nephew* (brother's son) of the deceased attends to the performance of the necessary rites.

At the birth of a son, the mother, besides other congratulatory blessings and benedictions, receives the surname of

* In the English language there is no word to distinguish the brother's son from that of a sister. The Bengalees have different words to define every relation distinctly. They have words to denote strictly wife's sisters, husband's sisters, his elder and younger brothers, the father-in-law of son, the children of the mother's and father's sisters, &c.

"herā beoonēe," mine of jewel. The sacred shells which every family has in its possession, to blow thrice in the evening, and on the holidays, are now sounded; the father brings some gifts to the baby; the family barber is sent to the friends and relatives with letters for each, containing the glad tidings, and in return gets valuable presents from them; the shoemakers, whose business is to sound trumpets, come immediately with their drums, flutes, and cymbals to play on them. The neighbors crowd the house to congratulate the family, and it is believed that the very site of the family lifts up in joy fourteen times, symbolizing the pleasure of the fourteen deceased ancestors. In short, the whole family assumes an aspect of ecstasy. But in honor of a poor female baby nothing of this sort is held. A conflict between prejudice and affection fills the mother's heart. With heaviness on the one eye, and tenderness on the other, she caresses her child, while the elderly women, wiser than herself, comfort her with the following remarks: "Do not weep, child. Let your disappointment be driven away by the thought that no human power could overrule these things. If we could, we would afford some remedy, but it is the will of Kristo that it should be so; and we all know that our fruits will be either male or female; female is child as well as male in the eyes of him who is their maker." In fact everything seems so sad, so quiet, that a foreigner standing in the very yard of the house would hardly know that there is a baby in the house, unless she herself, by her innocent smiles and occasional cries, lets him know that there is. The rich father, at the birth of a son, sends presents of a brazen jar or pitcher, a piece of new cloth, some sweet things to thousands of Brahmun families, and to the low castes simply sweet things and a little money. On the evening of the sixth day, the Hindoos believe that Broh-mò will come to write on the child's forehead all about its future destiny. Everything is kept clean and purified for the reception of the supposed presence of the god. The Brahmuns and other friends are invited; a member of the family walks round with a plate on his hand, to take a little dust from each Brahmun's foot, with which they touch the child's forehead, and when this has been done, each person goes to his respective home, with some confectioneries given to him. A poothee, sacred manuscript, an inkstand, and a pen are kept on a piece of board, near the child's bed, during the night. On the evening of the eighth day comes the feast of eight peas, "aught corie," on which occasion all the children in the neighborhood are invited. The order of the exercise is as follows. As the custom is for a Hindoo mother to stay twenty-one days after her delivery in a separate room where none but the nurse is allowed to enter; children stand in the yard and put some funny question, in poetry, to the nurse, who sits on the door-stone to answer these merry folks. The meaning of their questions is the inquiry after the baby's health, ending with some jokes upon the father. Eight boys hold a coolo or bamboo fan (of which there is mention in the Gospel of Matthew, iii. 12) in their left hands, and in their right hands the sticks. Now, when everything is ready, according to the order, one of them asks thus: "*Aught corrie bought* corria, chāla ancha valo?" and when the nurse has given her answer, saying, "Vālo," nicely, they beat the fan with the sticks which they hold in their right hands. Sometimes the boys meet with a very disagreeable experience on his occasion, especially the less smart ones, for amid the universal excitement, and by reason of darkness, they hit each other's hands. Suffering twice from the merry sticks of the boys, my hand bearing the doomed fan, I came to the conclusion never to join the party again.

But this decision, however, proved impracticable; the friends interpreted my unwillingness as based upon cowardice (for it was truly so), and the girls would hurl jokes and shame me, saying, "Had we a right to join them, we would right off." At last some kind but cunning boy furnished me with some prudent advice, that I must take my left hand away in season. I obeyed and was safe. When the storm has a little abated, they throw away the broken fan, over the roof of the baby's room. The second exercise is the scattering of large quantities of small sea-shells or copper money, cents, over the yard, which the children pick up, knocking and falling upon each other. At the close each person present, young or old, male or female, gets a sufficient quantity of confectioneries, pop-corn, peas, &c.

On the twenty-first day, which is the day of purification, the mother comes out of her room to present her child unto the gods and goddesses.* Of the latter, Shustee, guardian of infants, is worshipped with great reverence.

It may not be deemed improper to notice here about the dress and trappings of the children. Hindoo parents dress their younger ones with gold and silver ornaments, but not always with clothes. The reason is, that, in a warm climate like India, the children can hardly keep clothes on except in winter; moreover the Hindoo dress is merely long pieces of cotton cloth, untouched by the jaw of scissors, and unpinched by the point of needle, without any buttons or sleeves; consequently it would be childish if any should attempt to clothe a child with a dress like this. To dress in Hindoo fashion is very like erecting a house without nails, tacks, or screws, and that surely would require ingenuity. To say nothing of others, I myself did not learn to wear my

---

* See similar custom among the Jews, Luke ii. 22.

cloth neatly, according to the fashion, until I was nearly eighteen years old.

When the child has attained the age of nine months, its parents perform "*un-no pra-shun*," or the ceremony of rice. On a fixed day, before a large audience of guests and relatives, the father or uncle of the child puts one or two kernels of rice in its mouth, after the usual offerings to the gods. On this occasion it is customary for the guests to offer some gifts to the child. On the other hand, they, as well as intruders and beggars, are entertained in a grand feast.

CHAPTER III.

EDUCATION. — SANSCRITH. — CHALK IN THE HAND. — PATSHATA, THE TEACHER. — THE DISCIPLINE IN THE SCHOOL.

I WOULD, in this chapter, treat of the education of the Hindoo boys. But ere I commence this, a little description of the Sanscrith language seems desirable. It is universally observed that the Indians were known for their advancement in literary pursuits and for their language from a far remote antiquity. Their sublime literature with abundance of gold and jewels stands unrivalled even to the present day. As far as the fame of the learned Brahmuns has spread, in what estimation they were held among the nations around India, may be obvious from the following story. A Persian monarch had sent his messengers in search of the richest jewels and diamonds in India. They came in, and, after an earnest inquiry, returned to Persia with the most valuable articles that could be found. The monarch smiled at this mistake, saying that he did not mean *those* by jewels in India. Go, said he, to the court of King Becromandith, and you will find nine jewels there. Indeed, this Becromandith had, we read in the book, "*nobō ruttner shobha,*" society of nine learned men, jewels of rare value, of whom the celebrated Kalidass was the presiding genius.

The Sanscrith was then the current language of the people, and every class, high or low, had access to it. I do not mean to affirm that every class had access to the sacred books, but that various other able works were open for the instruction of the people. The members of the lowest caste could then discuss the difficult points on logic, rhetoric, mental philosophy, who at this day cannot talk on common things without grammatical mistakes. What a change these few hundred years have wrought! The beauty of Sanscrith, which could have been found in work-shops, is now strictly confined in the chest of the Brahmuns. The Sanscrith tree used to grow on the wayside, now it is found in the Brahminical soil only. Out of the thirty-four castes, only three have the right to study it comparatively. Brahmuns and Aucherjeăs can go through all the mystery of the language, while the physician can study as much as his profession would require; hundreds of their medical books being written in the Sanscrith, a good knowledge of this is necessary to understand them. It would seem absurd to a Christian to see the degree of reverence the low-caste Hindoos pay to this language. A priest can cause a large audience of the low castes to close the ears by uttering aloud a few words, such as "*om*" or "*gănētry.*" Even a Brahmun woman is forbidden to utter or hear them.

As there is no female education there at all, I will speak of the mode, the peculiarities of training the Hindoo boys. At the age of five, the boys begin to "touch the chalk by the hand." It is the custom of the Hindoos to fix a day, after consulting the stars and planets and days, to enter on the beginning of anything. A man would not leave home on any day of pleasure; a woman would not come to her husband's house at his or her own arrangement, without consulting the "*poujeeka,*" almanac. Thus they do on every occasion. In the common printed almanacs these things are stated thus:—"The Monday, 24th of April, *sooc-clo puckho*, white fortnight, *tha-thosee*, twelfth day of the moon, at $10\frac{1}{2}$ A. M., is a favorable time to go towards the east or north, or to undertake some other affair." Now when a day has been appointed in this way, the young boy is anointed and bathed. "Shurresh sutty," or the Muse, is worshipped, then the father or some one marks letters of the alphabet on the floor, which the boy writes over with a piece of chalk. By and by he is sent to the "*patshālā,*" the place of instruction, where the "*gooroo-moha-shay,*" sir teacher, gives lessons in writing, reading, and ciphering to some fifty or more boys. The boys write on palm-leaves before they are advanced enough to write on paper. The reason is, palm-leaves are long and smooth, and may be used anew after washing, in the same way as slates are used. There are no chairs or benches in the *patshālā,* but they sit on the carpet: sometimes the boys bring a piece of carpet or mat nearly five feet long and three feet broad, which they fold round their palm-leaves and pen of reeds. The *patshālā* has no regular term, but keeps throughout the year, holidays excepted, which come almost every month. The Hindoos know no Sabbath nor Christmas. The school opens at six in the morning, and again at three in the afternoon, giving, in the mean time, a recess of four hours. The boy who comes first has a dot for his number, and the names of the rest are written as they come respectively. Now when it is time to close, the teacher strikes on the hands of the boys according to their number. Thus, he who keeps the record, being the earliest of all, gets merely a slight touch of the teacher's whip, the second two, the third three, and so on. This is simply to enforce early attendance, because the first exercise in the *patshālā* is the reading aloud the prayer to the Muse, and repeating the multiplication-table. The late boys, of course, lose these exercises. A deep and unsullied reverence for the teacher is considered the best element in the life of the scholar, and very essential to his success; hence the Hindoo boy bows down to the ground before "*gooroo mohashoy,*" saying "*bi-tha thau,*" grant us knowledge. To serve him a little is worth several hours' study. The pupils are required to bring tobacco for him, which most of them get at the grocer's in exchange for the written banana-leaves, which he uses to make packages for salt, sugar, &c. If a boy be absent often, four smart boys are despatched to bring him by force, which errand they perform with great skill and courage. If the absentee be a real truant, and have a grudge against some boy, in this case you would find his enemies would go to bring him as the best chance of retaliation. He is brought into the *patshālā* in the way that ants carry a crust of bread into their hole. As they bring him, they sing thus:-

> "Gooro moshoy, tomar pōrō hazir,
> Achē-dundo chārā dow jol Khaia ashe."

In English, "Sir teacher, your pupil is come, and give us leave for a few minutes to go out and drink some water," &c.

The patshālā does not give thorough instruction in grammar, history, or philosophy, for the children of the privileged classes learn these in Sanscrith schools.

Under the British administration the old native system of training the youth has been almost done away in various parts of India, and English rules of discipline have been established, as far as it could be done without directly interfering with the superstition of the Hindoos.

There are high-schools, colleges, and numerous mission-schools in Calcutta and in other places in India. A university, a civil-engineering college, and a "School of Industrial Art," have of late been established. Nearly fifty years ago there was not a decent school in Calcutta. Mr. David Hare, of Edinburgh, laid the foundation of regular schools in India. He gave his money and his whole energy and life for this one philanthropic object. His tenderness, fatherly care, and earnest attention towards the students are proverbial. The Hare's Academy, the Hindoo and Sanscrith Colleges with their gigantic pillars and the intelligent and learned Bengalees openly speak of his disinterested love and Christian philanthropy. His mortal remains now rest under a marble slab, which may be seen on the College Square.

Indeed, one of the great blessings India has received from the West, and especially from England, is the system of educating her children in general. In her past histories (legendary age excepted) we do not hear of regularly organized colleges, where the children of all the castes could be instructed. The wretched condition of the low castes and their predecessors verify the fact. But I do not mean to say, as any of my dear countrymen should understand, that India had not trained her children before the English system was introduced. On the other hand, I wonder that she could produce illustrious poets, metaphysicians, logicians, astronomers, &c., without regular places of instruction.

Here and there, as we have observed before, there were Chow-Baries under the supervision of the Pundits, who in fact were the pastors, teachers, and guardians of the children of the privileged classes. No goldsmith nor washerman's son was seen to breathe the philosophic air of these institutions or drink of the silvery stream of the Brahminical literature. Again, even the great learning of some of the philosophers, poets, astrologers, is attributed to the miraculous agencies more emphatically than anything else. The Mohammedans, who ruled India before the British, did not direct their eyes towards the Hindoos of the lowest castes, for their education, or regeneration. To raise the fallen, cheer up the depressed, exalt the low, enlighten the ignorant, is the peculiar mission of Christianity, and the nations which profess it, breathe its influences, carry its blessings wherever they go. Thank God, that England has done her part in some measure, shown the spirit of Christ in seeking prosperity and providing education for the despised low castes, — the "lost sheep" of the Hindoos. Besides the public schools and colleges established directly by the government, where all the castes might go for instruction, provided they pay schooling fees, there are thousands of "Government Aided Schools" lately instituted by the East India Company.

The condition on which the *aid* was given is something like this. The proprietor of a school, desiring aid of a certain sum, must raise a like amount by fees from the pupils and other private donations, and spend the whole for support of his school. Among others, a philanthropic Brahmun, Baboo J. K. M. (the landholder) of Ottor Parah, near Calcutta, established more than twenty-four primary schools in different parts of his estate, defraying one half of the expense from his own treasury, and drawing the other from that of the government. These schools prepare the boys for the college, where they go after passing the junior scholarship examination, which entitles them to prosecute their studies free in the higher branches for one year, and draw a monthly stipend of five dollars. Those who fail to go successfully through the examination have to pay for their instruction of course. The standard for the junior and senior examinations is not the same every year, but varies according to the general progress of the schools, and the discretion of the Directors.

The year before I left Calcutta, the "standard for the junior scholarship examination comprised the following books: Cowper's Task, Tytler's Universal History, Paterson's Zoölogy, Stewart's Geography, Grammar, Mechanics, first four books of Euclid's Geometry, Algebra quadratic equation, Arithmetic whole, and other Bengalee studies." The candidates who pass this examination are from sixteen to twenty years old. The sphere to move about for the successful students is broad and honorable; they may continue their scholastic course in the Presidency College, study medicine, or teach schools where the branches of study are low. Let it be said, to the credit of the Bengalee boys, that hardly a primary school fails to send out annually three or four students to the higher colleges, from its first class, which scarcely makes room for fifteen.

I do not know exactly the studies in the senior classes in colleges, nor feel able to fathom the depth of the acquirements there. I would use another's tongue to show how much the Hindoo young men could do in their scholastic career. A writer in the Christian Examiner quotes from an able article on British India, in the London Quarterly Review, the following, which fitly answers my purpose:— "Young men (Indians) who have received an education, and have passed an examination, scarcely inferior in the variety and difficulty of its subjects to those of our English universities," &c. I do not exaggerate the intellectual powers of my countrymen, when I affirm that their aptness to learn anything set before them, their capacity to improve, are remarkable. These are not however their borrowed faculties, but their native, a part of their being. The same article I quoted above says:— "No race, perhaps, shows a higher intellectual development than the Brahmins of Western India or the higher castes in Bengal. Their thirst after knowledge — whether for its own sake or for the object of obtaining employment — is unbounded." India of to-day can show her pearls and jewels in her children, beside the celebrated R. M. Roy.

To speak nothing of her other cities, Calcutta alone has her numerous highly-educated sons; — the Reverend Messrs. K. M. Banerjea, G. C. Mitter, converts to the Episcopal faith; L. B. Day, of Free-church Institution; Baboos R. N. Sickdar, V. D. Banerjea, C. C. Singha, R. M. Mitter, P. C. Mitter, P. C. Sen, K. C. Mitter, R. G. Ghose, and others too numerous to mention. There was a short notice of the last-named gentleman in the Boston Journal: — "Baboo R. G. M., a native merchant of Calcutta, delivered, at the receipt of the Queen's proclamation, an address that causes him to be called the Bengalee Demosthenes."

Though the English schools are open to every class, high and low, yet the lowest classes do not send their children to them, under a mistaken idea that they have nothing to do with book-knowledge. Living in a degraded condition for a long time, they have lost entirely the right and claims of human beings, as it were. The miserable, pitiable state in which they live and die, and which is the effect of the despotic caste system, is regarded by them as the will and decree of God; consequently they dare not try to get rid of this yoke.

Most of the Brahmun young men study English as the money-making language, while others devote themselves to their professional studies. All the ancient Sanscrith books are written manuscripts; the pages are long, narrow, and colored. Some are written on palm-leaves, and "roogee pathroo," bark of a tree. Every student under the tuition of the superstitious priests, is obliged to transcribe a book as he makes progress in his studies. But in the Calcutta Government Sanscrith College, printed books, beautifully bound and gilded, are used.

The Hindoos are averse to female education, and suffer their daughters to live in entire ignorance. The popular belief among Hindoo women is, that, if a girl should learn to read and write, she would be a widow. The widowhood in Bengal is the saddest part of female life, and its consequent sufferings are such as have caused millions to prefer death, by being burnt alive on the funeral pile of the husband. But experience has falsified the idea in a measure. Here and there one out of ten thousand of women knows how to read a little, and enjoys connubial life. There are other difficulties to be considered and removed which prove strong obstacles to the education of the females in Bengal. The Hindoo women have no free intercourse in speech with other men beside their husbands, father, and brothers; their faces are covered with thick veils immediately after the marriage, and from that time they are not allowed to walk out of the house. Unless these customs are rooted up, there is no hope at all for the regeneration of the female in Bengal. As I compare a woman in Bengal with one in America or England, I see plainly the difference between Christianity and Hindooism. Nothing but the divine influence of Christianity has ennobled the female condition in Christendom. May the Christian women be ever grateful to God for his peculiar blessings unto them, and pray for the rescue of their sisters in the bondage of ignorance in heathen lands!

CHAPTER IV.

THE SECOND BIRTH. — BRAHMUN CONSECRATED THREAD. — DISCIPLINE AND PRIVILEGES OF THE BRAHMUN'S LIFE.

IN the interesting conversation of Christ with Nicodemus, St. John iii. 3 – 7, we hear him say, "Except a man be born again, he cannot see the kingdom of God." Again, "Marvel not that I said unto thee, Ye must be born again." This doctrine or command, whatever name may be given it, has been known to the Brahmuns from time immemorial, and even unto this day it is considered as the vital part of this dispensation. How little does a Brahmun differ from our Lord in the importance of a second birth! Christ says, "born again," the Brahmun says, "thejo," second birth. There is a difference between Christ's views and the Brahmun's on this point, which shows the superiority of the former over the latter. Christ did not prescribe different modes of spiritual birth for different nations. "Man," he says, "must be born of water and of the Spirit," assume a new life of holy actions, of purity, of devout trust, of practical brotherhood, of disinterestedness, and of unsullied love, so as to make himself worthy to tread in the steps of the Saviour, and breathe the balmy odor that comes from the celestial groves; taste the fruits of the *removed* tree of life, drink the water that issues from the great Fount of all bliss, dress in the robes of immortality, join his voice with the sweet, swelling chorus of angels, and enter into the promised mansions, to rest at the feet of the God of all.

But the Brahmun does not include the whole human race, as being under the necessity of a spiritual birth. He cares for one people, and even among them he prescribes different rites. As the ceremony for the second birth of the low castes is not very important, I will omit a description of it, and direct the attention to that of the three privileged classes, namely, Brahmun, Aucherjea, and Boitho, physician.

When a boy has attained his twelfth year his parents fix a day, to make him "thego," by offering him a piece of consecrated thread to wear round his neck. If, on the day previous to the fixed one, it thunder or rain, the ceremony is postponed for eight successive days, and if it should rain again, the same measure would be taken. On the morning of the day appointed he is anointed and bathed, within an enclosure made of four banana-leaves stuck into the ground. He is conducted to the altar, where the priest, after the preliminary services, cuts three locks from the hair of his head. He comes down from the altar for the first time to undergo other ceremonies. Now the family barber shaves his head all over, and passes two gold rings through the lower part of his ears. Here a merry fun is practised. The boy, when he sits before the barber, holds a banana in his hand, with which he is required to strike him when he has finished his duties. Sometimes the boy holds a green, and consequently hard, banana in his hand, so to warn the barber to be very careful in his operation, that he might not suffer afterwards. When all this is ended he comes up to the altar, where, besides the family priest, his father or uncle is required to take part in the ceremony. After invoking the presence of the deities and presenting offerings to the spirits of the fourteen ancestors, the father first puts a cord, made of hairy leaves of *shur* (a kind of white reed), round the boy's neck, which lies on his left shoulder, and, hanging round the left arm, makes a fold thereby. Then a *pobithoo*, consecrated thread, made of three stitches tied into a knot, which symbolizes the holy, mysterious union of the three, Brohmo, Bishnōō, and Shibă, into one. A piece of *shabor*, skin of deer, is tied with that thread. He wears a yellow or red robe, holds in his hand dundŏs, two staves, one made of Bāle wood and the other of Baoor or Bass. The leaves and fruit of the bāle are the chief favorites of Shibă, so much so that a dry bāle leaf is acceptable to him before a thousand varieties of odorous flowers. (In fact, almost every Hindoo deity is peculiarly fond of some especial leaf or flower, without which their worship is invalid. Thus Shibā loves *bāle leaf* or *tri-pothro*, "three leaves in one stem." Toolshēē, a leaf of a plant, is the favorite of Bishnōō; joba, a kind of large red flower, Kallee is fond of. The Shuresh-Shuttee likes *bakus* and gholghasa, the sun is fond of Corobēē, oliander, &c.) The mother of the boy comes first to give alms — a little raw rice, money, and a piece of thread — to the second born, who takes it in a yellow bag answering the purpose of a contribution box. The hundreds of guests who are invited in on this occasion are required, by their religious custom, to give gifts of a little money and a piece of thread. Occasionally some virtuous woman manages to offer the first gift, by paying all the expenses that accrue in the whole ceremony, which secures her the position of god-mother to the *thejo*. They then cover his face with a thick yellow veil, and conduct him to the room where he is to stay three or five days without seeing sun, moon, or the face of any one, except Brahmun. Henceforth he is a Brahmun, which means the "worshipper of Brohmo," or the "knower of Brohmo."

The discipline of a Brahmun life is grand in some respects, and in others tedious, dry, and fanatical, while its privileges are great and numerous. I will here briefly describe both. A Brahmun is to bathe early in the morning, regularly every day (if sickness does not interfere); worship and pray three times a day, — before sunrise, at noon, and in the evening; take one meal while it is day. The Hindoos do not use any table, china-plates, knives, forks, or spoons. When they take their meal they sit on the floor, put eatable things on marble or brazen platters, or silver, if they are rich. In place of knives and forks the fingers are used, which are furnished by Nature.* But over and above these, a Brahmun observes additional peculiarities, with which other castes have no concern at all. A Brahmun, when he sits to eat his meal, takes a drop of water on the palm of his right hand, touches it by the end of his tongue, saying "omrithō posthurnŏ moshee shō hă," pours it on the ground, puts a little food five times to his mouth, saying: 1. "Pran-a-ishohā;" 2. "Opānā ishohā;" 3. "Shomānŏ ish oha;" 4. "Otha noish-oha;" 5. "Banaish-oha;" finally, he spares "hundred rice" at his plate, even if he has not enough. This I understand as charity taught in an indirect way, for the little remainder on his plate is for the ants, flies, &c. But what is most trouble-

* They do not use knives, forks, and spoons at the table, not because they are ignorant of their services, but they do not need them. So is the case with the table. They sit all separate as the custom requires, and wash everything, even the floor, after the meal. They use the right hand for food, and the left for the drink. If rice or any boiled food should fall on the clothes, they will be washed after the meal. Owing to these peculiarities, the Hindoos do not use table, knives, &c., like Christians, who hardly wash themselves after the meal as the Hindoos do. I have occasionally used the "*table*" in the place of floor, in order to follow the English idiom.

some of all is the silence enjoined in the ceremonial discipline of a Brahmun's table. He must not speak a word; if he does, he is to suspend his eating immediately, by taking out if there be anything already in the mouth, and going without food until after the evening prayer. A very small number of the Brahmuns observe this all the days of their life, though they are required to do so; but all observe it for a year or two. It is a difficult task to put aside the long-contracted habit at once, and begin a contrary one in its place. The peevish, talkative boys suffer a great deal. They speak at the table, and thereby lose the meal. Not to speak of others, my own experience has taught me to dread this ceremony, and though I was very mild and careful, yet notwithstanding all my carefulness, I had to go without my meals five or six times in the course of every month, especially during the first half-year of my Brahmun life. The very day I became *thejo*, at meal-time, my mother requested all present to leave the room, lest any should attract my attention, and make me speak. She herself, also, went out, slamming the door and giving me enough for one meal. Unfortunately, I wanted a little more milk, so calling my mother, by a new language, not by the use of the organs of speech, but by striking the floor with my left hand. Nobody understood my singular language, and reflecting awhile on the result of the new discipline and the advantage of talkativeness, carelessly, I sung out "Ma." This sound reached her with the velocity of lightning. She rushed in, saying, "What is the matter?" "A little more milk, mother," said I. "Poor child; to-morrow by this time you shall have plenty." So saying, she took the plate away, with everything in it, charging me, if I wished for water, not to drink any until I had washed my mouth. I gazed around in vain. The yoke of superstition is really too heavy to bear. In desiring to have something more, I lost even what I had already!

The privileges of a Brahmun are great. His person is sacred. It would be a sin if any one should dare to touch him by the foot, for the foot is a profane part of the body, as they believe. The caste Soodras, rising from the foot of Brohmo, became the lowest. When one priest accidentally touches another by the foot, he asks his pardon, saying, "*Bishtŏ-bă* nōmō." It would be considered a real favor if a Brahmun should tread on a physician or barber, or other low caste.

The religious Hindoos daily drink "*pathuck joll,*" before the first meal of the day. Pathuck joll is a little water, which they take on the palm of their hand, in which the Brahmun dips the end of his right toe. Especially do sick persons drink this water, hoping to be cured from the disease that troubles them. I have heard a great many people say that they have been entirely restored to health simply by drinking "*pathuck joll,*" or eating a little dust from a Brahmun's foot. After a little acquaintance with the Christian doctrines, knowing what I owe to God and man,—that I am as sinful as others,—I abdicated the supremacy I had, and would not give the dust of my foot to any. As the consecrated thread which hangs round our neck distinguishes us from the other castes, and draws the sick and mistaken folks towards us, I used to hide it somewhere, under my clothes, in the streets of Calcutta or elsewhere in foreign places. Unfortunately at one time I had forgotten to hide it, and an old woman of nearly sixty came along and stretched forth her right hand towards me. Of course I understood what she meant by that, and in a loving tone said: "Mother, I cannot put my foot on your hand." "Why not, child?" she replied. "I am not a Brahmun, according to your idea. I am no better than you. We shall both stand on the same level before God." The old woman was ignorant and besotted, could not understand my meaning, and, in vain looking at me for the blessing, cried aloud in an angry tone, "If not a Brahmun, what are you then? A shoemaker, I guess." Though I noticed her dim old eyes flashing fire and a color of indignation visible on her wrinkled cheek, yet I ventured a few words more. "There is no disgrace in being a *moochēē*, shoemaker. I would rather be a humble, meek moochēē, than a proud Brahmun."

Brahmuns enjoy "*brom-horthro*," free-lands, which have been granted to them by the ancient Hindoo sovereigns. The Moosulman kings, who ruled India before the British, did not encroach much upon this right of the Brahmuns, only here and there some Nabobs were eager to break this system, but to no purpose. Under the present government the Brahmuns enjoy their lands free of any tribute. But I must not deny that some priests possess several acres over and above what has been given them.

Some low caste people would sell any articles to a Brahmun at a low price, while others would not sell them to him, fearing he would not pay fully. When he touches anything by his hand, as fruits or vegetables, from a low caste's farm, he will have it at any rate for nothing, or by the payment of a little or no money.

We read in our Scripture that the Brahmuns had absolute authority over the property as well as the life of other castes, and over their temporal and spiritual affairs. Frequent mention is there of some sad cases, which, though incredible, loudly speak of their despotism. On the other hand, we read of their acts of generosity, disinterestedness, and love. Of the former, here are some instances. Copeel monēē consumed sixty thousand offsprings of Saugur in the ashes simply by looking at them in anger. Porickith, a Kaisth king, having insulted a "*monēē*" by putting round his neck a dead snake, died by the anger of the insulted Brahmun. The king Corno sawed his only son of five, by the command of a Brahmun. Various instances could be cited to prove the power of this high class of men, but I will soon illustrate some of their generous deeds. A *monēē Augusth*, by his sanctity and power, put an eternal check on the monstrous cruelties of two giants, and relieved the millions of the poor victims from injustice and death. It is an imperative duty for them to entertain the guests of any caste, relieve the needy, restore peace, check injustice, and share one half of their sustenance with him who is without it.

"How are the Brahmun priests supported?" "Do they have a regular salary for their services?" &c., — are the inquiries frequently made to me. So I think it worth while to answer these questions fully here, although they have been partially explained, and will be elsewhere. As the priesthood, the parish, the religious services in Christendom, are quite unlike those in India, it seems necessary to consider them briefly in order to give the Christian reader true ideas of them. In this country an energetic preacher can draw round him a large congregation. The people visit church after church in search of good, weighty, or sentimental sermons, and wherever they find what is agreeable to their taste they hire a pew, and become members of the same. Thus the father goes to the brick church, the mother to one of stone, the daughter to a wooden one, and the sons, not finding theology in either, spend the time at home. But in Hindoo countries everything is fixed, binding, and must be attended to. The priesthood is hereditary, gods the same, the theology is well protected, contrived, authoritative, and religious services uniform, mechanical, and pleasing. They do not and cannot seek after a change; wherever they go, they see the same god, worship in the same way, the lamps are lighted, flowers scattered over the altar, incense burning, &c. In order to be settled over a rich people, the Brahmun depends little upon his "pulpit eloquence" or spiritual career; let him have, so to speak, "Abraham for his father," and plenty and comfort will be his. After the death of a Brahmun, his parish, containing any number of families living in the same village, or scattered around the country, will be equally divided among his sons like other property of the deceased. In case one of the sons proves unworthy of the charge, unable to attend to the religious ceremonies at the houses of his people, either being engaged in some other profession, as most of the Brahmuns are now, or owing to his ignorance of the services, his people cannot go away from him and settle another over them.

A rich, free-thinking farmer in my village, being guided by a party feeling, and detecting his priest in some acts of deception, bade him farewell, and sat at the feet of his brother. In a few months he was summoned to appear before the Priest of the priests, where there are no idols, on the throne of reality. His bereaved family interpreted his sudden death as owing to the visitations of the gods, feared that the children would fall victims to it also, and, after a season of entreaties, became reconciled to the old priest. As the people are not required to congregate together for the purpose of receiving instructions from the priest, or joining in worship with him, they dwell in different villages, and the priest visits them personally when his presence is needed by especial events, such as death, birth, marriage, or any private worship which the Hindoos observe now and then; and on general holidays he sends out his agents, himself being engaged at the house of some one rich Jorzman, parishioner. He has no monthly salary, but gets certain sums of money from each family under him on the day of worship. His income must be more or less in proportion to the wealth of his people. Sometimes one family gives him more than twenty could together. I know a rich Brahmun family, of low order, residing in a town four miles or more distant from the Calcutta Government House, who gave to the wife of its priest a lac of rupees ($50,000), because the gentleman of the family felt very much ashamed to hear his priest say his wife has not seen a lac of rupees at once. In this country the parish pays the preaching; in India they pay the priest.

There are numerous Brahmuns without a single family to attend to, yet they have an income. The very name Brahmun is a *sea*, and the rivers, channels, pour into it from various directions. It is customary with the Hindoos, especially with the wealthy ones, to distribute a certain sum of money, clothes, or useful metallic articles to each Brahmun family in the place, at the birth and marriage of the children. If there be more wealthy persons in a place, the Brahmuns will get more. Again, these rich men give annually winter clothes or summer dresses to the Brahmuns, this being part of their religion. By receiving these gifts continually, they keep the substantial things for their family use, and exchange the rest for what they need. Thus a great many buy fine brass dishes in exchange for goblets, or give napkins or clothes as the price of salt or sugar. The people bring fruits, vegetables, fish, milk, &c. to the Brahmun family, no matter whether they are their priests or not. During my stay in this country, I have noticed such practices carried out here in some degree. The farmers bring butter, potatoes, eggs, to the pastor; the difference being, that these bring presents to the pastor alone; the Hindoos do to the Brahmuns in general. Besides what they receive from these sources, the Brahmuns teach their children in secular studies, which secures employment for them in merchant or government offices.

Now almost everything is going on disorderly, as a forerunner of a great and good change I hope. From what I know, I should think the Brahmuns themselves (the most orthodox, conservative portions excepted) have little of that strong adherence to their profession which once characterized their predecessors.

My teacher, a Brahmun by caste, once remarked, that some priests would be willing to sell their sacred books, to buy Murray's spelling for their sons with the price.

CHAPTER V.

The Marriage.—Polygamy.—Koolyn and Moulick.—Marriage.—Age.—Selection.—Agreement.—Anointment.—Bachelor and Maiden Feasts.—The Joy-Cakes.—Bridegroom starts for Bride's House.—Reception.—Discussion.—Twelve Friends Party.—Throwing Stone Party.—Ceremony.—Good Interview.—Dining-room Plagues.—Distribution of Money.—Return.—Reception.—Bridal Feast.

This chapter will be devoted to the description of Hindoo marriage with all its numerous peculiarities. It assumes such a different aspect from that of this country, and contains such a host of absurd forms quite new to the Christian people, that I should like to detail it distinctly as it is. Marriage is regarded by the Hindoos as a sacred condition of human life, and essentially necessary to meet both our temporal and spiritual wants. Notwithstanding all the benevolent and charitable acts of life, the sanctity of the heart's thoughts and all the purities of the soul, a Hindoo requires something else to redeem his spirit after death. It is believed that after the departure of the last breath from the body, or, in a Hindoo mode of thought, after the return of the five elements which compose the human body to their respective homes, the vital spirit invisibly walks round the house until some one of the male members of the family exorcise it by a peculiar ceremony. Hence arises the need of matrimony and its efficacy as tending to the spiritual benefit of man. In India a man and woman must marry. It is expressedly a divine ordinance and a violation of it is by no means an act for commendation. The ceremonies performed by every male offspring are requisite for the redemption of the Hindoo parents; hence when a man sees his wife the mother of girls only, or of no children at all, he is required by his religious law and for the safety of the soul to marry more wives until his demand has been met or ambition gratified. But it ought to be observed here, that the necessity of offspring does not entitle a woman to marry a second time, even in her widowhood, for her step-son would do just us well for her spiritual wants. Sometimes we see a man here and there who spends a bachelor life, either through an inability to support a family or from some vicious character of his own or his parents. For if a single member of a family should be found guilty of some abominable practice, such as adultery, theft, murder, irreverence to the Brahmuns, intoxication, or violation of caste regulations in eating or marrying low caste, the family would be outcasted; people, even the nearest relative, would withhold any social intercourse whatever in order to avoid the equal fate of the sinner. To intermarry with an outcasted family is out of the question; even the family barber and washerman withdraw their services. How far this contagion troubles our people, the following incident will show to the curious and inquisitive. A young Brahmun married a girl, in our village, whose mother was the daughter of a Brahmun of a low order, or more distinctly a priest of the fishermen, and whose poor father was outcasted on that account. In course of time, through entreaties, the Brahmuns took pity upon him, and agreed that he should be allowed to dine with them provided he should sit at a distance from them, and, what is the greatest of all favors, that *they* would eat confectioneries at his house, but not rice of his family cooking. This favor which they conferred upon him was for this especial reason, to marry his daughter, who had already attained the proper age; for, as I have before said, it is a sin to live a bachelor or maiden life. Again another thing is to be considered here, a man can marry at any age or as many times as he desires, but the girl is to be married under or at the age of twelve, and only once in her life. Now our friend, the young man, was not acquainted with the stain of his father-in-law's family, and unfortunately did not inquire properly about it. The fact became publicly known, and his father, uncle, the priest who officiated, and the friends who attended the ceremony, were all outcasted, until some of them regained their former rank by undergoing some penances, which will be represented in the second part of this book.

Now to the point: I have spoken of the Hindoo regard for matrimony. I will ask the reader's attention to the description of that monstrous system, polygamy, which has painted the Hindoo community with a dark hue, and is the mother of manifold disorders, immoralities, and vices. We hear that some Brahmuns had fifty wives, — some three-score; but even at the present day there are thousands, each of whom is the husband of a dozen wives! In order to enable the reader to understand distinctly this horrible system, I will furnish him with a large amount of information respecting its origin. Ballŏl Sen, a Hindoo king, in order to regulate the overflowing number of the Brahmuns, to check wickedness, to encourage learning and piety, divided them into two orders, Koolyn and Moulick. There is a beautiful definition of Koolyn in the Sanscrith language, which reads thus in English: "Good behavior, modesty, learning, popularity, visitation to the pilgrimages, force of will, means of support, devotional habits, and charity, are the nine essential characteristics of a Koolyn." One wanting these godly qualities was called Moulick. The king, no doubt, was prompted by good and prudent motives in this classification, which every one will see as manifested in the very definition just cited above. After his death this system unfortunately underwent some modifications, which handed down the privileges of Koolyn, which were great, no doubt, to the heirs, and could not always give the qualities thereof. The peculiarities of the Koolyn order are these: they would get money if they should eat at a Moulick's house, or marry a daughter, either Moulick or Koolyn. They would not drink a tumbler of water even in a clerk's or a physician's house, and if they should marry their daughter to a Moulick, they would lose the rank thenceforward and forever. As a Koolyn must marry his daughter to one of the same order, sometimes one accepts the hands of scores, partly for the want of a sufficient number of bridegrooms, and partly as an act of virtue and generosity to unburden the parents by marrying their daughters. These men do not *always* support their hosts of wives, who frequently stay in their father's houses, and occasionally receive visits from them. I know of some unfortunate women who never saw the faces of their husbands more than once!

Early marriages are prevalent among the Hindoos. There is no fixed age for the marriage of a man, he can marry when he pleases; but if he be a Brahmun, he cannot marry under twelve, that is, without being "*born again.*" The marriage age for a girl is between six and twelve. You would scarcely see a girl of thirteen, out of thousands, unmarried. She is known (if there be any) as a real *thoobree*, spinster, and there is little hope of her ever being married without difficulty. My poor younger sister, only eleven years old, was I am sorry to tell it) dragged to the altar to marry a man of the age of her grandfather, and of little refinement.

Among the Hindoos of the present day there are no such things as courting and engagement. In olden times the system was quite different from what we see now, and was called "*itcha boree*," or marriage of choice. But I do not mean that they of old used to know each other well, attend to the meetings on holidays, or enjoy the grand spectacles and music in theatres and operas. No, nothing of this sort was known to them. They used simply to glance at each other's accomplishments, both external and internal, in the shortest time possible. This, though a little defective to the Americans and English, at any rate is far better than the present fashion of no acquaintance and no interview until at once before the altar. Shith-ă, Drou-pothe, Doymonthee, and other renowned women, have married in noble ways. The caste system does not allow the Hindoos to select their own brides. For, suppose a young man found out a girl of promise, how will he know that she belongs to that peculiar caste or order from which he is to have his wife? There is another obstacle. There are no promiscuous gatherings of the sexes in Bengal, either in the temples or in the dwelling-houses. Hindoo women of high caste rarely come even to the outer department of the house in which they live.

Reading the Christian customs concerning weddings in the English books, I shrank at the thought of marrying one whom I never saw. How many times have I prayed to God in behalf of the blind ones of Bengal. I have had to contend against my mother's will, for she of course wished me to marry a girl of ignorance in the ignorant way. Do the Bengalees really know what a wife is, and what social pleasures are? They are at once cut off from *that* society over which the gentler sex presides. It would be considered an act of shamelessness if a young wife should manage to see her husband in presence of any living creature. Twice a day when he takes his meal she can see him, if her eyes are very strong, through the meshes of her thick veil; or would she dare to draw her veil aside, the attendant girls or young women would hurl some rebukes at her. Poor thing, she cannot look at her own treasure! The plagues of some sort or other ever attend her, to trouble and put her to shame for trifles, which are neither sinful nor improper. Thus, while young, I troubled my good aunt for nothing serious. It was in the night, when the full-grown queen of the sky was shedding all her splendors on those Oriental regions, that we were standing in the yard of the house near the dining-room, where the gentleman of the house had entered to take his supper. We two were in the room, but at the approach of my father and uncle, she was obliged to come out. I too came out to cheer her loneliness for half an hour. But what did I? Just the contrary! There were two pairs of shoes on the dining-room steps, for the Hindoos do not carry into the room things made of leather. As the pair belonging to my uncle were elegantly embroidered with gold threads, and studded with small stones, which were dazzling as baby moons in the moonlight, my aunt took a fancy to thrust her feet into them and walked a few steps in the yard, with difficulty no doubt, for not being accustomed to wear shoes, and being so large that her feet seemed swallowed, as in small skiffs. Not knowing how to manage such a heavy pair, she made a horrible, rattling noise with the silver hoops round her ankles and the shoes, as she walked along. "What is the matter? What is that noise out there?" my uncle cried out. "Nothing, sir, only aunt was trying to walk in shoes." "Walk in shoes!" he cried, "walk in shoes! A woman, and a Hindoo too! She is going to be a *Kristan* (Christian), I guess." Who can describe her embarrassment? She sat down senseless, and for several days could not show her face to her friends!

When a girl has attained her seventh or eighth year, the father engages a *ghotuck*, procurer of his own caste, who is well acquainted with the different orders of the castes. It will be worth while in this place to speak of the *ghotucks*. They keep a record of all the marriages of the Koolyns in every part of Bengal, which they commit to memory and furnish as an interesting study to their children, who of course shoutd follow the same profession. Let a Koolyn tell a *ghotuck* his father's name, and he will trace his genealogy several generations back. Thus once we were sitting in the outer hall of my grandmother, a *ghotuck* came in and asked for some money for his travel homeward. He asked my brother's name and also my father's; then he repeated like a parrot the names of our several ancestors, and where and when they were married. Indeed he did it with as much precision as if he were repeating his own children's names. Now when the *ghotuck* has found out a young man of the right order, the parents of the opposite party come to each other's house to examine the bride, and the bridegroom in turn. On a fixed day they assemble in the gentleman's parlor where the girl is conducted by a female servant, dressed in fashion and with taste. To ascertain whether the girl is dumb, lame, or disfigured, or not, one from the bridegroom's party says, "What is your name, dear?" "Gollaup (Rose), sir," in a low mild tone. "What did you say your name was? Please speak a little clearer that we may all hear. There! there you see the venerable gentleman, do you? He is very fond of sweet voices, but unfortunately he is a little hard of hearing." After an exchange of jokes between the opposite parties, the girl, having regained confidence, in a more distinct tone, says: "My name is Gallaup, sir." "What, Gallaup? O, how pretty! how sweet the name is! Gallaup in name and in looks also. Walk a little, will you?" Whereupon she walks, and the eyes of all are turned to watch her motions, whether they are graceful or awkward. The presiding member of the opposite party puts a gift of money into her hand, which she acknowledges with a salutation. Now comes the examination of the boy. This is conducted in the same way, only it is extended a little further, namely, to see what there is in his mind and head. His handwriting is produced, and his knowledge of letters is fathomed. This is done by some high castes only, for the men of the low castes who come to the boy do not know how to read or write themselves. Even among the Brahmuns, some possess but little book-knowledge, write so awkwardly that nobody can read but themselves, and read a page in an hour, spelling each word they find.

The older brother of my brother-in-law, who came to preside over the arrangement, being required to sign his name, began to tremble, and, with much embarrassment, wrote down his own name on the paper with one mistake! Some cunning fathers, before the coming of the girl's friends, provide a room magnificently for his son's study, borrowing a pile of books from the boys in the neighborhood, and, in fact, arrange everything so nicely, that it is hardly possible at first to tell whether the room is the boy's study or merely a bookstore.

When both parties feel satisfied each with the other, they enter into a written agreement called "*log-no pottrica*," which records every arrangement respecting the marriage. In the evening of a fixed day, the parties meet at the house of the bride, where the family priest is required to write the instrument, and an astrologer to appoint a day for the wedding ceremony, and the other friends to be witnesses. Before commencing to write, the priest marks the paper with dots of red and yellow powders, writes the name of "*Doorga Ramà*," &c., on the top, and other things below. The following is the form of the agreement or "*log-no pottrica*":—

"SREE SREE DOORGA."

"THE WELL-WISHER, RAM CHUNDER DEB.

"Hereby in this happy writing, I promise to marry my first son, Sree Deno bundoo Deb, with your second daughter, Sree motly Modhoo Bindoo Debee, on the 24th of June, 9½ P. M., 1859. I promise, also, to pay all the expenses that shall occur on the occasion, provided you will give all the gold ornaments to your daughter, &c."

The father of the girl writes a similar one, answering to and approving the points suggested in the other, and congratulating the proposed *Bai-ba-hick* * with a good will.

My American and English friends know very well what is to be done, i. e. what arrangements and preparations are to be made two or three months before the marriage. The Bengalee do just the same as far as the preparation is concerned. Among the former the young man secures a home, furnishes the parlor with everything to render both the short summer and long winter pleasant and comfortable, drives over to Chickering and Sons for a best, well-tuned piano-forte, and brings home all the newly-composed music that possibly could be procured in the music-stores. The

* Means the son or daughter's father-in-law.

friends of the young lady seem very busy in knitting, seaming, sewing, embroidering, &c. Among the latter, no separate house is required at all, for it is considered greatest of all earthly pleasures to dwell under one and the same paternal roof. If the young man should remove somewhere, even after the death of his parents, in order to live with his wife, the children in the neighborhood would ridicule him as the slave of his wife, and her as the author of discord. Hindoo parents, on their death-bed, charge their sons not to have their food cooked in a different kitchen, but to dwell peaceably in the same house, helping each other. I know a Brahmun family in my village, Bātli, which contained thirty souls at the same time. The house that sheltered them is something like a fortress, enclosing an acre of land. There is no need of separate houses from various reasons. A newly-married wife in Bengal is more fit for a primary school in Boston than for housekeeping. Again, if her husband be absent for half a day even, she would not go to the next house to ask for help if absolutely necessary. Shopping and singing are out of the question. Thus, while very young I was sick, and the physician, not finding my father at home, put a few pills on a plate, and requested my mother, who was then by the side of the door, to get some *coorchēē*, bark of a tree, and mix its juice with them. Though in the next house there were several persons, yet she could not manage to get any *coorchēē*. In the afternoon the physician came, and feeling my pulse, said, smiling: "Madam, you have not applied the medicine, nor given your boy the prescribed regimen. I know why you have not: brother Gangooly is not at home." Going a few rods out of the house, he returned, calling my mother, saying, "Madame, here is the *coorchēē*, which grew on your own lot."

Now about the necessary preparations for the wedding. Nothing is to be more cared for than a good, faithful goldsmith, who is to make ornaments of various shapes and sizes. Three days before the marriage, both the bride and the bridegroom are anointed and bathed in their respective homes, by a dozen married women. The widows are entirely excluded from this and other ceremonies pertaining to the wedding. I have before observed, that the women cannot associate with men, and the question would naturally suggest itself, Do the married women anoint and bathe both bride and bridegroom? I will here be more distinct in portraying the scenes, for they are all new and different from those of my Christian friends. The women are for the most part elderly persons, and composed of sisters, aunts, and the like. This exception is made on an occasion like this. The bride and bridegroom are requested to keep a *jathee*, scissors, with them until the marriage ceremony is over. The relatives and other friends send valuable gifts, and entertain them in their houses. This mode of entertainment is called "the bachelor and maiden feasts." The evening previous to the wedding is celebrated the feast of "joy cakes." These cakes are made of cocoa-nuts, sugar, and rice-powder, and are cooked with much ceremony. When the raw rice is washed, they sound the sacred shells, trumpets, flutes, cymbals, &c.

As the couple will be joined in a fixed moment in the evening, the friends are very careful to reach the bride's house before that time. When the bridegroom starts he dresses in red silken cloth, wears a hat made of cord and other glittering, fanciful material; then his mother, or in her absence, aunt, comes near him, and inquires, "Child,— where are you going?" "To bring you a female servant, mother," he replies. If he be the son of a rich man, hundreds of persons go with him. The bands, both native and English, play before him all the way. Some young boys, a hundred or more, dress in uniform; walk with colored flags in their hands; the hired dancing-girls dance on the platform, carried by men on their shoulders. Various fancy things, such as hills, houses, halls, and churches, made of bamboo sticks, beautifully covered with paint and gilded paper, are displayed, — fireworks of various sorts are burned, — streets leading to the bride's house are splendidly illuminated. When the bridegroom reaches his place of destination, he is received in an outer hall, accommodating hundreds. A party of twelve young men come and demand some money, which they get from every man who comes to marry in their place. This they dispose of at the public worship. Some little boys come, also, in the name of the "throwing stone party," for some money, which they spend for a feast or other amusements. The priests of the opposite parties enter into a discussion of various topics, embracing mental philosophy, astronomy, poetry, scriptures, &c., while the schoolboys do the same, questioning each other in geography, history, grammar, &c. Some dull and less active boys sit apart on the cushions with the pretence of headache or something else. Sometimes the boys of the bride's village disturb the others very much. I know of many instances in which they cut the best cashmere shawls to pieces, threw fire on them with a pretended carelessness, and painted the face of some poor dull boy with ink, who might happen to sleep at that time. Again, the "twelve friends" sometimes practice much violence if they do not get the exact sum of money they demand. I, unfortunately, once went to attend the wedding of our priest's son, in a town nearly twenty miles north of Calcutta. The party above mentioned proved so troublesome that we were obliged to fly by the back door in the night, through bamboo forests, tired, hungry, and afraid lest they should overtake us, and we be handled roughly.

Now the appointed time comes; the bridegroom is conducted into the inner department of the house, where no persons are allowed to enter, except his father, priest, and the barber. As he passes through a narrow entry, the young women throw at him a copious shower of pastry made of raw rice and molasses. The place for the marriage ceremony is furnished thus: two painted seats of board for the bridegroom and the bride, — some other aushuns, small pieces of carpet, for the priests and the parents, — a set of all sorts of household furniture used by them, — and a small throne, containing some images of their gods. The service is conducted in the Sanscrith language, which none but the priests can understand. After the preliminary service the young couple look at each other for the first time, which is called *Shooblo dirstu*, good interview. This good interview, or rather first interview, relieves the young man from his doubts and fears in regard to the bride, and she, too, feels a like anxiety. Her face is covered with a veil, and she cannot see her husband, — she only knows that she is going to marry some one, and her definite knowledge of him ends with this fact. They require the bridegroom to stand on a piece of painted board, then the bride is brought, sitting on a similar seat and supported by two or four men, as the case requires. By them she is raised in the air, and as the bridegroom looks eagerly at her, the face being then unveiled, some young women give blows on his back, sides, and shoulders. Receiving the first-expected blow from the gentler sex, he turns to the direction from whence it comes, and others favor him with more from various quarters. He, no doubt, feels very badly, and greatly confused, and if he be a stout and grown-up young man he bears these blows with manly fortitude, and if not, he cries a little. I have heard of some boys, who, unable to bear these invasions, looking up, cried aloud, "Ma! I shall not marry." They then exchange two flower garlands, which can be done in Bengal all the year round. The priest then binds their four hands with a cord made of flowers, and causes them to recognize each other as the lawful husband and wife. The guests remain sitting during this part of the ceremony, and the father of the bride, her uncle, or mother, is required to take part in the ceremony and dedicate her to the bridegroom. At the conclusion the priests receive their fees, according to some fixed order. For instance, if the bridegroom pays five dollars to the priest of the bride, her father is required to pay double the sum to the other priest. The entertainment of the guests then takes place in the yard, hall, porticos, and other places. The Brahmuns sit in one place, the Shoodras in another, and thus each according to the rank held in the caste system. Some difficulties yet disturb the bridegroom in the dining-room. The women contrive various sorts of fun to plague him. They set cakes made of rags, rice made of white corks, on the plate, and milk composed of white chalk and water, — good things are, of course, given by and by, but these he dare not touch lest there be other hidden difficulties. In order to give some distinct idea of the fun the young women practise on this occasion, I would mention the sad case of my uncle. They dug a vat in the floor, four feet square and as many feet deep, purposely to perpetrate a joke upon him, a piece of shaggy carpet was spread for the seat, supported by frail sticks. Poor uncle! unconscious of the hidden trap, sat on it, and down he went! In order to add more to his embarrassment, there was water at the bottom of the vat. Judging from these, and witnessing other kinds of plagues, I should say the marriage night is a rather hard time for a Bengalee bridegroom.

The "*bashar ghor*," or bride's chamber, is crowded with women during the night, who entertain the married couple with songs, make the bridegroom sing, and answer, if he can, some puzzling questions, enigmas, &c.. The reader will notice that here there is allowed free intercourse in speech between the man and the women. But it should here be explained that these women must be sisters of the bride or her brother's wives, near or distant relations. Her mother or aunts, who in law would be such to the bridegroom, do not enter into the mirth of the "*bashor ghor*." The next morning his father has to pay some money to the following persons, the policemen of the village, the man who teaches in the school, the Brahmun who teaches free the Sanscrith scholars, the men who take care of the temple, images, &c., the poor, low caste people, and a generous sum to the women who entertain, or rather plague the night previous. He then starts for his own village with his wife and some of the servants. Both she and her mother bathe in tears as they part. Being received at his house, he stands in the yard on a painted seat, and the girl before him on a dish with milk in it. She holds a live fish in her right hand, and he stretches out and puts his hand on her head. Seven married women walk round them seven times, blowing some *shunko*, and pouring water on the ground from a pitcher as they walk. Then comes the "bride's feast," at which hundreds from different castes are invited if she be a Bramun. The persons invited from the relatives and friends see the face of the bride, and put some money in her hand. When they see her, the attendant maid takes off the veil from her face and she closes her eyes. This mode is very good indeed, for nobody can notice the color and size of her eyes, whether they are dark blue, brunette, large, small or cross. When her own caste sit at the dinner, she brings a little rice to some of the leading men.

The *full shorjai*, or bed made of flowers, together with a large quantity of spices, confectioneries, fruits, and clothes, are sent by her father on the third day after the marriage, which are distributed to the families in the neighborhood. After staying through eight days she returns to her father's house, and occasionally goes to her new home until she attains her thirteenth year, when she commences a regular married life. As it is my desire to relate the scenes of Hindoo life, its manners, customs, and peculiarities as faithfully as the rules of propriety will allow, I should say that there is a second marriage which occurs during two or three years after the first, which I forbear to describe. I cannot close this chapter without making some remarks on the Hindoo marriage. Escaping the maladies of superstition, and standing under the light of true religion, with feelings of love and refinement in my heart, I shudder at, and clearly see, the defects in the system we have considered. The very thought of marrying a person whose joys and sorrows I am to participate in, who is to become one with me, without knowing her character and seeing her face at all, makes me shudder. How many hundreds in Bengal are spending their days in wretchedness! There, with many, the affection between husband and wife is rather compulsory than heartfelt. True love does rarely grace the connubial life of the Hindoos. Their children do not know what innocent social comforts are. Vice, with its thousand branches, twines round their lives. Faithlessness to the married relations, discord between, and separation of two who are required to be strictly one, are the defective features of the

Hindoo families in general. As there is no system of divorcement or a second marriage for the women, a hundred-fold is added to their deplorable condition. A goldsmith, a neighbor of mine, bleeds his wife almost twice a month for some trifles done, such as looking on the street through the window, talking with women outside of the house, &c. He being her lord and tyrant does as he has a mind, and finds no check to his brutal conduct. Of course the gentlemen in the neighborhood remonstrate with him for his conduct, but this affects him for a season only. He was fined several times, but not divorced, which measure only could save the unfortunate woman from future sufferings.

CHAPTER VI.

DEATH. — BOITHORNEE. — BATHING. — ANOINTMENT. — SHO. — BURNING THE BODY. — EXPRESSION OF MOURNING. — WIDOWS. — SHORATHO.

"NONE but the sinners die under their own roof," is the prevailing belief among the Hindoos. The person who dies at home, and on Tuesday or Saturday, is believed to be surely possessed of an evil spirit, *roth jonēē*. His ghost walks round the house and frequents the places where he rested in his lifetime. Hence, the moment the physician has declared that there is no hope of life for the sick person, the friends hurry him away to the ghaut on the bank of the river Ganges, where they lay him down in such a way that he may see and bow down to the sacred river. It must be observed here, that in almost every ghaut, either at the expense of the town, or of a single individual, some rooms are erected for the accommodation of the sick and their friends, because in some instances they linger a long time before death comes. In that case they all remain there day and night. If the sick person be a rich old man, having four or five sons living, a great many religious ceremonies are performed at the ghaut. In the morning and afternoon a priest expounds the sacred legends to a large audience, who come to visit the sick and hear the preaching.

"Boithornee" is performed at this time, either by the sick himself, if he is able to utter the words, or by his oldest son. It is believed that between the edges of this world and the other there is a river, Boithornee, to cross by those who go from this. There are no boats at all. Each one must provide the means for himself. Hence, at the point of death, or a little while before the departure from this world, the traveller dedicates a cow, and a large quantity of raw rice, pease, clarified butter, sugar, and clothes, unto the gods. As a compensation, the infernal spirit will provide him with a cow, which will carry him over to the other side of the Boithornee, and the eatable things will satisfy the spirits on the way. The reader will, no doubt, compare these with the funeral proceedings of the ancient Greeks, and see how nearly they resemble each other. Sometimes it happens that the sick man recovers after a while, and consequently desires to return home. This is a bad omen, and a sad case, especially if the man be aged. They would say the messenger of *Jom*, Pluto, had arrested him by a mistake, having the commission to take away another in the same family. Sometimes, through a mistake, they summon some one in the neighborhood!

When the man returns home, he closes his eyes on the way; the first thing he sees is an idol in the priest's hand, and calls any person he may choose by name, who is expected to go to the city of Pluto in his stead. Hence he calls an old person in the family if there be one, because it will be a comfort to him, and his death is lamented less. I was once posted with an idol in my hand to receive a young lady, who had been carried by the forgetful "peons of death." She opened her big, dark eyes, looked earnestly both at me and the idol (for this was the only chance for her to see a young man face to face), and humbly bent her head, saying, "Takoor, grant that no misfortune, consequent to my return, may befall the family."

When the men see the sick person breathing his last, they plunge his whole body up to his neck, and shout, "Gunga Nara onŏ, Brohmo om Ramŏ." But if they be Sudras they omit the word *om*, which is too sacred for them to utter. The reader will easily imagine how soon the last remnant of life flies from the body under such treatment, and, to add to the sufferings of the last hour, a man pinches very tightly the great toes of the sick until he dies. They then erect a pile of wood, which is nearly six feet long, three broad, and six high, on which they lay the dead body. Before doing this they anoint the body, and put a cross on the forehead with the sacred mud from the Gunga. When the corpse has been laid down on the wooden pile, the oldest son of the deceased walks seven times round it, with a blazing torch in his hand, repeating some words after a Brahmun of low order, who performs the funeral service. He then touches the mouth of the dead with the fire of the torch; the friends help him in this, and in the course of five hours they burn the body to ashes. If any one should touch a person of the funeral party, he must stay with them until the end of the service. They take a piece of the burnt body and enclose it in a mud cup, and throw it into the river. The Hindoos, as a people, burn the dead bodies of their friends; but to give the reader true information about this custom I should say, however, that there are some low castes, *Potto* and *Jugēē*, who burn or bury their dead as circumstances permit. Again, the children under one year of age, of any caste whatever, are buried on the river's side; but no tablet or monument is erected on the spot. The reason why the infants are buried is, I believe, the unwillingness to put fire to their delicate frames.

They then wash the funeral place, remove the ashes, and bathe themselves before they leave the spot. The leading man of the party, i. e. the son of the deceased, erects a pole nearly eight feet long on the place just washed and cleaned, also sets there a *colser*, or water-pitcher, and a *shora*, or earthen saucer, with eight small sea-shells upon it, and slightly strikes the pitcher with a shovel, and turns his face in the opposite way. As he leaves the place he does not turn back to see the things behind him, for it is said, if any should dare to look back, he would see hosts of evil and infernal spirits dancing and feasting on human flesh. I have often thought I should like to ascertain the truth of this, by doing what is thus forbidden, but I had no opportunity, because, when my father died, I was young and superstitious, and the second son. Now, being outcasted, I have not the privileges of a son, consequently, even in the absence of my older brother, some one else in the family will burn the body of my mother when she dies.

The party then walks first to the house of the man that died, slowly repeating *Horēē Cōle*, touches some fire, cuts *nim* (a leaf having a little taste), and chews a few grains of raw rice, which are purposely kept on the street near the house.

The expression of mourning is shown in various ways. Those bearing the same family title, such as Gangooly, Mookerjea, Doss, &c., will not shave their heads, cut the nails, anoint the body with oil, nor use any sort of animal food, for some fixed time. If the death of a Gangooly be known to hundreds of Gangooly families, they would all observe these rules, and one additional, namely, they would not offer prayers or worship the idols. The Brahmuns and astrologers observe these mourning customs ten days, the physicians fifteen, and others a month, during which time the sons suffer a great deal. They all dress in white, go with wet clothes after bathing, eat rice, boiled potatoes, peas, &c., once in twenty-four hours, and sleep on the floor on a carpet, quite separate from wife, children, or any friends.

There are some peculiarities in boiling the rice, the only meal of the day. Almost every one is required to cook for himself at this time of mourning. The earthen pan is placed on three large iron nails driven into the ground, and the fire for the cooking is made of dry cocoa-nut leaves.

During those days of mourning the sons of the deceased call on every family in his native place, high or low caste, rich or poor. Entering into a gentleman's house, they thus address him: "Sir, to-day is the sixth day of my father's departure from this world. He has received the grace of Gunga. I am ignorant of a great many things, inexperienced, and know not what to do. I earnestly entreat you to be kind enough to go to my house, superintend everything necessary, advise me and others interested in my case, receive and entertain the guests in my behalf," &c. It is customary to give some pecuniary aid to them, especially if they be poor, for it costs a large sum of money to perform the ceremony, and entertain several hundred persons, at least. The day before the ceremony,—which comes, as before stated, on the tenth day to a Brahmun, the fifteenth to a physician, and the thirtieth to the low castes,—they all shave their heads; the women simply cut their nails and bathe in the river. The oldest son, who is the chief actor in the scene, offers *thus pindoo* (made of rice, butter, [*ghee*,] and bananas) to the spirit of the departed father, as food for the ten days. Now, on the next day, comes the *Shrawthō*, or grand ceremony. The invitations, through letters and by messengers, draw immense crowds of relatives, friends, priests, monks, and beggars. In an open spacious place, either in the worshipping department of the house or outside of it, an earthen altar is erected, and *brisho kastō*, or funeral post, is placed near it. This post is carved out from a piece of wood, either *bale*, *nim*, or *jug-go doomur*, a kind of fig-tree. The priest marries a calf and a young bull before it, while it serves as a pole to which cords are fastened for the purpose of binding the queer bridegroom. They brand both sides of the bull, so as to make him conspicuous all the days of his life. A peculiar caste is hired to do this, because to burn *go churmo*, cow's skin, is a profane act. Hindoos have different castes to do the profane as well as sacred part.

All sorts of household furniture are dedicated to the gods, and then distributed to the Brahmuns. Some choirs, composed of common men and women of ill repute, come to sing the legends of Krishno, for which they receive some compensation. Sometimes twenty, more or less, different choirs come, and the people know not which to hear. In such cases, however, they hear the leading ones, giving them a liberal sum, and sending others away with but little. But it ought to be mentioned here that the choir having a handsome young lady, well dressed and ornamented, as its head, will secure a hearing at any rate, and, the whole time being occupied with feasts and entertainments, she is engaged to sing again, when all will be quiet.

Three days after this ceremony, they all anoint themselves with yellow powder and oil, and form a long procession of singers, priests and relatives, carry the funeral post on their shoulders, and stick it into the ground by the side of the river. Every year, on the same day, the children or grandchildren of the deceased are required to repeat some part of this *Sha-ahho*, and entertain as many persons as their circumstances will permit. Hence a Hindoo gentleman entertains people in feasts nearly six times a year, in honor of his departed forefathers. Even a poor man is bound to do this, otherwise he will be regarded as an infidel and a sinner.

There is a Brishookasto, or funeral post, in the Salem Museum, where curiosities from India are placed for exhibition. There is also another at the room of the American Unitarian Association.

It seems necessary to me to give my Christian friends some idea of widowhood in Bengal. The very day a girl becomes a widow, her colored clothes, silver and golden ornaments, are all taken off, and a mark of red powder, which every married woman wears on the forehead, is rubbed out. Henceforth she is to dress in white, and wear no ornament of any kind whatever during her lifetime. Her daily meals are reduced to one, and that is prepared in the simplest way possible. She is strictly prohibited the use of any sort of animal food. This restriction has been carried to such an extreme, that, if a scale of fish be found in the plate of a widow, she must immediately stop eating and go without food the same day. Each widow is required to cook her own food, and to abstain entirely from food and drink two days, *aka-thusly,* in every month. There are other fasting days for this class of wretched women, but the young ones feel satisfied with observing the two fixed ones. Who can witness the sufferings, the sighs of the Bengalee widow of thirteen or fourteen years, on the fast-days, without pity? In the warm days of April, when the burning sun dries up the ponds of their water, scorches the leaves of the trees, these poor victims to the rigidness of superstition faint and pant in hunger and thirst. If they are dying on the *aka-thusly* day, a little water will be put to the lips, merely to wet them. In order to escape these continual sufferings, it has been the practice with many widows to burn themselves with the corpse of the husband,

and though the subtle Brahmuns inculcate various rewards for the burning of the Shuttee, yet I cannot see anything more weighty than the putting an end at once to all their troubles, even at the guilt of suicide. They have no hope of ever cheering their widowhood in the world. A learned Brahmun, the principal of Calcutta Sanscrith College, is earnestly engaged in redeeming the condition of the widows by introducing the system of widow marriage. Having a deep knowledge of the national literature, also the Scriptures of the country, he traced back its customs and institutions, and wrote a pamphlet, in which he succeeded in proving that widow marriage had been known to the Hindoos of old. His reference to the ancients, his able arguments and pathetic discourses in behalf of the wretched millions, were met by the people with the ferocity of lions. Nearly sixty pamphlets were published by the enemies of the widows, against this great reformer. Amidst the heavy shower and thunder of reproach from his blind countrymen, this noble child of God, with a few friends by his side, with the love of humanity in his heart and the smile of his Father upon his head, stood firmly, and, summoning all his forces, maintained the honor and superiority in the field. With an elaborate work he answered his opponents, confuted their mistaken reasonings, and, to their great mortification, married a young Brahmun widow of sixteen to a suitable bridegroom. May he be successful in instituting this wished for system, which will save the females of Bengal from manifold sufferings and sins!

It ought to be observed in this place, that no widow is asked or forced to die with her husband. She who voluntarily takes up her cross and follows after her beloved husband of life, is welcome. Every preparation will be made to help her in this act of mistaken devotion. I have heard of some widows, who made all the necessary arrangements for this mode of suicide while their husbands were living. As it would be a disgrace to the family in case of her failure, the people ask her to consider the matter well, and, finding her firm in her position, bind her and her dead husband together with some cords, and lay them both on the *Chitta* or funeral pile, where she is burned alive amid the praises of the spectators. In many instances, the devoted widows, forsaking their little ones, and committing them to the care of others, have followed after their husbands. It is a heart-rending scene indeed to behold the wretched children, who, with horror unspeakable, witness the death of their two dearest relatives on earth, — the one taken away by the natural death, the other, yea the sweeter, the tenderer of the two, a victim to superstition, a martyr to her conviction of the mistaken precepts of her priests.

My sisters in Christ, be grateful to your Father for the light you possess. Learn to appreciate the thousand blessings which crown your heads, and, comparing your privileges, your comforts, your associations with those of Indian females, thank heartily the great Giver of all. O, do not carelessly tread on the pearls cast so lavishly before you, but prize them, feel their influence, and make good and right use of them! Remember that to whom much is given, much will be required from the same. Pray for yourselves, and pray in behalf of your sisters in the bondage of superstition, pining and mourning in ignorance. God raise the hearts of the people of this country, especially of women, that some daughters of God, like blessed Mrs. Judson, Mrs. Mundey, and others, might take pity on the dismal condition of their sisters in the bright, yet dark, heathen India. Noble Christian men and women, who send only their male missionaries to India, do not know that the female India, which is the better and larger portion of the country, has no chance nor allowance to hear them. So the women grow up and die in ignorance, yea, entire ignorance, of the only wise God. Their lives are spent in the worship of the ideal gods and goddesses! In the dark days of their widowhood, which lasts with life, there is nothing to comfort them, no hope, no promise to calm their troubled spirits, no knowledge of literature, science, or true religion to draw instructions therefrom. Sad, dark, dismal, pitiable, their conditions are! Nothing but the lights of the true religion can emancipate them from their servitude, strengthen them in their weakness, and exalt them from the low and degraded surface they stand on. Let pity awake in your tender breasts, ye women of America and England, towards the suffering millions! God does everything by instrumentalities, you are the same in his hands. Work then if it be expedient, or send the female teachers to work in the harvest of your King. Behold, the harvest is great, but the laborers are few! Help them, and bless them with the light you enjoy, — yea, the light of the knowledge of the King eternal, immortal, and the only wise God, — and yours will be the blessings forever!

CHAPTER VII.

DOMESTIC LIFE, EDUCATION, ETC.

ACCORDING to their ideas of good and bad, the Hindoos teach their children in their early days to love the former and shun the latter. They are taught to fear the gods, love their parents, respect the aged, and adhere to all the institutions of their ancestors, social or religious. As the result of such careful, regular training, a great many children do and say what they have no conception of, like the birds which the Hindoos teach to utter words. With a view to give some idea of this training, I would first notice the early days of the Hindoo children, but feel sorry that I have to begin with something quite ridiculous. It is the fear of the Vooths or devils,—the spirits of men, women, cows, &c., dying under peculiar circumstances. The number of these wicked spirits is immensely large in countries through which the sacred Gunga does not pass, because its sanctifying influences drive them a great way off. Again, as it is believed that those who breathe their last on the lap of their "Mother Gunga" with the consciousness of their approaching end, and say, "This is Gunga, and I am dying," are conducted to heaven, almost all the sick persons are led thither to die. Hence there are only very few devils near the Gunga. The Hindoo mother sitting by the cradle of her baby sings the names of the demons as her lullaby. My dear mother had the following, which she was wont to sing when the children would cry and would not go to bed, or made any noise. "I am Ear-cutter, live on the palm-tree and cut the ears of the noisy children." Such songs always have immediate effects; the little ones stop crying and hide their faces under the arms of their mother. As these grow older and are able to understand words, the lullaby turns to be a story of devils, tigers, lions, &c. After dark the mother, father, or the servants gather round them a youthful auditory, and tell them long stories of the devils,—how they wander about in the night, especially on dark nights; go from one to the other end of the village by a single step; encounter bad men in their nocturnal rounds, and require them to recite their prayers. The men or children who cannot say their prayers meet with very disagreeable experiences from their hands. These stories, too, have great influence upon the children; they learn their lessons, prayers, and hymns, by heart before they come across a devil, who is pretty suré to examine them as to their acquirements. The devils have their castes and orders; the spirit of a Brahmun is Doithó; of a woman, Patné; of low caste, in general, Vooths; of a miser, Joc; of a glutton, Pisha, etc.

The children learn the names of the male and female deities, and thank them when they go to bed. The mother takes her babe to the temple, and bends its head before the idols, if it be too young to show voluntary expressions of reverence. Often we find little boys or girls going to the temple with their parents, holding fruits in their hands.*

* Foreigners have very imperfect ideas of Hindoo temples: they think they are public places where people resort for the purpose of worshipping their gods and also for hearing the instructions of the Brahmuns. The temples are for the former, and not for the latter purpose. In them are placed the images of certain gods, such as Shiba, Kallēē, etc., which are worshipped and taken care of by some Brahmuns, who either hire or own them. People bring (especially on some holiday) their gifts of fruits, con-

The discipline at the table is peculiar. The Hindoos do not use knives, forks, and spoons at their tables; but they teach their children to make good use of, and to handle delicately, the tools they have, viz. their fingers. The children must sit decently in their places, must not scoop away the contents of the plate at once, nor put their fingers into their mouths up to the whole length. To leave one's seat before others have finished their eating is regarded as an insult to the party. It is not only an insult, but more than that, as the party would not eat any more and would leave their seats accordingly. The Brahmuns do not touch each other while at meals; if accidentally they should do so, the oldest of the party ceases to eat, but sits quietly until the end, when he leaves his seat with the rest, and does not eat any cooked food till evening. Anything left on the plate, whatever be its quality or quantity, is not taken into the kitchen or closet in order that it may be used again. Hence they take what they can eat, and the remainder is given to the servants, who are always from the low castes.

Discipline at the school is as follows. Love to the teacher,

---

fectionery, money, clothes, etc. to the idols, and offer them by the hands of the priests. The low castes are not allowed to tread on the sacred floor, and they dare not do it. They are satisfied with the pleasure of standing outside where the priest comes out, sprinkles holy water on their heads, blesses them by putting his foot on their hands, and returns them their trays, baskets, etc. in which they bring their offerings. These are the leading features of the services in Hindoo temples.

As the gods are presented to the children as irritable, fault-finding, powerful, and fierce, the children fear, but do not love them. When a mother would not have her child touch any eatable, let her only say, "It is for the gods," and that is enough. But still there are several little ones who by not being allowed to put their hands upon some tempting fruit or confectionery, because it belongs to the gods, hate their idols, now and then. My own younger brother, a boy of four years, remarked, "Mother, you say it belongs to Shalgram, that pineapple belongs to Shalgram. I know that your Shalgram is a mere pebble."

respect to his person, obedience to his commands, and attention to his teaching, are strictly insisted upon in our scholastic career. The Hindoo boys (for the girls are not sent to the schools or anywhere else for instruction, there being no such thing as female education) are taught first of all to regard, or, I might say, to idolize their teacher. To refuse him a service, or to speak a word before his face in the spirit of defiance, is a sin. Pupils really prostrate themselves before him, and offer prayer to him, as a personification of knowledge. So much confidence is put in him that the boys sometimes pay more attention to his words than they do to those of their parents. For obedience to and confidence in a teacher are preludes to scholastic success. Under any marked circumstances, for instance like the late school question in Boston about reading the commandments, in which the parents and the teacher were opposite parties, each demanding of the child submission, a Hindoo boy would obey the teacher while under his instruction, his sacred position awakening respect. I have known a boy who cared so much for the wants of his teacher, that he would not listen to the paltry excuses of his parents for not meeting them. The teacher had told him to bring his schooling fee, which he wished to remit to his family by a man who was to leave the place the next morning. The boy asked the money from his parents, but did not get it; they said, some time during the week they would forward it to the teacher. This did not satisfy the boy, who, in the absence of his parents, took away a heavy brazen jar, pawned it at a neighbor's, and brought the money to his teacher. Being desired to give the reasons for his conduct, he replied, "The teacher ought to receive his fee when he needs it, and especially when he wants to send it home, and in due time; and that if they really wished to pay him during the week, they might just as well recover the jar then." As most of their books are manuscripts, and liable to be torn, spoiled, or lost, the boys are taught to "love them as their friends, and watch and bind them as their prisoners."

If, carelessly, a boy drops his book on the ground, he picks it up, dusts it with his cloth, bends his head before it, and kisses it with reverence. The judicious care which ought to be taken of books, writing-tools, etc. has grown into a superstition. When a boy touches his book, pen, or inkstand carelessly with his feet, he thanks Shores-shutty, and begs her pardon.

Duty is exacted towards all in the different domestic relations. Parents and all brothers and sisters are objects of reverence, and it is the first and great duty of a child to honor his parents by words, deeds, and affection, as by mouth, hand, and heart. The Hindoo children prostrate themselves before their parents, and, taking the dust of their feet by the hand, put it on their heads,—a way in which the Hindoos show their humiliation towards others. They do not take the names of their parents on their lips, unless it is for the information of others, and even then two or three respectful terms are used before and after each name. It is regarded impolite to inquire the name of a married woman. A separate term of honor is put before the name of a departed father, uncle, etc. To call a person by his name, who is older than one's self, is an insult to him, as well as a sign of a want of good training in ourselves. In the family, the young boy does not address his older sister or brother as sister Mary, brother George, by their names, but uses, "First brother, First sister, Second brother, Second sister," etc. A married woman does not, on *any account*, utter the names of her husband, his eldest brother, her father, and mother-in-law, etc., nor sound the very letter which begins their names. For, instance, she whose husband's is Shiba, uses F in the place of S, making *Fiba.* *Goguth,* being the name of a god, is a common name among the Hindoos, and thousands of women say, "Forguth-nauth" when they bow down to the celebrated Jugur-nauth. A man must not touch the person of his younger brother's wife, unless compelled by some emergency. If he does so in seeming carelessness, he brings the world's odium on his head. It is not respectful to laugh wildly, and make loose remarks, before father, mother, uncle, aunt, brothers, sisters, cousins, or, in short, before other grown-up persons. In conversation, to look or stare at the face of the person (especially if he or she be older) whom we speak to is very impolite; on the other hand, it does not look well to gaze at a person while he speaks to us.* Singing, or playing on any instrument, before grown up persons, especially if they are relations, is improper; hence, pianos or other musical instruments are not household furniture in Bengal. The music is made among persons of the same age, and where no father, uncle, or elder brother is present. This, however, is confined only to the males; Hindoo females do not sing to men or even to themselves. Occasionally, you will hear a girl singing, in a tone sweet yet so low that you will think she has just recovered from a dreadful fever; while her female hearers are on the look-out, — lending one

* Being brought up under this etiquette, I did not look at the face of Mr. Dall or of good Captain Hendie in conversation with them. When I first came on board the ship, Mr. Dall, because I looked aside, before leaving us wrote down in my handbook the following: "When any one speaks to me, my first duty is *to look at him* with respectful attention." At any rate I did not lack "respectful attention" to the speaker; but his age and *our* idea of reverence attached to it bent my eyes downwards, that I might hear his words by my ear, receive them on my head, and obey them with my might.

ear to her song, and the other to catch the step of any one who might be coming. Proficiency in music or dancing is not an accomplishment to a Hindoo woman; her accomplishments consist in keeping silence before, and speaking gently to, her friends; in abstaining from wild laughter; in paying attention to the regulations for her sex; in offering due regard to others; in her familiarity with the art of cooking, and her reverence for all holy and pure things. Dancing is strictly forbidden among the males or females of any respectable standing whatever, and it is thought to be degrading, a savage practice, to move about or stretch the limbs with measured steps before an audience. In India, dancing men and women always belong to the disreputable class, who sell their services to the public. The Hindoos believe that the custom of dancing by both sexes originated among the savage people; although it is a main source of pleasure among the enlightened. A Hindoo father would rather see his children walk on crutches than waltz before anybody. Confined as the dancing is to the disreputable people, it is itself a difficult art; every one cannot dance according to rule, unless a systematic instruction is received. There are, I presume, more than forty different kinds of movements. When a girl dances, she imitates the sounds of the music, by means of the ornaments round her ankles. As she gently glides along before you, you will hear the low ringing noise of her ornaments, in perfect harmony with the sound of the music, and this designates the kind of the dancing. But it is to be observed here, that even the disreputable public people do not dance together, male and female leaning against each other's bosom, and putting their arms round the waist. Among the high castes, any sport requiring the exertion of bodily strength is excluded.

The chess, cards, and other games, similar and superior

to backgammon, are the prominent ones. But here, again, age and relation are to be considered. A gentleman does not play with his brother or children, or any nearest relation young or old; for it is impolite to play a game with or before grown-up friends; and, on the other hand, it is showing a shallow character to engage in a game with children. Again, the members of the low castes do not join in the sport with the Brahmun, lest they come so near his sacred person as to touch him with their foot, or to speak wildly to him in the heat of the action. Particular care is taken to teach young boys the art of writing letters to their friends. As each person is to be addressed by peculiar words, expressive of age, position, and relation, etc., there are some fixed rules which are consulted by the writer. In English, "My dear" answers almost every purpose, except in a lawyer's letter. It is applicable to father, uncle, mother, brother, husband, wife, sister, brother-in-law, priest, children, friends, debtor, creditor, etc.; but in Bengalee the system is quite different. The writer must discriminate between a father and brother-in-law, by addressing each according to the relation he holds to the one who addresses him. In writing to father, mother, uncle, oldest brother and sister, father and mother-in-law, and priest, the address is "Right adorable," and the writer's name in all cases is used at the beginning. The address to those younger in years is, the "Object of blessing." A man addresses the father or mother-in-law of his son or daughter by a distinct phrase, which *could not be* applied to any other. Low castes observe these rules while writing among themselves; but in case they write to a Brahmun, young or old, the phrase, "Most adorable," or, "Obedience to thee is my joy," etc., is used. The following is a sample of a father's letter to his son: —

"OBJECT OF BLESSING:—

"Know and accept my good wishes and blessing from this. For thy spiritual and temporal welfare I solicit the grace of God unceasingly, and in so doing consists my substantial joy," etc.

In order to take a long or short journey, especially if undertaken for some important business, a "fortunate hour" is sought for, which the priests designate after consulting the day and its planet (each day, being named after the heavenly bodies, such as Sun, Moon, etc., has its attendant planet). Before starting on the journey, a man prostrates himself before his parents, bows to them reverently, bends his head also before the idols or pictures of the gods, asks their blessing, recites a prayer or two, which are always creed-like and authoritative, and finally bids "Farewell, I come then." This is answered by, "Let success attend your steps," "Gods be with you," etc. If accidentally he should strike or touch his head against a door or wall, or if any one present should shout or sneeze, or if any one should speak to him, he would immediately take his seat for a few minutes. Such interruption is regarded a bad omen, and, if repeated, the journey is to be postponed.

In the streets, all the castes salute the Brahmuns as often as they meet them. The Hindoo would not let the priests go without his salutation. He folds his hands, holds them near his breast, and bends his head, saying, "Salutation to the feet of the Second Born," at which the Brahmun gently raises his right hand a little, uttering, "Be victorious!" or "Live ever!" or "Blessing be thine!" Unless there be a deep interest or settled familiarity between the parties, they do not speak to each other in the street. Some persons inquire of their friends, "Well, I hope?" "All well at home?" and are responded with, "As you see," or, "As you will," etc. The low castes do not walk close by the Brahmuns, nor tread on their shadow, if they can help it. To whistle, sing, or smoke in the street, is ungentlemanly. The very lowest castes are found to do those things. A Hindoo gentleman would not eat anything between his meals in a car or in a carriage. So, in India, the cry of "Candy, sweet oranges, apples, Stewart's gum-drops!" is not heard in railroad cars.

The tests of gentlemanliness are positive. From early years the children are guarded against falling into evil passion, fighting or quarrelling, etc. The grown-up, high-caste people *very* rarely come to blows, or even lay hands upon one another. Our parents, sisters, wives, would feel ashamed of us in the extreme if they heard that their children, brothers, or husband were fighting-men. Indeed, it would bring shame upon the whole family if one member of it were found making use of a club sword, or gun against his brother.

A Hindoo gentleman does not appear before any stranger without arranging his dress; again, *too much* fixing is regarded foppish. He does not use unkind words to others.

The daily routine of the men is as follows. After washing their mouths, early in the morning, the castes attend to their respective business. The Brahmuns go first to gather flowers for worship, and afterwards attend to the idols at their own houses, as well as at those of their "parishioners." A great many of them go to teach schools, or work in the courts, hospitals, or mercantile affairs, etc. But these are not all Brahminical. Other castes work until eleven or twelve; after that they bathe, offer prayers to the idols, and take their meals. In the afternoon they go to work again. The priests spend the afternoon in their studies, and in household affairs. Some of them occasionally meet, either in a parlor or in the open air, to play chess. The evening is spent in different ways. The good fathers gather their sons round them, inquire about the studies of the day, and give them instruction in parables and stories. Others go round visiting their friends, hearing music, or attending the meeting frequently held to consider local difficulties. At last, at nine or ten, comes the supper, which is served in their peculiar way.

As to the occupation of the females, I will speak only of the high-caste ones, as the head of the sex to which they belong. The first part of the morning is spent in attending to the sweeping of all the rooms, entries, yard, washing the kitchen, the marble or metallic plates which are used at late tea. These are done mostly by female servants, but as being of a different caste they are not allowed to come to that portion of the kitchen where the cooking-utensils are kept, or to the kitchen at all; the sweeping and washing here are done by the members of the family. The performance of the duties in the kitchen is a difficult one; for if anybody should touch a cooking-pan or a kettle before taking a bath, it would not be used any longer; so such things are placed beyond the reach of little folks. As the utensils are often liable to be touched, they are, however, mostly earthen-ware; so in case they are thrown out, as they often are, the loss is not great. After the sweeping has been done, the women get ready for the bath; anoint their bodies with oil common, or *foo lud* perfumatory, as circumstances permit. I have seen a rich, handsome, but vain Brahmun woman rub her arms and face with *Kheer* (thickly boiled milk), that a good fragrance might come from her person! They then go into the river or tank, where hundreds wash themselves together on some holiday. On their way home, the religious as well as elderly portion of them visit the idols in the temple; the young women, however religious, are not often suffered to go to the temple, lest they come into collision with young men who frequent them for this purpose. Reaching home, they help each other in the cooking. As the Hindoos do not set vegetables or fish whole on the table, and use highly seasoned and spiced dishes, great care is taken to dress fish, cut the vegetables, and grind spices. Widows do not eat anything touched by hands that have just dressed fish; so one takes care of vegetables, another of fish, a third grinds spices, and thus they pleasantly alleviate the labor which, if done by one, would be anything but easy, and of course would take more time. The Hindoo way of cooking things is really scientific; and it takes time and requires skill to do it. They do not think much of boiling, baking, frying; alleging, that only those who do not and cannot cook better feel satisfied with them.

Let a Bengalee woman prepare some common leaves or flowers, and, if you eat them, you will hardly know what you are eating. Out of *one* kind of fish and two or three of vegetables, she would prepare ten different dishes, perhaps, each differing from the other in regard to flavor, taste, and richness. In fact, in some grand feasts, the number of *Banjuns,* or curries, as called by foreigners, exceeds forty! In the legendary accounts we read of *fifty-four* Ban-juns used by the gods. As there is no fixed time for taking meals, the men dine when they are ready, either together or separate, and the women afterwards. If there be a female visitor in the family, the newly married daughter-in-law would not eat anything before her, and to meet at the table with *men* is out of the question. My lady friends, in this country, have often asked me, "Who presides at the table there?" "Who waits upon the gentlemen?" etc.

The mother or any other elderly female serves food to

the men, but she does not partake of it with them. If there be only a young woman present to help her husband or his brother, she skilfully manages to look at the condition of the plates, and acts accordingly. Sometimes she gives them what they do not wish for, or more than they can eat. The married women do not sit close by the widows, lest they touch them or their plates; in either case the latter are required by the religious regulation of their order to stop eating. Very commonly the widows do not eat *any* food cooked by married women, even if they were their daughters.

Immediately after the meal they go to the tank, which is always within a few rods' distance from the kitchen, for the purpose of washing their hands, mouth, and feet. Almost all young women go into the water and wash the dress they had on while at dinner. Now they use *meeshie*, a kind of black powder to clean their teeth a second time, which, as a national peculiarity, are bright and smooth as pearls. This powder is a preparation of three or four materials; and, although it is black, leaves no darkness on the teeth. It has also a fine taste. The little children, unable to resist the temptation, eat the powder while cleaning their teeth with it.

Then comes the toilet. The head is decorated, the hair fixed with much care and skill. One woman sits behind her friend to fix her hair, which is always dark, thick, flowing, and sometimes so long as to reach the knees. They do not use hair-pins or ribbons; some delicate stitches of thread made in braiding the waste hair are used to tie the *Kho-pă*, or knot, which, when properly made, looks "*splendid*," as the girls call it. A gay dress is worn, ornaments are put in their proper places, some attar of rose is sprinkled over the dress, hair, &c., and after this the young lady is all right,—ready to receive callers, or to go to parties, if it were customary. But they must see and enjoy praise, comment upon and find fault with each other's dress or personal accomplishments by themselves, as hardly any outsider, especially a male, gets any chance to see them. Sometimes the women living in houses adjoining assemble in one, where they spend the time in playing cards, telling stories, or feeding on gossip. The subjects of their conversation are the following, which they speak upon briskly, even within the space of a few minutes:—First, the dinner, how it was cooked, by whom, and of what it consisted. Now one regrets she could not succeed very well in cooking fish, and puts too much salt in it; another specifies every material of which the *Ban-jun* consisted. Second, the ornaments, the price and quality of the gold and silver which they are made of. Third, husbands, their tempers, affections, liberality, and age, etc. Fourth, the property, the dress, ornaments, bodily and mental qualities of the neighbors, etc. In some of these I perceive that human nature is everywhere the same.

In this country the women do not regard it as useless talk, while busy in knitting or sewing, to inquire of the lady with the pink bonnet who made her dress, who cut the pattern, or to speculate upon the wealth of the man Sarah is engaged to, etc.

The Hindoo women have no sewing to do; there is simply a long piece of cloth worn round the body in a graceful manner, forming gown, sack, bonnet, and all. They now and then make fancy articles, such as small baskets covered with broadcloth, and elegantly set with shells of various description, flowers with wax, rags, or paper, hanging sleeves studded and fringed with shells and silk, etc. But these they cannot make money out of, as it would be a disgrace to a family to hold anything made by the gentle sex for sale.

Some poor high-caste woman, however, may dispose of her things privately among her nearest relations. The meeting of the young women in Bengal is often marred with sad incidents; it is quite certain that some one will go home with tears in her eyes, caused by jokes or unkind words of her comrades. Then the friends of the injured take the matter into consideration, and do not hesitate to commit vengeance with fourfold rash words and cursing. As they are not taught to read or write, the rest of their time is spent in telling or hearing legends of gods, stories of demons, tigers, etc.

Now Christian women, only think of the daily occupation of your sisters in Bengal! How would you like to be in your room all the time, to speak to only a few of your own sex, to take your meals in a solitary corner of the kitchen, to consume the golden time in telling or hearing nonsensical stories, worshipping idols made of "wood and stone," and to die in ignorance and superstition? Would you be willing even for a day to lose the pleasure of reading your Adam Bede, Harper's or Atlantic Monthlies, or be deprived of the privilege or power to investigate the contents of envelopes forwarded by parents, friends, and beaux? Having had the pleasure of spending a couple of years among you, the knowledge that I have of your condition, privileges, abilities, and culture, I know what answer you would make. Let us then pray to our God and their God that in his good time he would ennoble the condition of his daughters beyond Christendom, and raise noble. earnest souls as missionaries to work in His harvest!

BOOK SECOND.

INTRODUCTION.

The chief object of the following book will be to treat of the religion of the Hindoos.

By religion of the Hindoos, I do not mean the genuine Hindoo religion which was prevalent in India in remote ages, — not the Hindoo religion as it was, but as it is; not what the *Bathŭs* taught, or the *Rheeshies* lived under, but what the Shastars, Poorans, and Tuntros teach, and the mass, both the Brahmuns and other castes, observe to-day, as the "life and light," and the absolute way to reach *Goluck* (pleroma of Krishto, Happiness). What mighty revolutions time achieves in the religious, moral, social, intellectual, and political conditions of men! Read the ancient Scripture of the Hindoos, observe the pure, sublime doctrines they inculcate, watch the Monees and Rheeshies in their cottages of light, attend the court of Ram, Kornos, or Joodhistres, and then come down to the Shastars and the Thejos of the present day. You will be surprised to see the spacious gulf of difference between them. A manifestation of sad change will greet your eyes wherever you cast them, — either on the religion, the language, the manners, or the customs of the people. This sad change has reached the very fibre and nerve of Hindoo life, both external and internal. A noble, large-minded Brahmun, the learned principal of the Government of the Sanscrith College, says in one of his books to this effect, that by careful examination we see the Hindoos of the present day appear quite different from those of ancient times, so much so, that they seem like a different race.

Look at the sad contrasts and corruptions. The ancients believed "*om ākŏ mabŏ thee te ung;*" in English, "there is *one* God, without a second." Now the people have hosts of gods whom they daily worship! There was no caste system, none such as we see now,—a system which forbids any close social relations between the members of separate castes. The Brahmuns often used to dine and intermarry with the Khatryas.

We read in the Hindoo religious books that the Brahmuns were often entertained by other castes, thus: Doorbāsha eats the food cooked by Throw-pothee; Krishto, in a Brahmun attire, demands hospitality from Koxmo. Ogusth dines at Hillol and Bathaw-bee's; Sacoontola gives her land to Doosh montha. Instances of a similar nature could be cited by hundreds, which would clearly show that the ancient Hindoos had no such religion, manners, and customs as those of the present day. The ancient Hindooism, though far inferior to Christianity, is superior to, and more rational than, the Egyptian, Grecian, or Roman paganisms. Yea, by careful examination, a candid man would see that even Judaism, just as it is, is inferior to the spirit of *Aurjā*.

As I compare carefully the instructions, the ceremonies, the mode of worship, the representation of the Almighty in those two ancient religions, I should suppose that modern Judaism was the corruption of primitive Hindooism, and that in falling into the hands of the nations round Judæa, who had comparatively a dark faith of their own, and on account of its being associated with Christianity, it became the object of their admiration. If the true worship is that which is free from forms, but is in spirit and in truth,—if neither this mountain nor the temple is strictly the seat of God or the place of worship,—if God does not care for sacrifices or incense, but chooses a true and contrite heart,—then the religion which prescribes such forms, no matter when, how, or under what circumstances, is not equal to one which is entirely free from any form or ceremonies. To bring this matter to the light, I would try to illustrate it with distinctness. There is a theory diametrically opposite in its substance to that which the Jews and the Hindoos receive of their respective religions. Even most Christians adhere to the theory, that in the world's infancy, when the children of clay were not prepared to receive a revealed religion, to digest strong food, the All-wise Creator gave the Jews the law, commanded them to build Him a temple, an altar, to offer sacrifices and burn incense unto Him. But the Brahminical theory is different. It says that Hindoos, in the Sootojoog, or the age of truth, built no marble temple to God, but dedicated the pure, the contrite heart as the seat of Brohmo; used no material offering or incense, but faith, gratitude, and love, in their worship of their Creator.

But in course of time, impurity and injustice increased "with the increase of human population," the mind of man learned to admire the things around him. His eyes were dazzled with the products of art in its various forms. The life of simplicity gave place to luxury; the pursuit of worldly pleasures so much occupied the attention of man that it seemed impossible for him to spend time in mere speculation concerning an invisible Deity. Shastars came forth to remedy these corruptions, by introducing substitutes for the lost faith. Temples of marble or of precious stone, altars covered with silver and gold, and dazzling images, filled up the length and breadth of the country.

The four great epochs, or the Zoogs, of the Hindoos, which show the peculiar features of the moral and religious condition of the people, have been treated of by several foreign writers. I would simply touch them in order to describe the changes therein. As I do not remember exactly the length of these Zoogs, how many years each contained, I would not dare to speak of them, but feel willing to bring out some leading points for our present use.

The first is called the Shorto, or the age of truth; the second is *Treta*, curiously called so, although it means "Third"; the third is Dwapur; and the fourth, or last, is Kolie, the age of darkness, sin, etc. In the Shorto Zoog, as we read in our ancient books, everything concerning the external or internal appearance of man indicated simplicity and peace. What we read of the simple, rural, righteous lives of Adam, Eve, and Abraham, was exactly so with the Hindoos of the first Age. Their dwelling stood upon peace, supported by pillars of brotherhood, and roofed by love. The inmates were simple in their dress, temperate in their food, childlike in their temper, pure in their affection, and strong in their faith towards God. The lion and the lamb met at the same crib in these cottages of love. No gods or goddesses were known or worshipped then except the Creator, "the Father of all." They used to address each other by the terms *debŏ*, *dabe*, god and goddess, and to treat, regard, and recognize each other as the creations of Krishto, or by another word, the image of the same. All had the right to draw from out of the great source of spiritual comfort, the sacred Bāthɔs (Vedas). The loving Father, "Bisho Pitha," the good spirit, "Porom Aut-on," was alone worshipped, loved, held as sovereign, recognized everywhere and in every circumstance. Nothing was more earnestly and at first sought as the pearl of unspeakable worth, yea, more than that, as the true destiny, than the true manhood of piety, the path of righteousness, which leads men safely to the great terminus of our career, — the "Shorgo," the Heaven of God. Other objects of life received but slight attention; the thought, What shall we eat, what shall we drink, and wherewithal shall we be clothed? did not overwhelm them, for they believed in their own proverb, "Those who walk in the path of righteousness get their bread even in midnight;" that is, they know no disappointment, and have hope and faith forever. It must be remembered here, that this proverb of the Hindoos is a parallel to, or at least conveys the same spirit, as that of Christ's saying, "But seek ye first the kingdom of God, and his righteousness, and all these things shall be added unto you." They were not indolent, however; they did not wait until ready-made "manna" would fall from the sky, but attended to husbandry, developed and used their energies to help each other, and at the same time lived a pious, unspotted life.

The following anecdote gives a fair idea of the life of the people of that pure age. Krishto once sent his brother to seek out a poor Brahmun, that he might give him some alms. Accordingly he started on his sacred mission, and encountered a Brahmun in a rice-plantation. He was diligently engaged in picking up the stray grains of rice that had fallen down to the holes in the ground, by means of a stick with some glue on the end of it. Boloram, the brother of Krishto, watched his proceedings a few moments, advanced towards the Brahmun, and addressed him in the following words: "Deleō! (god!) may thy servant know the motive that leads thy hands to seek grains from the furrows in the ground, and not from the waving, golden stalks before thee!" "Child," the sage replied, "with little labor I can gather these grains from the furrows, and so I do. These stalks, as you see, I have reserved for those warbling tenants of the air, the children of the Most High, whose short bills would not reach the stray grains in holes." "Blessed sire," Boloram rejoined, "it will take a long time to gather enough for your daily meal. My brother solicits the hands of a Brahmun, to put some gold into them. Should thy hands leave the things here, and thy feet tread his court, thy servants would deem it a great favor." He looked towards heaven with deep reverence, and, turning his loving eyes towards Boloram, said: "Smile of Heaven, crown him who loves his fellow-creatures! Child, God has bountifully furnished me with all I need to earn my living. There are others who are not thus blessed. Go to them, child, and entertain them with your brother's charity." Krishto, having a curiosity to know more of this Brahmun, — his "piety at home," — determined to visit him in his cottage. Late in the afternoon, filling his basket with rice, the Brahmun came home; his wife washed his feet, and then cooked the rice. The husband came out to see if there were any guest at the door, and, not finding any, went in, bade his wife to sit at meal, and thanked God for the mercy shown unto them. In the same moment, Krishto, in the disguise of an old Brahmun, appeared at the cottage door and blessed the inmates. They did not touch their food then, but left their seats, and, folding their arms, with reverence addressed their guest. "Joy sheds its charms upon us, this floor is holy at thy touch. Welcome to it! Thy servants, with all they possess, wait for thy command." Krishto replied, "Peace be to your children!" It would please Brohmo to see us three dine together under this roof, and sing his praise." "As it pleases our lord, be it so," said the pious couple. They then divided the food equally among them, and partook of it with gratitude toward the Giver of all. Proceeding no further, I would stop here to speak of other *Zooga.*

The Zoogas that succeed Shorto present a different picture altogether. Men have in some measure departed from the state of simplicity, and have made the frolics of Krishto, with his sixteen hundred female friends, immortal by their genius. Like the Old Testament God he too chooses a favorite people, *Pandubas,* walks with them in their sojourn in the wilderness, brings them back to a land of their own, excites and helps them to fight with their enemies, etc. At one time he tries the faith of Korna, asking him to offer his only child of five years unto him, as did Jehovah of Abraham.

The present age is the Kolie. We who live in it know of course its leading aspect, the "house divided against itself," the children rise against their parents; unnatural affections and disappointments come thereby; ambition, injustice, selfishness, disregard to holy things, have attained their full power. In the place of one God, the Hindoo worships millions; temples, pagodas, altars, are seen everywhere.

This is the dark age of the Hindoos. The following is an anecdote describing the transition between the Zoogas. In order to teach his favorite servant the knowledge of things, and store his mind with various experiences, Krishto accompanied him to take a survey over the world. They came to a farm where two men, apparently tired, begged them to stop for a moment and help them to adjust a matter that was troubling them very much. The one was a Brahmun, the owner of the farm, and the other a laborer hired to work upon it. As the latter was ploughing the ground, he accidentally turned out a large jar with pearls and jewels in it. Thanking God for his mercy, he ran to the Brahmun with the utmost speed, and informed him of the treasure. He came to the spot and saw the tale was true. The Brahmun told the workman to carry the wealth to his own house, for he saw it first; but he would not, fearing it would be a sin to take away the money found in another's land. Thus both exhausted their logic in their attempts to convince each other as to his lawful right to the treasure; but to no purpose. Krishto did not mind their appeal, and proceeded on his journey. Shortly after, he returned, and saw both the Brahmun and the workman fighting and bruising each other. Each claimed the wealth. The Brahmun says it was found on his farm, therefore it belongs to him. The workman says he first found it, and it ought to be his. Krishto turned to his servant, and said, "Do you notice the change? It was just before the transition of the Zoogas that the man found the money. It was when *self* was little regarded; now it is another age when *self* becomes dominant and exercises absolute sway. The very man who refused the money then is fighting for it now. Look at the change, child."

The purity, self-denial, innocence, that once graced their lives and homes, now seem restless, as if disgusted with their abodes, and ready to migrate to some more genial sphere. Here and there the banner of ambition floats on the palaces. Luxury succeeds; display and injustice dethrone charity. The heart ceases to be the temple of God. Its every corner is occupied by strange, unchaste, delusive propensities, found where nobler aspirations once dwelt. The altars are to be seen here and there, the offerings of beasts are dedicated unto the gods, ritualism takes the place of the worship in spirit. The great actors upon the stage are Rama and Rabōna, one a god and the other a monster. The conduct of Rabōna was such, that it filled the earth with fear. Both the Shoors and the Oshoors (gods or good men, and the monsters or cruel tyrants) trembled at his presence. The complaints against him grew universal; the gods solicited protection and the interposition of the great Rama, who alone had the power to check the tyrant Rabōna. Accordingly the incarnation of Bishto appears in the world to pour out a healing balm over its injured people. Now it was foretold that the age of Rama will be called Trita, the Third, but the condition of the world demanded his advent earlier, so the age he lived in, though second, being the immediate successor of the First, or Shoto, retained the name Trita, fulfilling the prophecy thereby. We are introduced to Dawpur now, which means the second. What the world sowed in the age previous is coming up luxuriantly in this, but the harvest is by and by. The Trita sows the seeds of confusion, injustice, impurity, ambition; the Dawpur waters them, and the Kolie gives the increase. Among others the chief actor on the stage is Krishto, another incarnation of Bishto. His mission in this is rather delicate in its nature. After the display of heroic deeds to relieve the world, which was groaning under the heavy yoke of Rabōna, he feels tired; perhaps comes to refresh himself, and spend his time in marriage, music, and romance. Handsome in person, a god in nature, active in movements, a good musician, he casts a net of charms around a host of young women, and draws them all out without breaking the net or sinking the vessel. Hindoo legends say that the prime object of his learning to play his Banay was to sing the praise of Radha, wife of Awe-an, and who is also his own wife from eternity.*

How much Christianity is needed to regenerate the Hindoos will be shown when I treat of their idolatrous worship, festivals, etc., in the following pages. The great mass of the people, properly speaking, have no idea of God, true humanity, and a future life. In this country, I notice the death of men does not excite so great a horror as it does among the Hindoos. A Christian mother calmly resigns herself to the decree of her God, and commits her treasures to His safe keeping; for she has hopes of meeting them again in her "Father's mansion." But I have seen Hindoo mothers who in their ignorance beat their breast, and curse their gods, at the death of their children! They believe that death breaks the chain of love and affection forever! My mother is in the habit (as is common with the Hindoo women) of weeping over the sad remembrance of her lost children and brother: and I used to comfort her by saying, there is a future state where they from the east, west, north, and south will meet in their common home. Indeed, Brahminism is dry, mysterious, sensual, contradictory in itself, and, with its various forms, pleases the senses, but does not meet the thirst of spirituality. It does not, or rather cannot, guide the mistaken, humble the proud, comfort the sorrowing, and teach us in all the vicissitudes of life to repose our trust in the saying, "*Thy will be done.*" It has sanctioned the worship of *thirty-three million* of gods and goddesses, most of whom you will find in this world, and in the sky. Of course the Brahmuns say they do not worship these

---

* The Hindoo Scriptures have a long story showing how Radha at once became wife of Krishto and of Awe-an. It is hardly possible in this connection to recite it. But let it be known that the Hindoos have some reason to produce in defence of their faith, which they hold dear.

hand-made idols; these are only the representatives of the unseen deities; but the lower castes, the large portion of the people, take them for the gods themselves. I admit the Brahminical ordinances have some hidden beauty underlying them; but the time has come when everything which aims to promote the temporal or spiritual condition of man ought to be as clear as spring, as accessible as air, and as bright as the sun. Certainly the time has come for the dim lights, here and there, to be absorbed by the great salutary Light,—for the return of the erring children to their Father's home, that they may bend their knees before the throne of Grace.

Being born and trained in a Brahmun family, I well know the magnitude of its superstitious life. Almost every day you will hear of the institution of a new mode of worship, and the discovery of some new idol. The people, especially the young men, are tired of these things. Being educated in the missionary and government schools, under the influence of European knowledge, these young men prove strong obstacles to the bigoted Hindoos in their discovery of new idols. I know hundreds who used to drag the images from their seats, and place them somewhere in the road, fields, or some dirty places. On my way to a friend's house, with an image of Shal-gram, I looked at it to see whether a trace of divinity or life could be seen in it or not; and finding but a round, smooth, black pebble, I dropped it on the ground. The poor senseless thing fell into a bush, and I had to hunt for it nearly ten minutes. Not only enlightened young men do such things, but some priests themselves place and replace idols for their own interest. In Krishto-poor, a village nearly twelve miles northwest of Calcutta, there is a stone image of Shiba, which they say is full of life, power, and compassion.

Whether it is naturally so, or carved to signify this, I cannot tell. It has a rough, thorny surface. A story says that the "*mool-shun-ash*" (head votary) had been sick of small-pox for several days, and in the night before the Shun-ash, the god, took the small-pox in his own body, enabling thereby the sick man to join the festival. Some one, hoping to secure the living idol in his own hand, and to trouble its former priest, stole it away in the gloom of night, and it was not seen for years. They erected another in its stead, but lately the old fellow, tired of seclusion, lone and home-sick, came again to his former place.

Now I will begin to treat of the Hindoo worship, religious festivals, and ceremonies; and, to aid the reader, I will describe the circumstances which gave rise to these things. Foreign writers describe them as they see them outwardly. Each of them has some meaning, good or bad, rational or foolish. To narrate these things in order and precision, I will begin from the month Bois-ak, April, which is the first month of the Hindoo year, and will describe the holidays, festivals, worships, etc., that come in the successive months. It ought to be said here, that, owing to the changes in the almanac, the increase or decrease of the days in the month, the holidays sometimes vary their time; thus the car of Jugger-nauth is drawn on the 27th of June, or sometimes early in July.

CHAPTER I.

BOIS-AK, APRIL.

THE NEW YEAR'S DAY.—THE CHANGE OF ACCOUNT-BOOKS.—SACRED CHOIR.—DEDICATION OF WATER-PITCHER.—WOMEN'S CEREMONY.—WAY-SIDE HOSPITALITY.—THE IDOLS IN WATER.

ALTHOUGH there are months many and days many, the Hindoo regards some with peculiar reverence, believing they have in their very nature some efficacy and sacredness which others have not. The acts of benevolence, charity, and devotion performed in them will be of more value than the same things done at any other time; thus a gift to a Brahmun in the day of full moon would be more efficacious, bear more fruit, than at any other time. As I have determined to state the significance of some of the Brahminical institutions, I would ask the reader to fix his eyes on the prudence and somewhat innocent cunning of the learned priests. As Brahminism regards *faith* as fruitless unless manifested in deeds, it joins some acts of charity to every form of worship or devotion. Now the poor people cannot possibly offer gifts or bring sacrifices to the temple often. For their convenience some especial months, days, or hours have been selected that they might do something, which is, after all, "better than nothing."

Three months out of the twelve are regarded comparatively sacred by the Hindoos; viz. Bois-ak, Kartic, and Magh,—April, October, and January. Bois-ak and Magh are the most sacred. The former commences the Hindoo new year, and everything assumes a new aspect. The merchants, the storekeepers settle the accounts of the past year, by paying their debts and receiving their payments. The stores and offices are fancifully decorated; the scales and weights are washed and worshipped; debtors and all customers are invited to spend the evening, &c. In the evening the store is beautifully illuminated. The head-clerk or the master himself sits on the cushion with a writing-desk and account-books before him, in which he enters the names of those who pay their debts in part or full. Some, as an expression of good-will, deposit money in advance; while others, on the contrary, cannot pay their real debts, and consequently miss the cakes, sweetmeats, fruits, and music with reluctance. However, on the whole, with the inability of some, and the liberality of other customers, the *book* commences the year cheerfully. On the head of the first page of each book two round figures are marked with red and yellow powders. Every day the book begins by depositing a little money to some deity, and at the close of the year this little money is accurately collected and disposed for the worship.

During the sacred month, a band of singers, composed of from two to six persons, comes to the door early in the morning to sing a hymn. They get some compensation at the end of the month. Sometimes two or three parties come at a time; and one sings while the others wait. It would be an irreligious act to turn them out; whether you care for them, and wish to hear their music, or not, it would not make any difference. The fact is, the praise of the gods is to be sung at the door of each Hindoo. Sometimes a man or low-caste woman comes to the door to do what a Christian is strictly forbidden to do, that is, to take the name of the Lord in vain. One hundred and eight times the name of Krishno is repeated in different ways!

Dedication of Water-Pitcher.—On the first day of this month the Hindoos of all castes dedicate *ghut*, or pitchers, to the gods, deceased forefathers, &c. These *ghuts* are earthen, brazen, or silver, according to the circumstances of the dedicator. The common belief of the people is this, that the ancestors, long since dead, feel thirsty in the hot Bois-ak, and the water thus dedicated by sacred words (*mon-tro*) will be beneficial to them. The ignorant mass believe so, otherwise they would not do anything of the kind. But the prudent priest will tell you that in the honor, and to the name of, and as a token of respect to, the deceased fathers, we dedicate these and distribute them to the Brahmuns. There is no particular number of the *ghuts*. It varies from three to any indefinite number. They are all placed in rows, with trays full of fruits on their tops. The first is offered to the favorite god; the second, to the dead or living pastor, *gooroo*,* of the worshipper; the third, to the father, if he is dead; the fourth, to grandfather, &c. In this way, following the thread of genealogy, they go, step by step, to a great distance back, both on the paternal and maternal side.†

* A peculiar religious ceremony, like that of *baptism*, is performed for every Hindoo. The Brahmun who does it, and selects a male or female deity for his disciple, is called *gooroo*, or pastor. The disciple, *Shis-ho*, can on no account change his *gooroo* or the god he furnishes. The *gooroo* exercises absolute sway over his *Shis-ho;* just as the "*infallible Pope*" does over the Romanists. Gooroo has the power to send his Shis-ho to heaven or hell as he pleases. Without a passport from him, the "gates of heaven" would not admit the Shis-ho.

† It is customary with the Orientals to commit to memory the names of the distant ancestry. Among the Jews it was th custom, and is so still, I presume. Matthew and Luke traced the genealogy of our Master a great way back.

In this month, the Hindoo women perform religious ceremonies of various sorts. These differ according to the age of the females. The maids, that is the girls under seven, eight, or nine, perform those of an elementary character, which initiate them into higher grades of religious observances. For the amusement of my Christian sisters, I will narrate some ceremonies performed by my sisters in Bengal. "Jom Pooker" (Pluto's Tank) is a vat dug in the earth, nearly three feet square and one foot deep; some water-lilies are planted in it, small alligators and sharks made of earth are put in also; the images of Pluto are placed on the four corners of the tank. Before breakfast the young girl comes, to worship the tank, with flowers. Sitting by it she pours a little water into the tank, then puts flowers on the head of the Plutos, offering prayers in poetry. Here is the translation: "I worship this tank of Pluto. As a reward, I will feed on cream-cakes on plates of gold, and wear *shun-kho* forever." In the afternoon is the worship of *Shā jooty*. There is a large collection of drawings on the floor. This custom is good, in one respect at least, for it requires the girls to draw the pictures of houses, animals, rivers, boats, trees of all sorts, carriages, temples, gods, sun, moon, &c. every day.

The accompanying plate contains "Sha Jooty," with the pictures as drawn by the Hindoo girl. She uses prayers in rhyme, and I will translate one which she offers to *Shiba:* "O, good Shiba, grant that I may not fall in the hands of a dunce."

Now I will leave the girls and see what the married women do in the sacred month. To speak of the matter intelligently, I must proceed in order, because they observe a great many ceremonies from the morning to the afternoon. Where do those women go, with flowers in their little baskets and small pitchers in their hands? They go to bathe in the river; let us follow them and watch their proceedings. See, they take a little water in their hands and sprinkle it over their heads before they go in. The reason is, they deem it sin to touch the sacred Gunga by the foot; but as they have got to go in, they put a little water on the head as a token of reverence, and slowly say, "Mother, forgive!" There you see they turn their faces towards the north as they dive. There are reasons for this too. In the north there is the mountain, Hymalaya, from which the river rises; and, again, it is desirable to have the sun on the right. Facing north, they pay respect to both sacred objects at the same time. What do they put flowers in the water for? That is the way in which the Hindoos worship their gods. Look at the right, a little way off, and you will see the men are doing the same. When I was a little boy, I used to go to bathe with my father, and pick up the beautiful flowers, the rose and lotus, as they floated on the silvery water of the Ganges. But there are other ways of getting flowers; you need not take the trouble of picking them up; simply take one flower from the water, set it on the basket, and the basket with its contents will be yours. Or you may do this: touch the basket with your toe, or smell a flower and drop it over the others. I hated to do such things because it would only trouble the worshippers as well as show our own indecency.

The women have done their bathing and worship; they are filling their brazen and copper pitchers with water; not for their own use; you will see in a minute what they do with it. Strange! why do they walk round that large tree? And what a splendid tree is that! That is the Bannian. I dare say in your geography there is mention of this sacred tree of the Hindoo. They call it *Burr*, and hold it sacred, for in the time of the universal deluge, their god, Un-un (*the Endless*) had floated on a Burr-leaf. The fact, although merely a poetical one, has placed the tree in the rank of the gods. The Hindoos, as you have seen before, worship it, adorn the stem with flower-wreaths, paint it with all sorts of powders, and water the roots with great care. They do not cut and use the bannian wood for fuel. When it grows old, decays, or dies, only one Brahmun out of hundreds would be willing to use it. The laws of the Hindoos protect it, and a fine or some other punishment is inflicted upon a person who should chop it with an axe. But a Brahmun can do it without experiencing any trouble. I think it is an admirable law which protects such a shady tree as Burr. The learned men call it a natural curiosity. Those cord-like roots, now hanging in the air, will, a few years hence, reach the ground and form new stems.

We have followed the Hindoo women back to their houses, now let us patiently witness the rest of their superstitious observances. There, you see, as they go they bow down to the gods of "wood and stone," which crowd the sides of the streets and highways in India.

The servant brings a cow, which these mistaken women would worship, as you will see. First of all, the worshipper pours water on the feet of the cow, as she cannot wash them in any more convenient way; then she puts some oil and yellow powder on her forehead; and gives her some fresh, green grass and bananas to eat. The reason why they worship the cow is this: it is believed that "Doorga," the great goddess, once took the form of a cow, at another, the form of a hawk, and, again, the form of a jackal, and the Hindoos worship them on that account. How much reverence is paid to the cows, and with what care they are treated, will be described by and by.

Fol go-chāno (*Gift of Fruits*).—This religious act is performed by giving some kind of fruit, a *poetha*, and a little money to a Brahmun. This ceremony has its order. In the first year the girl offers a nut, a banana in the second, a cocoa-nut in the third year. After the expiration of the term, the Brahmun who had received the first nut will be entertained at dinner and get a suit of clothes.

Boisak Champaka receives its name from the month in which it is observed, and the flower *champaka*, which is put into a Brahmun's hand to smell. The women take a vow to feed a Brahmun luxuriously every day in this month. As they are forbidden to eat or drink anything until the Brahmun has been fed, and as it often happens that he is not to be found, they secure him by the invitation the day before. Sometimes a Brahmun gets several invitations in one day, but he accepts only the one which comes first. When he comes in, his hostess washes his feet, wipes them with her *un-chol*, the border of the dress, and leads him to a room where he is entertained with all the dainties of the season. Frequently a funny affair at this time takes place in the dining-room. As the custom is for a Hindoo woman to keep silence and veil her face before almost all persons, and as it is a natural desire in young men to see her face, or hear her voice, especially if she is young, the Brahmun guest plays several tricks to accomplish his end. He would not eat heartily, but merely put his hand on this and that, or cut a piece of cake with his teeth as if he had no appetite; hoping his youthful hostess would beg him to help himself. In such cases, she who is faithful to, and a sincere observer of all the rules and discipline of her sex, goes out for a moment to bring some elderly woman with her, who acts her part, though to the utter disappointment of the guest. But if she be regardless of the regulations, and wants a pretext, in that case everything goes on very nicely. He then washes his hands and face after dinner and sits down to rest a little, when she gives him some money to pocket, a few flowers, *Champaka*, to smell, and fans him for four or five minutes.

Matha Bantha comes in the afternoon. Each woman invites one to visit her house, whom she entertains in the following manner. In the first place she anoints her guest with perfuming oil, combs and fixes her hair, and gives a lunch of cakes and confectioneries. The guest is always from the Brahmun caste, but no widow is entertained on the occasion. There are others of the same kind, but I omit them, for, as I fear to increase the bulk of my book, I would use a limited supply of my materials.

The Way-side Hospitality.—It has been observed before that the Hindoo religion teaches some truth, and inculcates acts of charity, in various ways, which at the first appearance look mysterious and foolish. Thus the dedication and distribution of the water-pitcher, fans, umbrellas, etc., in this fiery month, has some visible good meaning. We can see the loving heart of its founder underlying them all. But I am sorry to observe that most of the charitable acts of the Hindoos do not fall like the dews of heaven, blessing the widows, the orphans, and the needy in general. A man desiring to give alms out of his limited means, would pass "the poor, the lame, the blind, and the halt," unnoticed, and offer his gift to a Brahmun, whether he be the true object of charity or not. *The way-side hospitality*, as an act of love, deserves commendation. Although it is a "respecter of persons," it assumes an aspect of universality, and sheds its light over people of all classes, colors, and creeds; even the irrational creatures, the beasts of burden, are recipients of its blessings. Cottages are built by the side of the roads, where the tired passengers refresh themselves, by means of the hospitality of private individuals.

Each cottage has a hired host who asks the passer-by to walk in and be rested. The Brahmuns very rarely go to such places, for it does not seem respectable to them to partake of a charity so public. Low-caste passengers resort to these places, and are entertained with sugar, wet peas, and cold water. Large tubs with water in them are placed outside of the cottage for the cattle and other beasts of burden.

The Hindoos bathe their idols every day in this month. The reason for doing this will be easily known. In this warm month, the Bengalees (most of them at least) bathe themselves twice a day; the young children swim in ponds; even the cattle are led to the water and are bathed. The Hindoo is taught to "serve others like himself," — "*auttio buth sabā*," — so when he feels hungry, thirsty, tired, sleepy, warm or cold, he believes the idols do the same, and he ministers to them under these circumstances as he would like to be ministered to. Hence the images have warm clothes for winter and thin for summer; they are provided with all the necessary comforts of the season. The mode of bathing the idols is the following. After offering the dinner to the gods of stone or metal, the priest puts them on a copper vessel, burying them under fragrant flowers of various kinds, and another vessel with water in it is hung right over the whole. This has some small holes at the bottom, through which water drops on the gods below and keeps them cool thereby. Toolshee, a favorite plant of Krishto, is treated in the same way, only it is not put in a copper vessel. The priest, who has the care of a great many idols in different places, walks round in the evening to take them out of the water, wipes them with towels, and offers them some luncheon to eat. In wealthy families this meal is very luxurious, capable of feeding twenty persons with all the varieties of fruits and confectionery. As this lunch is sent to the Brahmun families, the low castes cannot partake of its contents unless the receiver gives them a little. In a place where there are two or three fame-seeking rich men, the dishes compete with each other to the satisfaction of the Brahmuns, who, of course, get a great deal on this occasion. There are two ways of disposing of the contents of the dish; the one, as I have observed, in sending it to the houses of the Brahmuns in turn, and the other in inviting them to refreshments in the evening.

If the weather be insufferably warm in May, no water or luncheon will be offered unto the idols; the first and last days of April are two impassible limits, which seem to say, "Thus far shalt thou come and no farther." Again, the poor lowest castes cannot be the direct recipients of this charity. They carry the loaded dish by the cottage whose inmates are in poverty, fasting, and helplessness, and leave it at the door of a priest. As I reflect upon the inferiority of the low caste to the Brahmuns, and think that the Hindoos hate to set anything before them which belongs to the priest, I remember the saying, "Give not that which is holy unto the dogs." The low caste is just as polluted to a Brahmun as an unclean beast. If a Brahmun carelessly touch a dog, he will wash himself, and in case he touch a shoemaker or hog-keeper, the same precaution is to be taken!

Thus ends Boisak the first month of the Hindoo year, doing good to the people in general, but caring more for the favored caste, the Brahmuns. The heavenly wisdom says, "God is no respecter of persons." He maketh His sun to rise upon the just and unjust. It tells us to invite, not the proud, rich, and high, but the poor, the lame, the blind, the halt; for such are the true objects of our love and sympathy,— through these channels our love ought to flow like a stream, to soften the parched and dry ground.

CHAPTER II.

JO-ISTO, MAY.

THE WORSHIP OF SHUS-TY. — SON-IN-LAW INVITED.

THIS month has only a few leading religious observances which have no sanction in the Shasturs. The worship of Shus-ty, the watching goddess of the babies, is entirely a female affair. The men pay very little homage to her although they regard it as sacred and help the women in its arrangements. It can be easily understood why this goddess is worshipped, from the fact that the mothers and would-be mothers take much interest in the worship; the childless widows take no part in it. Shus-ty means *sixth*, from the day in which she is adored. It will be remembered that on the evening of the sixth day after the birth of a child this goddess is worshipped with much ceremony; and whenever her general worship comes, it does so on the sixth day of the full moon. Sometimes her image is placed in the water, at others in some conspicuous place in the house. This is quite different from other modes of worship, in regard to some of its peculiarities. A large quantity of plantain, some bamboo leaves and banian leaves are particularly needed.

At the house of some venerable matron, who is widely known for her devotion to the religious ordinances, the women from the neighborhood congregate, bringing with them their respective babies, that they may receive the benediction from the officiating matron. Each woman brings also some raw rice, a certain number of plantains, and a few stitches of cotton thread, which latter they color with yellow powder, and put on round the neck or arms of the children. The fashionable adults do not like to wear this clumsy wet thread on their arms; the mother, by persuasion or force, touches their forehead with this consecrated symbol, and wears it round her own arm for a fortnight, but often she loads her yielding child with the share of those who have refused. The thing which stands as the representation of the goddess is a churning-stick made of bamboo, or sometimes a mill-stone. In some villages there are statues of Shus-ty made of "wood and stone." The honored matron scatters flowers, green leaves, powders, etc., on the image, bathes it with Ganges water, and offers it food to eat, which it cannot do in any visible way. At the close she recites a legendary anecdote of Shus-ty's kindness to the children committed to her care by consecration, and her displeasure over those not duly dedicated to her. Of course, this fills the heart of Hindoo mothers with joy, — that is the thought of having had their children put under the protection of Shus-ty, whose blessing will help them to grow in stature and in life! * On this occasion, the Hindoos invite their sons-in-law to attend the worship. It is a general custom, from the highest to the lowest castes, to entertain their sons-in-law in their houses. It is entirely a matter of social pleasure in its very nature, but, being attached to the worship of the goddess, is considered as a religious institution. If a man has five married daughters he sends letters of invitation to their husbands. In case of one being absent from home, his por-

* Great respect is paid to the cat as the messenger of the goddess. They do not ill-treat this creature for fear of the displeasure of its mistress. Love for animals is taught here in this curious way!

tion of the entertainment, composed of a handsome present of dress and confectioneries, will be forwarded to his parents. Not only to the husbands of daughters is such hospitality shown; it extends in different ways to the husbands of cousins and nieces. When every family in the town has been crowded with these welcome guests, a neighbor invites his friends' sons-in-law. Thus every house wears a garment of festivity. The music and sports are everywhere. If it be the first visit to his father-in-law's house after his marriage, the young man is taxed very much. He is bound by the custom of the place to entertain a pleasure party in a feast. As the women do not meet with men in social gatherings, an extra arrangement is made in the inner department of the house for their satisfaction. It is worth while to observe how in these social pleasures and amusements the Hindoo cannot attain that degree of sociability and love which the Christians have. After eighteen months' stay in America, I can imagine the magnitude of the grand time which this people would enjoy on occasions like this of the Hindoos. In this country, the music, dancing, speeches from both sexes contribute much to the ordinary enjoyments of life, but among the Hindoos the case is quite different. In their festivities or social pleasures we see a conflict between the natural affection and artificial regulations. While one draws toward another with that brotherly love which is implanted in every breast by nature, — the caste system with its hideous features stretches forth its hand to keep them asunder. It spreads four seats, and sets four separate tables for men of four distinct professions. If a man of high caste carelessly treads upon the place where the low castes sit at the meal, he will bathe immediately.

CHAPTER III.

AUSH-ER, JUNE.

THE BATH OF JOGGER-NAUTH.—THE WORSHIP OF THE RIVER GUNGA.

It has been observed in the beginning of this book that the structure of modern Hindooism is the work of time. The fancy, ignorance, and interest of men have decorated its different parts with golden hues which fascinate the senses, and satisfy the minds of the weak. After the laying down of the corner-stone it has received abundant supply of forms and new institutions from various quarters, and consequently grown fast and bulky within a few hundred years. Although it has grown old it retains a healthy, youthful vigor, keeps on growing, and will continue to do so until the "pure and undefiled religion" shall strike like thunderbolts on its thousand cemented headstones, and reduce its tall form to the very base which stands on simplicity, truth, and love.

The bath of Jogger-nauth is comparatively a new institution, and owes its birth to a fictitious legend. There is a great temple of Jogger-nauth in Orissa on the sea-shore above Madras. The images of Jogger-nauth, Bollo-ram his brother, and Shoo-vothra, his sister, are costly, but very awkward, made of a peculiar kind of wood called *Nimbh*. All other Hindoo idols are beautifully constructed in male or female human figures, quite unlike these of Jogger-nauth and his friends, which look neither like man, woman, horse, nor dog. A great many of the Hindoos make fun of Bisho-corma (Universal Artist), who is believed to have built the temple and image of Jogger-nauth. Here is the remark: "The construction of Jogger-nauth has displayed the poor taste of Bisho-corma in delicate arts."

However, the homeliness of the image does not interfere with the reverence and love which the people have for it. I have heard the remarks of those who had visited Jogger-nauth, saying: "That when on our way, which is long, inhospitable, and uncomfortable, I said, Let not my enemy whose ill I seek after come this way; but standing before the gate of the temple, I exclaimed, Would that I had the millions of stars for my eyes, that I could see the 'moon-like face' of the god! O, let the mothers forsake their babies, husbands their wives, and wives their husbands, and come to feast themseves on the sacred graces of Jogger-nauth." It is very natural that they should say so, for there are two ways which guide us in our decision in regard to beauty and accomplishment. To some the external beauty of an object takes the place of an internal accomplishment; while to others the inward accomplishment, tenderness, and purity of character stand instead of the outward beauty of the casket. When we are quite pleased with some charming object, we are apt to take for granted what is not visible in it. And again, when we see an object through the glass of love, it stands before our eyes, if not before the world, with a charm which is rarely visible to others. There is a fine anecdote illustrative of this. A handsome Bengal young man was ridiculed by his friends for his love of a homely woman, whose fine mental and moral culture was unrivalled. The young man begged them to see her through his loving eyes.

The Hindoos sincerely believe that Jogger-nauth is the

great god of the universe, and is full of mercy, grace, and goodness. Hence they overlook the outward defects, and are satisfied with what there is within. An eminent Bengalee gentleman of Calcutta, in one of his books, says: "What a pity it is that a diamond of inestimable worth should sparkle on the forehead of an ugly idol of Orisa." For the information of those who might not have a chance to see a Jogger-nauth, I would describe it just as it is, for it is invariably constructed in the same way everywhere. Its face is circular, and contains an area which would hold almost its whole body; the place where the nose grows is as level as a prairie, his eyes resemble pretty much the Indian snow-shoes in shape, and his arms are mere stumps. I have said before that Jogger-nauth has great influence over the Hindoos, even the obstinate caste system prostrates itself down in his presence. Myriads of men and women visit Orisa annually to attend to the bath and the car of Jogger-nauth ceremonies, which follow each other within a month's interval. The Jogger-nauth, no matter what it is in substance, is a name of significant meaning, "the Lord of the Universe." Jogguth, with various endings, is the common name of persons in India, thus: Joggo Bundhoo, Friend of the Universe; Joguth Chunder, which is my name, means the Moon of the Universe.

Within the enclosure of the temple there is no respect to castes; and that which destroys caste is freely recognized. In the "aunundho bazzar," *market of joy*, which is within the enclosure of the temple, the Hindoos of every caste would eat of one dish, and what is more surprising than that, is to see them walk with rice-curries in their pocket, and putting some into each other's mouth as they pass. But I am sorry to say, that, though brotherhood, the sense of equality, the disregard to castes, is felt and allowed within the walls which surround the temple, no sooner do the people come out of the enclosure than this levelling influence dies an instantaneous death! I have often asked of my Hindoo friends, that if it pleases Jogger-nauth to see love and equality cherished in us for one another, why cannot we do that wherever we live, — at our homes in Bengal as well as in his temple in Orisa? Wherever be our bodies, we are before his presence; the walls cannot hide us from his sight. If he is God Almighty, his eyes will easily penetrate the massive walls to watch his children without.

The bath of Jogger-nauth, as a public religious institution, was unknown to them of olden times. The following circumstance gave rise to it. Jogger-nauth, in disguise of a boy, had come to bathe in the sacred river Ganges. He chose Mahesh, a place fourteen miles above Calcutta, for his appearance. Taking some refreshment at the store of a confectioner named Kalli Shunker, he gave him a golden ornament in exchange, and in a minute disappeared from the store. As a testimony to his divine presence there, a large Nimbh tree bore blossoms of Champaka. The people were surprised beyond measure to see such a miracle wrought on the tree, but none could conceive of the agency which thus manifested its power. The priest of Jogger-nauth not finding the ornament in the person of the god, began to search the temple, bed-room of the idol, etc., for it. Careful inquiry was made in the temple; some junior officers were suspected as having stolen the "sacred property." In the night the chief Panda, votary, saw Jogger-nauth in a dream, and heard him speak as follows: "I had been to bathe in the Gunga yesterday, where at the store of Kalli Shunker, I exchanged my ornament for my lunch; that the fact might be a memorial to the succeeding generations." The story affirms that they found the ornament in possession of the confectioner, which circumstance, together with the Champakas on the Nimbh, proved the affair to the satisfaction of all. Hence is the origin of the institution of "Stau Jatra." From the fact of the god's appearance in Mahesh, although there were hundreds of places on the Ganges, it received great renown as the chosen, favorite place of Jogger-nauth. A wealthy Bengalee gentleman of Calcutta has built a temple and a car on the spot with the outlay of an immense sum of money. The bathing is performed on a high altar made of brick, in the midst of a wide field, which groans under the feet of myriads on this occasion. It is the next exciting scene to that of Orisa, but it excels the other in its licentious shows and amusements.

The next general worship is that of Gunga. Very few images are made of this goddess. They offer the sacrifices on the bank of the river. Every Hindoo family sends offerings of flowers, incense, eatable things, and clothes to her. Its water is believed to have a greater degree of purifying influences on this day than on any other, so that almost every one who can possibly avail himself of this opportunity, bathes in the river. I have seen several men wash their dogs, cats, and birds on this day. It is also believed that the venomous serpents lay their eggs to-day, and if it should rain, the amount of poison would be less dangerous! "Monsha," *the goddess of the serpents*, is worshipped, as her favor is regarded as the only sure protection against poisonous creatures.

There are several noble rivers in India, and why should the Hindoos regard Gunga as sacred so much so that the intrinsic sanctity of its water can redeem men from their sins, however dark they are? A prayer offered universally by the Hindoos to this noble river, reads thus: "Ready

Redeemer of all iniquities, Destroyer of all distress, Giver of happiness and salvation, O Mother Gunga, thou art our only way." Why they hold it sacred above other rivers in Hindostan, is a question of importance which ought to be answered. As the legendary origin of the sacred river of the Hindoos is known only to them, I would venture, having the true knowledge of the same, to describe it, and thereby solve the mystery to those unacquainted with Hindoo mythologies. But earnest as I am to communicate it to my friends, I find a great difficulty in my way. It is a long channel of a story, with tributaries coming into it from various directions. I hardly know where to take it up, and where to leave it, and at the same time to convey the true, distinct knowledge of the origin of the sanctity of Gunga to a Christian reader. I shall not, however, fear the absurdity of the story, as I do not believe it myself, nor ask the reader to regard it as true. Odd as this may sound to any one, it shows him the Oriental method of treating truth, in rich, glowing allegories; the truth is hidden in their bosom. The river Gunga is another representation of the goddess Doorgă, the daughter of the Hymaloy mountain, and the wife of Shiba the Hindoo god. Look at the truth, figuratively expressed! Rivers issuing from the mountains are their sons and daughters, no doubt, as the Hindoos name them, and hence the Gunga is the daughter of Hymaloy. Let us hear the whole story. After the marriage of Shiba with Parboti (mountaineer) or Giriza (mountain-born), the daughter of Hymaloy, the god went to reside in Koylas, a romantic chain of the same mountain. The Hindoo poets call this place finer than any in heaven, which I doubt not that it is, otherwise the god would not have made it his favorite abode. The soil is golden, the trees bend under the weight of delicious fruits, while others smile with bright, fragrant flowers; the breeze is balmy, and the birds handsome, merry, and singing. On a certain day, Doorga was sitting on a golden throne with Shiba, when there appeared a crowd of male and female figures, some with hands broken, others with legs badly bruised, and the rest had their faces turned backwards; in short, all of them were disfigured, maimed, and hurt in the extreme. Shiba smiled at them, at which his wife asked him: "Lord, who are these that stand before us? Their unhappy fate enlists my sympathy; my hands and heart are ready to serve them." Thus, the god replied: "If it would please thee, goddess! to hear from me the names and the circumstances of this injured group before thee, lend thy ears then to the sad story. These are six male and thirty-six female tunes. The children of the earth had attempted to sing them, and not being able to manage harmoniously, have left them a quarter or half-finished; even those who have finished the song, could not preserve the harmony; for a song and a tune are two different things. Therefore, thou seest one is with broken wrist, the second is without nose, the third has his limbs broken, etc." The goddess wanted to know if there was any way of making them whole again. Shiba assured her that there was, and that in *his* own power too; "that these poor suffering *Tunes* had in vain sought redress from the renowned singers on the earth, and finding that human power could not confer upon them the adequate help, are now before me; I will make them whole." Accordingly invitations were sent round the heavens to the gods, and a large audience of the celestial beings was held at the pleroma of Shiba. A Sage invented a musical instrument for the occasion, which was called Tăn poorā, or Tune-perfecter.

I need not say anything about the singing of the god, which satisfied the whole gathering. Now Krishto being naturally mild, delicate, and pleasure-seeking, was so much moved at the music that he perspired. The astonished gods held a counsel, and commissioned Bromha to receive the perspiration that was dropping from his feet in his pitcher "*Comoondul*," and to preserve the sacred relic in his possession. So he did. With a heart overflowing with joy the Creator held his *Comoondul* under the feet of Krishto, for he knew that out of them issued the life and immortality for the Hindoo sinners. They called the *water* (perspiration of Krishto), Gunga. Here is the brief account of the birth of the Sacred River of the Hindoos, showing from what a sacred source it is derived, how and under what circumstances, etc. I will now turn to the fact which brought it into the world from the house of Bromha; which advent is looked upon by the Hindoos with as much joyous enthusiasm as that with which a Christian looks upon Christmas. For there is this point of resemblance between the mission of Christ and that of Krishto: Christ washes the sin of the world, however dark it is, with his blood; while, on the other hand, the perspiration of Krishto redeems the Hindoos from their sins, washes away the impurities that stain their lives, and brings immortality to the dead and lost. Indeed, to a Hindoo a drop of water of Gunga is itself a Life and Light, and the only way to enter into the everlasting joys in the Goluck of Krishto. Christ saw Satan fall from the sky; his advent took out the sting of Death, so we hear the stories of *Jom* (Death) complaining of the emptiness of his womb or cell. Frequently we read the account of the quarrel between the angels of Krishto and *Jom* touching the fate of a man who, spending his whole life in sin and unbelief, had thrown himself into the water of the Ganges in his last moments. The services of Ganges are more beneficent to the Hindoo than the blood of Christ to the Christian. We are taught to believe in Christ, — his holy mission, — his fulness of knowledge and sanctification; but it is quite a different case with a Hindoo. Even if he did not believe in the sanctifying influence of his religious nature, and the redeeming power of the Gunga, he goes to heaven, provided his body or ashes are thrown into its sacred water. Hence the bank of the Gunga has been a Cross to the Hindoo; it has been the best place for them in which to die that they may live again. Thousands — young and old, male and female, pious and sinful — are brought hither to breathe their last, to throw off corruption and ascend the Goluck of Krishto. To a Hindoo *death* in or near to his Sacred River is a *Gain*. The true end of his being is accomplished if he succeeds in dropping in and dying near the Ganges, or Gunga.

The following is an universally-believed account of the advent of the Sacred River of the Hindoos into the world. The Book containing it is read and expounded by the learned and eloquent priests to the listening crowds. The children read it in their school-books, and the Hindoo monks sing it from place to place. There was an illustrious family called Shoòjo Bungshoor, the Offspring of the Sun, and which has been made immortal by Balmica in his celebrated poem Ramayona, as being the tribe which Rama, the great god, chose, and of which he became a member. In this family there lived a king of the name of Saugor, renowned in and esteemed by his time. To use the Hindoo phrase, he was a terror to the tyrants and a friend to the peaceable, help to the needy and the delight of the age he lived in. It was customary with the ancient Hindoo kings to do "Ausho' med," a religious ceremony, to extend his power, peace, help, love, etc., all over the world. When a king has succeeded in this, has brought every country on the surface of the globe under his power and protection, the throne of Indra will be his reward. The throne of Indra had been aspired to by several kings, but none of them ever reached the prize, the reason being that he used to interfere with their plans, frustrate their precaution, and cause them to desist from the undertaking forever. The leading features of this ceremony of Ausho' med, and the ways in which it used to be conducted, are these: A horse, bearing on his forehead the inscription, "Let *him* who denies the power of the master catch the horse," was sent round the country to the dominions of kings and nobles, accompanied, however, with armed soldiers. The horse was sent about the land for the purpose of demanding submission from the world. In some places he travelled unmolested, and securing submission for his lord; and wherever the people did stop him, it was understood that they hated the yoke of dependence. The soldiers would immediately inquire distinctly the real motive of the man who stopped the horse, whether it was curiosity or a mistake or a purpose that actuated him. If it were a mistake, or fancy, they would pardon him, and recover the horse and unfurl the banner of their king on the spot. If otherwise they would resort to war. This Saugor, the celebrated king, forwarded his "sixty thousand" sons in a triumphal expedition, into all the countries known at his time.* They visited the uttermost parts of the world, ascended the mountains, crossed the rivers, proclaimed the

* It is surprising to learn that one man had "sixty thousand sons," all grown-up, reliable heroes at the same time; numerous as the sands on the sea-shore. The Hindoos say this host of sons was born to fulfil the prophecy of a Brahmun who had blessed the king, sáying, perhaps, "Be thou the father of sixty thousand male children."

power of the name of their illustrious father, and brought almost all the world into subjection. Arriving at a place near the sea, the princes congratulated each other on their success; and finding no place where to direct their steps, resolved to return home to their longing father, who, on their successful return, would perform the ceremony. Elated with joy at the success of their mission, they all sat down on the sea-shore to review their past adventures, while the majestic waves of the sea rolled before them, defying their power, and with thundering voice declared the power of Him who alone can tell them, "Thus far shall you come and no farther." The cool, balmy breezes from the neighboring forests blew upon them; their joyous spirits felt the weariness of the flesh, and one after another the veteran princes wore the garment of sleep; while the horse, incapable of musing upon the glorious career he had gone through and the victories he had won, bent his eyes upon the green, shaggy ground before him. The place was so remote from the populous country, that while it was mid-day there reigned a death-like silence; no "hurries and bustles," no sound of mechanics' hammer were heard there, save that the distant sea thundered now and then. The only inhabitant of the place was a Saint Copeel, who, retiring from the active, pleasure-seeking community, had selected this romantic spot for his hermitage, to spend his life in prayer and fasting.

Now Indra, the king of the sky, who had been watching the progress of these princes with an anxious eye, left his airy throne, descended upon the earth in the form of a man, and stood on the very spot where the children of Saugor unconsciously lay. "They have," he said to himself, "obtained victory almost over the whole world, and enlisted all the crowned heads as their subjects; there is no one under the sun to catch their *horse* or to obstruct their triumphal course. If they return to their father to crown him with the world's victory, to place the vanquished sovereigns as stools under his feet, Krishto would offer him the supremacy of the sky. I too, hitherto the lord of the gods, should become his subject. It is not too late yet. Let me seek a Brahmun's wrath to turn the course of the princes. Krishto's will be done," he said, and in a moment he held the rein of the triumphal horse. He led him to the cottage of Copeel, tied him by his side, and ascended the cloud for his palace, and from thence looked down at the result.

Now the tired sun seeks his home beyond the western seas, the singing tenants of the air bound towards their leafy homes, the wild beasts in yon forests return to their lairs, while others leave their dens; and the canopy of darkness is spread over the creation. It was then that the sons of Saugor rose from their grassy bed. "Early in the morning," they say, "we guide our steps towards home — the blessed spot on the earth! The greetings of our friends, the tender arms of our parents will receive us. The Aushómed will be celebrated in the presence of the astonished world; the vanquished kings will be invited, the Brahmuns worshipped, the poor entertained, the music, dance, and feast will be observed, and the earth will wear a garment of mirth!" Early in the morning they arrange their things to start for their home. "Bring the horse," one says, "where is he?" Some go after the horse, but do not find him. He has gone to the forest they think, and a party go in search of the beast. In vain they roamed through the woods! The horse could not be found. After a day's toil, they come near the cottage of Copeel, and, to their utter surprise find the object of their search, tied near the altar of the Saint. The venerable saint presented a curious sight to the princes. He had a piece of "tiger's skin" for his raiment, his hair flowing down his shoulders in graceful curls, eyes closed, hands folded. They took him for a horse-thief. Still as the rule of the *ceremony* would not permit them to recover the horse without the consent of the supposed thief, they called on him to answer for his conduct. But, alas! there was no sensibility in him. His heart and soul have bade farewell to the world's pleasures, and been fixed upon the throne of Krishto. He did not know what was going on around him. The princes grew tired of waiting for the answer from Copeel, and began to speak to him in the following way: "Friend, if you are really afraid of us, and feel sorry for what you have done, say so; we shall choose mercy and not sacrifice. We have sworn before the gods to protect the horse, and, wherever he is caught, not to recover him in secret. What object have you in bringing the horse here? Is it poverty, pride, or fancy that actuated you to hold the triumphal horse of Saugor? Return our horse to us, and we will pardon you, and give you other horses if you wish for them; or if you dare to be our rival, tell us distinctly, that we may take the necessary course." The entreaties, persuasions, reasonings, threatenings, effected nothing. It seemed as if they spoke to a senseless statue. Failing in their efforts to adjust the matter satisfactorily to both parties, and knowing it would be shameful to carry away the horse, one of them kicked the innocent Brahmun. The insulting touch of the foot to his sacred person broke the spiritual dream of Copeel; he felt this intrusion in the extreme; thought some evil spirits were trying to endanger his life; he looked upon the sons of Saugor in wrath, and they were instantly burnt to ashes.* The account of this disaster

* This, and kindred anecdotes, have great effect upon the practical life of the Hindoos, because they are thereby taught to believe that their own

reached the anxious king, who came himself to the spot to soothe the injured Brahmun with prayer and worship, and thereby to beg of him the salvation of his sons.*

The Saint Copeel took pity upon the king, and said that the only way to redeem the souls of his sixty thousand sons was the blessing of Gunga, then in possession of Bromho. Saugor returned to his own palace, and soon after joined his sons in the upper world.

Now the gods assembled in heaven to consider what was to be done towards the sons of Saugor or his family. As there was no male child in it to help its growth, the first and the last fell before the wrath of the Brahmun. This Bongsho (*Stock*) is to be preserved, or Rama will not come out of it for the redemption of the world. Accordingly a Monie (saint) was sent to this family of widows to bless and console them in their sorrows. At the presence of the Monie at the door, one widow came forward to receive him, and fell down on the ground to kiss his sacred feet. "Be thou the mother of a child, daughter!" were the words of

---

good or bad deeds will bring forth fruits for them according to their nature, — that by the mete by which they measure others will be measured unto them. They are thus taught the Divine justice, — that God is not a silent spectator of our proceedings: He notices everything, and meets us according to our merit. Again, such anecdotes have another influence upon the Hindoo mind. The Hindoos fear to insult a Brahmun, whose wrath is warm enough to burn the offender to ashes. But the Brahmun's wrath does not amount to any visible danger now.

* This teaches a beautiful lesson of the nature of reconciliation, although wrapped in the allegorical covering of superstition. We see that none but the injured can forgive us, — that we ought to be reconciled to him, and *redress* the wrong we have done if possible; for without reformation, mere repentance is nothing. The Hindoo idea is, that even the gods do not stand by the side of the offender if he does not humble himself and ask pardon, that is, if he be not reconciled to his brother whom he had ill-treated. It is something like the saying, "Make peace with thy brother while *he* is on the way," etc.

blessing that fell from the lips of the Brahmun. The embarrassed woman rose from the ground, and with tears in her eyes addressed him as follows: "Lord, thy daughter is a widow; how then should she be a mother? It has pleased Krishto to extinguish the family of Saugor, so at once the sixty thousand sons perished in the wrath of Copeel! Thou knowest all this, — the magnitude of the sad story, holy father!" "Be comforted, daughter, lament not," the Brahmun said; "the sons of Saugor will be redeemed and his family be continued, for Rama has chosen it for his incarnation. My words that have fallen upon thee *must* be fulfilled. It is the will of the gods that thou shalt bring forth a son for the redemption of the family. He will find favor in the sight of Gunga, who, leaving the house of Bromho, shall come into the world first to wash away the iniquities of the sons of Saugor, and then of the world in general." In due time the widow queen, at the visitation of the blessing of the saint, gave birth to a son, which circumstance brought universal joy to the world. The Brahmuns came to bless the babe, and called him by the name of Vogiroth. The child, owing to the peculiar circumstances of his birth, had no bones in his body; was a mere lump of flesh, could not walk or move about without making awkward gestures.* As he was busy one day in arranging his playthings, a Monie called him Oshto Bunko. (He was very awkward in his

* In the Hindoo poems it has been shrewdly accounted for why Vogiroth had no bones in him. I am well acquainted with it, but think it not of much consequence to detail. Again, there is another thing to be considered, the adaptedness of the expression to the taste of a Christian reader. Every nation has its peculiar taste in regard to the idiom and expression of thought; what is decent with one is immodest with others. I see some expressions in the Bible which are not permitted to be used to the English or American people. The Oriental nations understand their peculiar meaning when they use those phrases.

person, and crooked; so they called him by the name, "eight curves," his body being in so many places broken perhaps.) The prince, although only four years old or more, had been trained by his mother to salute the Brahmuns reverently, and to pay them the due homage. Seeing the Brahmun coming before him, he left his playthings in order to salute him, but, being without bones in his body, his movements enraged the object of his worship. The Brahmun thought the boy was making fun of him, by imitating his ungraceful gestures; and thus interpreting the child's innocent deeds, cursed him. "Proud prince, darest thou mock my awkward person, which Krishto has given me? In despising my person thou dost despise my maker. Let it be according to thy will; if pride has led thee to mock at me, be thou awkward like me; and if owing to some defect in thy own person thou didst make the irreverent gestures, be thou whole, and henceforth live a handsome child." To the joy of the child and his relatives, the "cursing of the Brahmun begat blessing," at that very moment he stood before the saint with a well-proportioned, stout, and handsome person!

At the age of five he was put under the tuition and guidance of a celebrated sage. Besides the mental and physical training, the sage took particular care to develop the spiritual nature of his pupil, to set his infant step in the path of truth, to inspire his simple heart with the love for the gods. His relations did not bring the knowledge of the great calamity that had befallen the family to the child's notice. Every precaution was taken to keep from his knowledge even the word *father*. One day, as he was playing with the young children in the neighborhood, he heard them ask each other's father's name. The turn came to him, and a boy asked him what his father's name was. A difficult question to answer, for he had never heard the name of *father* in his house, and never seen a *man* who was so related to him, except the teacher and other Brahmuns, who often came to console the widows with their kind words. "Friends," he said, "ask the names of my mother, aunts, teacher, &c., and I will tell you ; I do not know who my father is. In our house we have no such relative." The children burst into laughter, to the mortification of Vogiroth, and began to express their surprise in their childish way. The fatherless prince left his gay comrades for his mother, who he hoped would adjust the matter, and teach him to answer the questions of the children in future. The joke of the boys had pained him so much that his blooming face seemed pale. Embarrassment threw a thick veil on his forehead, and it looked like the moon in eclipse. His hasty steps trod the chamber floor, and drew the anxious household around him. "Mother!" burst forth the insulted child, "I was very much pained by unkind words of the boys, one of which I did not fully comprehend, so I came to you to have it explained. Strange words, mother, they uttered, which I alone among them was unacquainted with. '*Father*'*!* what does it mean? The boys asked me the name of my *father*, which I could not tell; where is my father, and what is his name, mother?" The troubled queen heard the sad recital with sighs; and, as the child seemed determined to know all about the mysterious term *father*, she could not keep the fact in secret any longer. "Krishto's will be done," she said; and reviewing all the circumstances that characterized the child's birth, unfolded the sad fate of the family to the eager ears of Vogiroth, — how the sixty thousand sons of Saugor were consumed to ashes by the Brahmun whom they had insulted, &c. Every word that fell from the lips of the queen penetrated the soul of the child, and filled his heart with deep longing about the redemption of his ancestors. "Mother, is there any power in the world that can redeem them from their cursed death?" "There is none, child! The insulted Brahmun has kindly told us that the sacred water of Gunga would wash their sins, if that could be brought into the world." "Where is the abode of Gunga, mother, and who is she that washeth away the sins of men?" Trusting to Gunga, as the result of these inquiries, the queen informed the child of the name and attributes of the goddess. The child seemed to be satisfied with these explanations. Calmness passed upon his stormy soul, but it was for a short time only. He felt anxious to know how the blessings of Gunga could be obtained; he believed it was his duty, as the offspring of Saugor, to serve the spiritual good of his family, and thereby blot out the stain which it had brought upon itself by insulting the Brahmun. But he was too young for the undertaking; a mere child of five, strong and manly as his will appeared to be. At the usual hour of the day, his tutor, the Brahmun sage, came to the palace, and the child took his seat at his feet. He could not recite his lesson with the usual facility; he looked sober, and that was enough to apprise the tutor of the sad state of his pupil's mind. Affectionately drawing him close to his breast, he asked him to tell him what ailed him, and was surprised at the recital. The child begged him to favor him and help him in the undertaking, as he had fully determined to obtain the mercy of Gunga, to redeem the children of Saugor, even if it would cost his life. He further desired the sage, in that simplicity and inexperience that are peculiar to his age, to inform him of the place of Gunga, — how he could arrive there, how long it would take, and how much it would cost, what kind of a person Gunga was, etc. The venerable sage attempted in vain to dissuade him from the enterprise, saying it was hardly possible for an ordinary man to have an interview with the great goddess in this world of sin; that the sages have spent their lives in prayer and fasting, away from home and kindred, amidst the wilderness and its ferocious inhabitants, without any material success; that the heavenly hosts — the gods — desire to see the goddess, but cannot. The child heard all these with much solicitude; and, instead of reflecting upon the discouraging aspect of the case set before him by his teacher, asked him one more question. It was, by what *address* he should call upon the Gunga, — what relation she bore to him? "She is the Mother of the universe," the sage replied, "and whoever wants to come unto her, will find that address appropriate and sacred." The child overflows with joy on hearing that the goddess is his mother; the dark prospect before him vanishes away, and he sees the path easy and sunny. "What," said he, "shall I fear to go to my mother? The sweet name! It will melt the heart of the goddess, even if it were made of rock. I do not know the way; but *faith* will surely offer its service and be my guide; the *Kanon* wilderness is infested with savage beasts; my *love* will charm them: there are other obstacles indeed; my firmness will surmount them all." Emboldened by such thoughts, and being determined to reach the prize, he revealed his cherished plan to the trusting heart of his mother.

After a long discussion, which, of course, took place on the occasion, she being assured by a "*divine voice*" of the child's successful mission, gave her reluctant consent. A Hindoo poet describes the parting scene to the following effect. The little pilgrim stood before the weeping household to bid them farewell. The queen, conscious of the happy success that will crown her son, and unable to resist the influence of her affection toward him, could neither bid him *stay* nor *go*. It required an effort to utter either. "Great Goddess Doorga," she prayed, "thy handmaid commits her babe — her only child — to thy protection. Let thy all-seeing eyes watch his steps, thy loving-kindness minister unto his wants. Mother Earth! whose name is Patience, do not take any offence which the infancy of my child is liable to offer unto thee! Lofty, wide-spreading trees! you whose branches form canopies over the earth and obstruct the sun's rays, shield my little one under your shade, — when he is tired, let him rest under your branches, — when hungry, feed him with your fruits, and when in danger, inform me of it by nodding your heads that reach the sky. Wild beasts! be ye friendly to him. Do not prick his tender feet, ye thorns; and ye stones, do not hurt them by any means. Day, when you bid farewell to the world, commit my child to the hand of your successor; and Night, when you retire, put him into the hands of Day; and finally, do you both, good Day and Night, return him safe to the anxious arms of his mother." The legend proceeds on with the young pilgrim, who bids good-by to his dear mother and other relatives, and starts on his journey into the wilderness.* The Hindoo poets paint the early part of this

---

* This is one of the leading features of Hindoo piety. In order to secure the blessing of a god or goddess, it is essentially needful to withdraw ourselves from the world, and take a vow to spend a certain portion, or the whole of our life in the wilderness; to abstain from food, drink, and recreation, and gradually to bring ourselves to that state in which we do not live by "bread alone," but by "every word that proceedeth out of the mouth of God." We read in the lives of the Hindoo sages the process they had used to subdue their bodies, by continual fasts and self-torture. In the early part of their hermit life, they used to take a little food once a day, then once in two, and after a while one meal at the end of the week. In warm weather their seat was surrounded by a blazing fire made on purpose, and in winter they used to immerse their bodies in water, and pray.

child's life in the desert with amusing colors. Wandering a few days among the wild trees, with no word save "Mother Gunga" in his mouth, he thinks the time has already come for an interview with the goddess; he encounters a wild beast, and taking it for the messenger of Gunga, addresses it in the following way: "Did you come from my Mother Gunga, to bring me hope and consolation? Glad I am to know that my prayers and tears have reached her gracious throne, and met with success. Tell me, noble friend, what message have you for me, the little pilgrim," etc. Year after year rolled away, leaving young Vogiroth at his altar in the wilderness. The goddess, although she was all the time walking with and watching him invisibly, did not bid his troubled heart be still. Now she sends her angels to tempt him, and try his faith and adherence to the undertaking, who now frown upon him with their hideous appearances, then urge him to go back to his home, alleging the undertaking was too difficult for him; sometimes they promise the world's supremacy, — the pleasures of the Kirnoras, — provided he will give up his cherished plans, etc. But he heeded little their temptations, and aiming at the mark, made his way through trials and temptations with manly fortitude.

At last pity awakes in Gunga's breast. She comes to bless the child, stands before him, puts her divine hands upon his head, seats him on her lap, and assures him of her protection forever. When the boy begged her to come into the world and redeem the children of Saugor, the goddess at first declined, but at the unceasing prayer and earnest entreaties of the child she consented to come. Now who should receive the sacred stream, as it flows down from the Pitcher of Brahma, was a difficult question, for it was feared the earth would be torn to pieces by the force of the sacred stream. Shiba, at the solicitation of the young saint, volunteered to receive Gunga on his head, when it should fall from the pitcher of the Creator; but the goddess, proud of her own strength, feared he would not be able to sustain its fury. He read the secrets of her heart, bent his head to receive the stream, and detained it for some time within his curls, thereby giving the goddess some idea of his astonishing power. It is to be observed here, that the sacred water, as it issued from the possession of Brahma, divided itself into *three drops*, or equal portions,—the one ascended to heaven in the name of Monda Kenū, the second descended to the region under the earth in the name of Vōgōbuthy, and the third, Wlluk-non'dā, remained on the earth,—thus at once sanctifying three different spheres. Now as, if the stream should run, it surely would wash away cities, towns, and whatever happened to be on its way, it was thought prudent to open channels in the earth, in desolate places, that it might course through them. Human power was too inadequate for the purpose. Oyrabut, the mighty elephant of Indra (King of heaven), was called upon, and by means of his teeth he dug a grand canal on the earth. The legend says, that as the compensation of his labor he demanded the hand of the goddess, and she in wrath rushed upon him, breaking his bones to pieces.

As the stream glided along, it happened to sweep away the Kasa of a Monie.* The Brahmun drank the whole stream, and drained the canal of its last drop. Vogiroth fell at his feet, told him the sad story of his undertaking, and begged him to return Gunga to him; because, without her water, his family would find no salvation.

---

* Kasa, a copper vessel used by the Hindoos in their religious services, to put water in, which they sprinkle on their heads and upon the idols also.

The venerable Brahmun complied with the prayer of the child, but knew not how to bring the sacred stream out of his stomach, as it would be irreverent and wicked to let it issue through either of the Nobo-dār, nine openings of the body.

Considering the matter seriously, he at last tore the skin of his Janoo, knee, and the river flowed out of the opening. Hence, another name of Gunga is Jarnovy. She inquired of the child how far there was yet to go, and where the ashes of his ancestors were deposited. He could not answer at all, so she became hundred-headed, and went in different directions in search of the ashes of the children of Saugor. Thus do the Hindoos account for so many mouths of the Ganges that meet the sea.

Such is the legend of Gunga, the sacred river of the Hindoos. It is universally believed to be a true account of the goddess. The place where the river meets the sea, particularly near the Saugor Island, is regarded as a sacred spot, and is visited by the Hindoos once a year, in the month of *Maugh*, or January. Here the assembled myriads bathe in and worship the Gunga. It being more than an ordinary bath, and performed in such a sacred spot as the Sungh-um — the confluence of Gunga with the sea — it is deemed by very many necessary to avail themselves of the opportunity, and make the best possible use of the occasion. Before plunging the body into water, the man stands near the Brahmun priest, and confesses to God whatever sin he has committed and can possibly remember.

This is the Hindoo mode of Repentance.

We are told of a real conservative priest of Eastern Bengal, who would have his people confess audibly and distinctly the iniquities they had committed, specifying them by their name, nature, and circumstance, and thus making the matter worse, after all.

But now the confession is made and heard by the individual sinners themselves; no ears of the priest or bystanders hear anything. It is believed that the goddess, who heareth in secret, shall forgive and reward them openly.

In conclusion, it would not be out of place, I think, to speak, in this connection, of the reverence the Hindoos pay to their Sacred River. The long arms of caste cannot reach a victim if he happens to be on its water. In sailing as well as in row-boats, which crowd on the Ganges, the members of all castes sit side by side, talk to each other, smoke their *hookas*, and take their luncheon; but these things *could not* be done in a vehicle on land. A Brahmun would eat his luncheon on a boat having a low-caste man, — a shoemaker, perhaps, — only a few feet from him, because the holiness of the river takes away, in some degree, the difference that exists between the two castes.* They sprinkle its water upon everything almost, for purifying purposes. Those who bathe in ponds drop a few drops of Gunga water on their heads. A Hindoo who would speak lies, or bear false witness against his brother, with a hard heart, if urged to do it with a cup of Ganges water in his hand, would keep his conscience clear, for he will not dare to speak lies then!

In courts of justice the witnesses had to touch the holy water in giving their depositions; now they are simply reminded of its presence. If any one should speak *truth*, calling the Gunga for his witness, it is regarded sinful. It often happens that when a rich man is robbed of his gold or

---

* When I speak of the low castes, I hope the reader will not feel sensitive, for I know the very classes of men who are high in Christian countries are low in India. A great many men engaged in shoemaking business move about as the "*upper ten*," and are high caste in this country, while among the Hindoos such persons, notwithstanding their opulence (which begets high caste here), are lowest indeed.

silver, and the police recovers it, he is required to claim it by *oath*, that is, by touching the water of the Ganges, but he would not. The very idea of swearing or taking oath in the presence of an adorable object is abominable to him; he would rather go away poor and suffering than retain or acquire money that way. In order that it might be regarded most solemnly, the Hindoos believe that when a man swears falsely in the name of a holy person or thing, not only he is condemned, but also "fourteen ancestors" suffer for it. There are, however, thousands who do not observe all these rules. I speak of the rules themselves.

CHAPTER IV.

SHRA-BUN, JULY.

THE ROTH JATRA, OR THE CAR OF JOGGER-NAUTH.

FOREIGNERS in general, misled by the reports of missionaries, have some incorrect ideas of the worship of Jogger-nauth by the Hindoos. They say that the Hindoos throw themselves under the wheels of his car, as a voluntary sacrifice, and are crushed to death. I do not agree with them in this assertion, although I have no sympathy with any of the forms of worship of my countrymen. The "Car of Jogger-nauth," as foreigners call it, is worshipped and drawn for a different purpose. The ceremony connected with it has its origin in the following legendary incident, which, to me appears a historical one. Krishno, an incarnation of Bishno, was the only child of Joshoda and Nuntho of Gocool, — the modern Agra. Kong-sho, the tyrant king of Mothoora, made a great Jogeo, — a religious festival, and invited the sovereigns and people of various countries to attend it. Nuntho, the father of Krishno, being the king of Gocool, was respectfully invited to appear at the court of Kong-sho, with his son, whose chivalry was then the popular object of admiration. As a token of especial honor, Occroor, a sage widely known for his eminent piety, was commissioned by Kong-sho to bring the young prince of Gocool to the festival. He accordingly went with a Roth or car

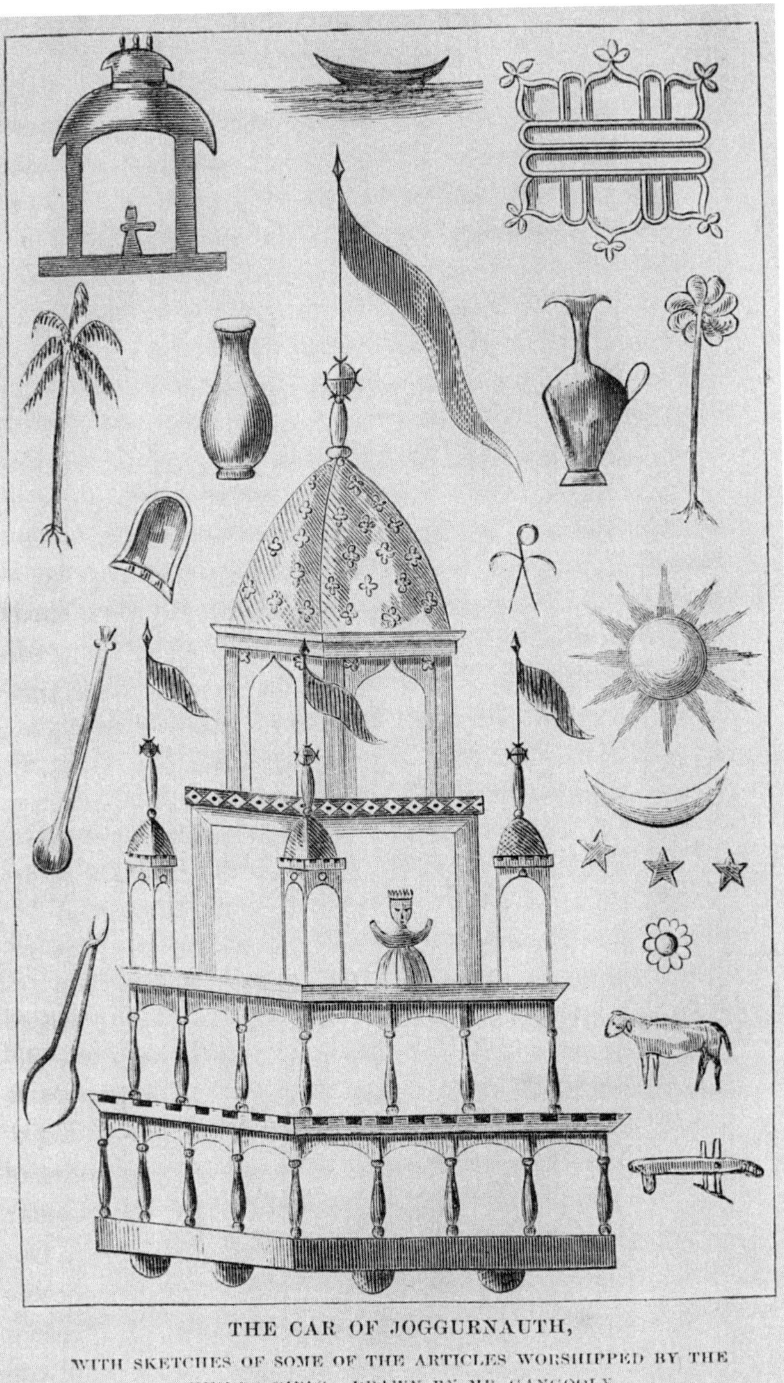

THE CAR OF JOGGURNAUTH,

WITH SKETCHES OF SOME OF THE ARTICLES WORSHIPPED BY THE HINDOO GIRLS. DRAWN BY MR. GANGOOLY.

for that purpose. Krishno went with the sage, and did not return to his parents again. Now to commemorate his departure from his native land, the "Car of Jogger-nauth" has been instituted, which is worshipped and drawn as follows.

The cars are constructed of different sizes, but the shape is always the same. They are of the form of a pyramid; square at the base, and become pointed at the top. Some are of stupendous size, being fifty feet high, more or less, and beautiful wooden statuary and paintings adorn them from top to bottom. A car has five, nine, or thirteen cupolas, the highest, or main one, is the seat of the idols. As it is drawn, the bells ring and silken flags wave on the cupolas. There are four cars in my village, and I will speak of them. The first was dedicated by a rich landholder, the second by the high-priest of the priests, the third by a dairyman, and the fourth by a rich Brahmun widow, who settled in our village a few years ago. Her car is said to be one of the handsomest, with nearly fifty statues, and a large silver *chuc-cross*, the throne and ornaments of the idol are of gold.

In the morning of the day in which the car is drawn thousands of people are entertained at the dinner, by the owner. In the afternoon the procession is formed before the car in the following manner. Men walk in rows with flags in their hands; the bands with hundreds of drums, flutes, cymbals, etc., — the Krith-on, or a band of singers who sing the praises of Krishno alone. The car in motion, drawn by hundreds, makes a tremendous noise, and grinds everything to powder that comes under its solid wheels. It is everywhere believed in Christian countries that the Hindoo devotees throw themselves under the Car of Jogger-nauth in order to be crushed to death. But that is not a true statement of the case. Self-torture is practised, sacrifices are offered, and in many cases even suicide is committed, to satisfy some Hindoo deities, but nothing of this nature is allowable before Jogger-nauth. He does not take delight in cruel, bloody shows. His love for his creatures is so great that no animal food is offered to him. His worshippers, a peculiar sect of the Hindoos, called Boish-tule, do not kill or eat fish, nor look on pictures representing scenes of battle, murder, or assassination. The loss of lives under the Car of Jogger-nauth is owing to the carelessness of the people. It is believed by them that he who pulls the ropes attached to the car will be carried away after his death, to the heaven of Krish-no by his Pooshpo Roth, — flowery car. Elated by the false promise of heaven, an immense crowd comes forward to give at least three pulls of the sacred car, and some among them accidentally falling down are trodden by the feet of men or crushed by the wheels of the car. I have seen four stout men go to heaven that way, being ground to pieces by the car of the rich widow mentioned above. Of course, while a Hindoo, I believed like the others, but do not remember of ever drawing the car at all. Being a Brahmun, and widely known as a sincere lover of the idols, I used to sit on the top of the car, fan the idols, receive the shower of flower-garlands from the crowd and throw them again at the men, women, and children below as a benediction. Such was my devotion and affection to the images, that while almost everybody deserted the car on account of a heavy shower, I alone sat by and took care of the idols, believing they would reward me abundantly hereafter! No worship of the Hindoos is free from some act of immorality or vice. The Brahmuns, especially the young ones, from the high seats on the car, find out, with keen eyes, and lustful hearts, some handsome females in the crowded street, or in the house-top, and hit them severely with the bananas.

There is no Scriptural reference to the place where the car shall stop. It is sometimes carried to the distance of a mile and is left there for seven days, during which time the idols are worshipped in some temple or house built or hired for the purpose. On the eighth day the car is drawn back to its former place, where it remains motionless until the next year. They make large eyes for the car with paint, that it may look at all and be careful not to crush any cruelly. After the death of four men under the car in my village it was found that the painter had not drawn the eyes on the top of the car!!!

CHAPTER V.

VAUTHRO, AUGUST.

THE BIRTHDAY OF KRISHNO.—FASTING AND WORSHIP ON THE OCCASION.—REJOICING OF NUNTHO; THE WORSHIP OF MONSHA,—A GODDESS WHOSE MESSENGERS ARE SERPENTS, ADDERS, TOADS, ETC.

THE Hindoo mythology relates the birth of Krishno as having taken place in this month, on the "eighth day after the full moon." He was born to redeem the world, which was then trembling under the feet of a tyrant. His parents were in a humble prison at the time of his advent. In the presence of the heavenly babe the fetters that bound the prisoners were broken asunder, the cell began to dazzle, joy and sorrow overwhelmed the unhappy parents. "A heavenly voice" whispered to the father to fly with the child to Gocool, across the river Jomuna, which was immediately done. The tyrant who sought to destroy the child felt mortified, seeing his precaution frustrated, and sent some messengers to kill all the infants in the neighboring places.

The Hindoos hold this day sacred, and spend it in fasting and worship. They abstain entirely from food and drink for more than thirty hours, at the end of which Krishno's image is worshipped, and the story of his birth is read to the hungry worshippers. In connection with the birth of Krishno comes Nunth-sobe,—the rejoicing of Nuntho, the king, in whose palace the infant Krishno was left in the shade of night.

On this occasion the Hindoos anoint themselves with all

sorts of perfumatory oil, attar of rose, etc., and spend three days in grand festivities, music, and dancing.

On the thirtieth of this month is the worship of Mōnshā, which, on account of a singular feast that accompanies it, is quite different from others of the same sort. The name of this feast is Ur-run-thun. Cooking is strictly forbidden on this day; no fire is to be put in the oven. They cook all their food the evening before, with much care and ceremony, such as offering prayers to the goddess, sounding the sacred shell, etc.

In the morning of the thirtieth, the cactus trees are worshipped, which grow high in India. The stem is washed, and anointed; flower wreaths are hung on the branches, the sacrifice of a he-goat offered, etc. As the messengers of the goddess are serpents, and cannot be conveniently handled, their pictures are worshipped with due respect and awe.

CHAPTER VI.

AUSHEEN, SEPTEMBER.

THE DOORGA POOJA.

THIS is the grand worship of the Hindoos. Men of humble circumstances cannot bring the image of Doorga into their houses, because it requires a large amount of money to make the necessary preparations. The image itself is always the largest and most expensive; to speak nothing of other things which, though economically arranged, demand a large sum. Fifteen days or more before the worship, the whole country is in excitement. Men who, under various circumstances in life, spend their days as exiles in distant places, come home on this occasion to greet their dearest relations once more. The distribution of presents to, and reception of them from, the friends and neighbors is universally observed. Even the very poor, low-caste man, who can barely clothe his children in winter, and must go barefooted all the time, would buy new dresses, shoes, etc., for his little ones, in the Doorga pooja holidays. The rich, charitable Hindoos give Barshick — an annual gift of money and new clothes — to the Brahmuns, as well as to the domestics and poor people, that they may not appear naked and grieved before Doorga, their common mother. The amount of the sale of all sorts of articles is proverbial, — "The very dust of the Doorga pooja market is dear;" "There was such a crowd at the store that you could crack twenty heads by one stroke,"—such are the phrases they use to describe the market in September. The mechanics, the artists, the jewellers, the farmers, bring the results of their respective labor and skill to contribute to this occasion. But notwithstanding the joyous festivities, the presents and profusion, I am sorry to say the thing has a hideous feature. Those who spend their means in wicked and riotous living desire more than usual, on these days, to satisfy their own sensual appetites, and those of their wicked companions; and, failing to do it, resort to unfair means, and act as thieves, pirates, and murderers. The penitentiaries are crowded with these unfortunate people, who, hoping to spend the holidays merrily, live wretchedly under the strict regulation of the prison and the weight of their fetters! A sad contrast indeed! Before I describe the image, the preparation, and the worship, I will consider who the Doorga is, whom my country regards as the great goddess.

Doorga was the only child of Hymaloy and Manoka, who ruled the mountainous region of India in times of yore. There is a great deal of mysterious conjecture in regard to the name and nature of Hymaloy, the father of the great goddess; and I would bring them to the notice of my Christian readers. A story universally believed by the Hindoos, says: In ancient times the mountains were living, movable bodies, endowed with the use of senses, and could fly in the sky by means of wings, and this Hymaloy was their king. In course of time, these mountains grew very troublesome to their fellow-creatures, the men; and, jealous of each other's power, they began to make inroads upon the cities situated on the side, vale, or top of their antago nists. They did not use any arms in their warfare; but, to accomplish their end, used to fly in the air, and aiming at a certain doomed place, fell upon it, and buried thereby houses, trees, men, women, and all! To put a stop to these outrages, Por-oosh Ramah,* a deified king, cut off the wings of all the turbulent mountains, which thenceforth lay as immovable masses of earth. As I write this, fancy carries me to the top of the Rollstone in Fitchburg, Mass., where I saw a heavy boulder, which they say is an entirely different species of rock from the Rollstone. I think (in fun though) that the statement of the Hindoo legend is true; this boulder, if not the son or grandson of the old hill, was perhaps the child of its neighbor, came there to make a call, and, amid the general slaughter by the god, who spared neither age nor sex, lost its wings, and consequently has lain on the bosom of the Rollstone ever since! The legend deserves another remark. It was a noble, heroic act in Por-oosh Ramah to cut off the wings of the injurious mountains which were then filling the world with horror and devastation. But it is a hard thing to stop the course of nature. The naturally cruel mountains, having lost their wings and unable to fly about and tyrannize over others, now and then open their monstrous jaws, and send forth fire, ashes, and melted lava to the neighboring places, and destroy everything therein. Thus the beautiful cities of Pompeii and Herculaneum were destroyed by the cruel Vesuvius.

Now to the point: I think the father of Doorga received his name from the mountain Hymaloy, or the mountain from him. It was, and now is, the fashion to name places, mountains, and rivers, after some distinguished persons, or the persons after the places. Thus, we have Alexandria from Alexan-

---

* There are a great many anecdotes of deeds of valor and of generosity attributed to this king. He is said to have destroyed the Khitrias three hundred times. I should think it was the same Por-oosh who had fought with the Macedonian hero on the frontier of India.

der, Rome from Romulus, St. Louis, St. Lawrence, Mount Washington, and Scipio Africanus, etc.

Let the Hindoos believe whatever they will about the parents of Doorga, she herself was, beyond question, the delight of her subjects, and the pride of the age she lived in. Her popularity among the people, her wide renown of noble, generous character, as painted with the dazzling hues of Oriental imagination, had made such an impression on the minds of the people, that, in succeeding ages, the ignorant but grateful posterity deified and made her the "Great Mother" of the universe. Her worship rose from the following fact.

It is the custom of the Hindoo females to visit their parents once a year, at least. Doorga was married to Shiba, the Destroyer. At the invitation of her parents she forsook the pleasures of Hoylas,* and came to cheer up their lonely hearts by a kind visit in this month. She came only for three days, for her husband could not come with her, nor live in her absence. To commemorate that event, the Hindoos construct her image, and with great rejoicing worship it for three days.

Here I will describe the image, with all its peculiarities. I use the technical term of the Hindoos when I say "the image," or "Prothima," for it contains nine different idols, although they call it one.

I am sure the description of the goddess will be amusingly absurd to the Christian reader; but I will represent it just as it is, and finally show that, far from being the real representation of some deity, it is merely an ideal thing, — the contrivance of Fancy.

---

* Hoylas, the paradise of Shiba, is said to be a golden mountain, similar to the Olympus of the Grecian deities. There is a mountain of the above name in Thibet.

The goddess is like a young female of sixteen, with ten hands, three eyes, deep yellow complexion, and stands in a posture placing her right foot on the back of a lion and the left on the shoulder of a monster. The monster, "Mohisha Soor," comes out of the neck of a buffalo, in whose body the lower half of his person is deposited. He has a sword in his hand with which he meant to strike the goddess. On her right are Shoreshotee and Gonesh, — the one the goddess of poetry and music, and the other the god of success. On her left are Kartic and Lock-hee, the god of the babes and the goddess of riches. These four are the children of Doorga. Besides these she holds a serpent by one of her left hands, which bites the monster, — the enemy of its mistress. Looking at the image carefully I perceive it is nothing more than the embodiment of all the necessary comforts, pleasures, hopes of life. We want relief from the overwhelming sins which beset us in every direction; the monster is the representation of them, whom the goddess is cutting asunder. We want wealth, learning, success, children, and behold there are the symbolical representations of all these in the names of the sons and daughters of Doorga. Thus the ancient Brahmuns have painted whatever they have touched with philosophic colors, and arrayed before the people hosts of deities, which are essentially the painted, clothed, personified attributes of One God. The system was well adapted to the capacity of that distant age, — the age of figures, allegories, and sentiment; but the present age demands a clear, simple, and intelligible faith.

The worship commences on Shop-tomee, — the seventh day of the full-moon, — and occupies three successive days. Early in the morning of the first day is the bathing of "nine leaves," of which the banana is the chief. This is done with much ceremony, in the presence of thousands; the bells ringing and trumpets sounding by hundreds. They place the "nobo-pothrica," nine leaves, by the side of the image, dressing it like a female.

As the Hindoo mode of worship is almost always the same, and quite different from that of the Christian, I will here detail it in full, instead of describing it partially here and there. The image is placed in the middle of the hall, facing the main entry into the house. Two Brahmuns officiate at the same time; the one conducts the practical and the other the theoretical part of the ceremony; in other words the former does what the latter tells him to do. Thus the first, the head priest, sits before the image with a pile of flowers and perfumatory powders on his right, and a bell on the left; while the second takes his seat only a few steps from the first, with his sacred Scripture laying open before him, which he reads to direct his colleague how to proceed. The priest, first of all, is required to purify himself, the place he sits on, and the water he uses in the worship, by some ceremony. The doctrine of self-purification is good in its nature, and a Christian one too. Christ inculcated such on his disciples. But what a sad contrast stands between a Brahmun's and a Christian's mode of self-purification before worship! A Christian is taught to search the innermost parts of his heart, and bring out, if there be there, any impure, selfish, or passionate inclinations; and, leaving the sacrifice before the altar, go and make peace with his brother, or in some other way expel evil thoughts, and then pray. A beautiful process of self-purification indeed! But the Brahmun repeats some Sanscrith words, puts a flower on his own head, and turns his hands round his head, for the same purpose. This symbolism takes a prominent part in the Brahminic dispensation.

Lest the sprinkling of water and the shower of wet flowers might soil the dress of the idol, or wash away the painting, a copper tub is placed between the priest and the image, into which he casts flowers, pours water, etc. Some prayers are offered to the children, the friends, the servants, the messengers, even to the ornaments and household furniture of the goddess.

The offering of Noi-bitho comes in course. Hundreds of wooden or brazen trays are loaded with wet, raw rice,* fruits of nearly sixteen kinds, and other sweet things. These eatable things are set on the right hand side of the image, with the belief that it will cast its glance at them. The priests entreat the idols to accept the offering they bring, and drink the honey, milk, and water, etc., which they place before it. After these have been accepted by the goddess (as they believe), they are distributed to the Brahmun families.

Then comes the sacrifice. The Hindoos cherish the same notion of this offering as the ancient Hebrews did. In the Old Testament we read of the peace-offering, and the burnt-offering, and of the children of Adam bringing lambs, vegetables, etc., to the altar of the Almighty. The difference is, then, in the choice of the beast for the offering. The Hebrews used to kill oxen, which the Hindoos do not. The latter slaughter goats, sheep, and buffaloes, of the male sex, in presence of their idols; and, at the end, cut sugar-cane, pumpkin, etc., into pieces.

The place where the beasts are slaughtered is the middle of the yard, where a wooden block, with a jog on its top, is

---

* The rice is made in a peculiar way, and called "authup." The usual way of bringing out rice from the husk is, first to boil, then dry and thrash it. But this is not boiled at all, only dried and thrashed. Hence the particular care taken in preparing this kind of rice increases its price to some degree.

stuck in the ground. The blacksmith is the only caste to kill the victim for the others, although some Brahmuns do that part, to the displeasure of others.

The executioner, his scimitar, the block, the victims, animal or vegetable, are all washed and purified with sacred water. Nobody is allowed to lean against or touch a pillar, wall, or anything else. All stand straight, separate, and silent. One holds the hind-legs of the he-goat by his left hand and its fore-legs by his right, places its neck on the block, and then the blacksmith lifts up his fatal weapon, and the people shout aloud, "Victory to thee, O Mother!" The moment the last word, "Mother," has been uttered, the head of the victim falls bleeding on the ground, the bells ring, trumpets sound, the people jump in joy, and clap their hands. There is no precise number of the animals for the offering; it may be more or less, according to the circumstance and the inclination of the worshipper.* If the man fails to kill the beast by one blow, it is regarded a mischievous omen. Hence, at the successful blow, the master of the house takes the executioner by the arm, puts flower garlands round his neck, and presents him with some money, clothes, etc.

In the afternoon is the "vogue," — dinner. It is to be observed here that the Hindoos of all castes do not offer boiled food to the idol, — such as rice, vegetables, fish, meat (of the he-goat only). They make various distinctions between boiled and fried food; some is allowable, and others not; for instance, a Brahmun would eat cakes fried by a confectioner, but not rice boiled by him. The Brahmuns only present rice, vegetables, and other cooked food, to the idols, which are offered in the same way as the fruits, speci-

---

* The term worshipper, in the Hindoo sense, denotes the man who spends the money, brings the image, and entertains the people at his house, no matter whether he himself officiates and offers prayers or not.

fying them by the name. When they bring these to the hall, they sprinkle the river water along their path, on which the Brahmun with the dishes in his hands treads. When the goddess is supposed to cast her glance at, or to indicate an acceptance of the costly dishes, the screens are hung so that none of the lowest caste can see what is going on behind.

The invited guests, as well as other poor low-caste people, take their places in the order of their castes, and the Brahmuns serve them at the dinner. O, the pleasant task! although, personally, I had neither faith in nor delight at the worship of the idol, and stood aloof in the hour of sacrifice, burning of incense, and offering meat to the senseless deities, yet I used to come at this time and offer my services in distributing food to the people. But as a disciple of Him who blessed, loved, and ministered to the poor, neglected, and low, I was particularly mindful to serve and wait upon such as rarely received much care and attention from an orthodox Brahmun. Thus, during these three days the people dine at each other's houses, and all at the house of the Brahmuns who are highest and first in order. In the evening, the hall, the parlor, the entry, and the outside of the house, are all illuminated with chandeliers, lanterns, etc.

The priest performs the "aurothee," or moving of "four lamps" before the face of the idol. While he is thus engaged, ringing a bell by his left hand and moving the lamps by his right, some burn perfumatory incense and fan the idol, and others devote themselves to silent prayer; the band also plays in the yard. At the close, every soul present is on his knees or breast, prostrating before "wood or stone." I was often found on the outside of the house, away from the idol, at this time.

The guests appear again, and are entertained. The invited guests, the men of wealth, offer a present of money to the idol, when they come to the outer piazza of the hall. Beautiful it is to see men of different ages and circumstances visiting house after house, in crowds, in the excited, festive, superstitious Bengal. Would to God it was for some other occasion, and not for the worship of the idols.

Late in the evening begin the music, singing, dancing, theatrical shows, etc., quite different from those of Christians, both in regard to time, process, and substance. The usual hours for these are from eleven in the evening until six or seven in the next morning. On other occasions, when there is no idol to worship particularly, the music and shows extend twelve hours, without intermission. During these hours the people sit still, sometimes go out, promenade, chew spices, smoke tobacco, etc. The yard of the house, accommodating several hundreds, is the place where the theatrical plays and other amusements are held. For the information of the reader, I should describe in this place the musical entertainments of the Hindoos. They are far inferior to those in this country, in regard to the gorgeousness of the scenery; but far superior in point of elegance, taste, and composition, either of the tune or the play itself. A visit to the Boston Theatre, and the splendid spectacle displayed therein of "Faust and Marguerite," have made me think the Hindoos are superior in their intellectual displays, while the Americans excel in scenic representations. Dancing in India is regarded in a contrary light from what it is in this country. Hence, those who dance in the public theatre or private parlor are from the lowest castes, if they be men, or public prostitutes, if women. For the Orientals deem it a shame, an improper act, for women to sing or dance before men. The dancing of a young girl in the above theatre in Boston, and of others in the *polka*, would well confirm the Oriental estimation of female dancing. The spectators do not gather promiscuously, and pay the admittance fee, as they do in this country. The music, dancing, or shows, whatever they might be, are open to all,—but it is in a rich man's house, where the heads and backs of persons glitter with gold and jewels; the folks with cotton are not welcome. However, they have other places to go to, where every attention is shown to them. A Bengalee proverb says: "One door is closed against, while hundreds are open to us." I said there is no promiscuous gathering; I mean the gathering of both sexes. The women sit apart behind the screens, from whence they see everything without being seen. But this is not the case with all. Sometimes a young woman, with vain heart and handsome casket—body—manages to thrust out to the public gaze her pretty hands, glittering with costly ornaments. Thus the first two days of the Doorga pooja pass by, and the third or last is before us, with its singular, absurd amusements. It is *katha matie* amusement with clay. After the usual sacrifices have been offered, they wet the yard, and men of every age fall upon each other, singing and dancing in abominable ways. Some songs are purposely composed in vulgar words and sentiments, to be sung before the goddess, their Mother! This mistaken band of men and boys, with instrumental and vocal music, visit every house in the neighborhood which has the image within it. As a token of respect, the master of the house, or his representative, cordially receives this foolish party, and joins their number. You must join them, otherwise they will run after you, put clay on your clothes, and make you come at any rate. As they pass by, it is difficult to recognize them by their faces. Their clothes and whole bodies are so covered with clay, that at the first sight you will take them for some strange creatures, or John for James and James for Charles! Christians, who have no faith in the foreign missions, think the Hindoos are well off. Come! O come and see this single abominable, adulterous amusement of these men, the sad, the mistaken specimens of humanity, and you will find a great gulf lies between you and them. Thank your God and be grateful to his mercy. Spread the light abroad that has been committed to your care, that millions of the Great Human Family may see their course through the precipitous way of life!

Now, on the fourth, or last day, the image is thrown into water, with absurd ceremonies and costly shows. Agreeably to the order of exercises performed when a woman leaves her father's house for that of her husband, the women walk round the image, put some lunch in her hand, and entreat her to come again the next year. The men write their names on some *bāle* leaves, and deposit them at the feet of the goddess, hoping she will remember them by their individual names.

In the afternoon the bands play, the flags are waved, the guns fired, and the image is carried to the river Gunga. Some people throw the images into the water, while others take them on board of boats, and thereby give the goddess a good sail. While young, I used to cry for this treatment toward the "Mother," and ask my father why it would not be better to send her home by carriage, than sink her into the water. When it becomes dark they return to their homes, the bands playing a melancholy tune.

The benediction is offered by the priest at the place where the idol was. A jar with water in it is placed on the same seat which the goddess occupied, people sit on every side, and the priest sprinkles the "peace water" on their heads. Lest the sacred water should fall on their feet, which are regarded profane by the Hindoos, they cover them with their clothes, while their heads are exposed to the shower from the priest.

After this is performed what seems to me the best part of the worship, i. e. the greeting of each other with salutations. Each person takes a quantity of sweet confectionery with him, and goes round from house to house receiving or giving salutations, according to his position. I will describe this more distinctly. The Brahmuns do not salute other castes; and the grown-up people receive homage from their juniors, but do not give them any. Thus, a young man prostrates himself before his older brother, and both before their parents, uncle, aunt, etc. They put a little confectionery to each other's mouths, and embrace each other. On this occasion they use an intoxicating drug called "Vang;" with the exception of this, I like the proceedings of the evening. Thus close the Doorga-pooja holidays; doing some good, at least to the poor, for they are well cared for, entertained in feasts, and admitted to the fine shows in the splendid houses, where they are not allowed to enter on other occasions. Besides these, they get such a quantity of expensive eatable things as they never tasted before, and which they enjoy for a week or more.

CHAPTER VII.

KARTIC, OCTOBER.

"THE LAMP IN THE AIR." — THE GODDESS KALLEE. — TORCH-FESTIVAL. — RED MARKS ON THE DOOR-POST.

IT has been observed before that the Brahmuns attach some degree of sacredness to the months of April, October, and January. The month at hand is October, and is a sacred one, and we will see how the Hindoos observe it. There are a great many common religious ceremonies which are not of much consequence; hence I will omit them, and direct my attention to the four marked ones which are the subjects of this chapter.

From the first to the last of this month, a lantern is lit and sent aloft on the top of a bambo, or a high pole of any other kind of wood. As each house thus lights a lantern in the air, the number becomes very large in populous places, and it is amusing to see them burn like stars in the lower firmament.

The goddess Kallee. As I have determined to treat of the origin of, or the causes which gave rise to, the Hindoo worship, I will briefly describe the legend respecting the goddess. She is the wife of Shiba in another incarnation of Doorga.

Under different circumstances, or to accomplish some personal or universal good, Doorga the "great mother" appeared in various incarnations. The legend tells us the following. There were two Oshoor brother-rulers * of a kingdom. The world in their time suffered much.

Of all the worldly riches which allure the selfish adventurers, and cause them to explore the uttermost parts of the earth, there was something very peculiar which these two princes were wont to seek after. Neither the burning gold, nor glittering jewels, nor the absolute sway over the world was the object of their ambition. Human beings whom some people call their "property" were the objects of their ambition, and upon them the attention of these princes was fondly directed. By their craving human beings, I do not mean that they used to send a ship somewhere to the coast of Africa which would import human "property" for their farm or plantation. No! Their ambition was romantic, although not without sin. The fairest women, whom the poets describe as the gems and the life of society, were the tempting treasure to the eyes of these Sovereigns. It was a fixed determination in them to place the most handsome female on the throne as queen. They had servants to explore the vales and the groves of the female world, in search of such flowers. Wherever an accomplished female could be found, her parents would be requested to give her up to the throne, either shining gold or reeking sword being offered as an inducement. First persuasion, then violence were the methods to which they resorted to secure their end. Discontent grew up and was universally felt.

The poor, insulted parents, unable to cope with the tyranny of these wicked kings, appealed to the goddess Doorga, the great Mother. She took pity upon these sufferers, promised them relief, and determined to put a stop to the

* Oshoor means monster, or opposite to Shoor-god. The men of cruel characters, feared for their wicked deeds, are called Oshoor by the Hindoos.

wicked life of the kings. Agreeably to her promise, the goddess descended from her Koylas. In order to encounter the servants of the King Shumbhoos, who were in a certain place in quest of handsome females for their masters, she betook herself to a grove which they must pass by on their way home. A Hindoo poet describes her beauty in the following way. As she entered the grove her divine presence, her unrivalled charms, her sweet graces, filled the place with solemn grandeurs. The bees and the butterflies forsook the flowers, and, taking her for a blooming lotus, began to hover round her person. The members of her body created discontent among the inmates of the forest. The white, fragrant lotus, hitherto the pride of the flowers, seeing itself surpassed in beauty by the goddess, fled with shame to lodge in the water forever. Her delicate, graceful neck drove the swans away into the ponds, lakes, and rivulets. The pearls finding their pride sadly broken by the bright teeth of the goddess, hid themselves in their shells at the bottom of the oceans. The wild deer ran frantic to see her eyes far superior in grace to its own.

In the ecstacy of his poetical imagination, the poet thus describes the countenance of Doorga; that the Bromho, desiring to imitate her face, created the full moon, and finding it, when ready, not half so handsome as the face of the goddess, broke it into pieces in fifteen days! Vain labor; he forms and breaks the full moon all the time! Hence are the phases of the moon.

It happened as she expected, that the messengers of the king came that way and were surprised to see the grove dazzling with her beauty. They approached near, and asked: "Thābee! may we know whether a god or an angel is mourning at thy absence? Is it a region in the sky which is dark, being deprived of thy radiance? Who art thou that walkest alone in these groves, fearless as a lioness, free as air, sweet as roses, and mild as the moon? Or is it possible that thou art here, forsaking the airy regions, to shine upon the earth for a season?" Thus the goddess replied: "Noble friends! you are welcome in your kind inquiries. Indeed, my address will surprise you more than anything else in the world, for it is so singular, so romantic, so noble, and so bold. Formerly I was a great princess, now an orphan, poor and helpless, having no place where to go, and no kind friend to stand by me."

The messengers here interrupted her, when they knew the object of their earnest search was before them; for the goddess declared herself an orphan, poor, and helpless, and they hoped she would accept their invitation, and become their queen. Again, her helplessness made them sure of success, for if she did not comply with their request, they would take her by force. "Thābee," said they, "thy night of sorrows is spent. Behold, the dawn of happy day is breaking upon thee! Follow us to the throne of mighty Shombhoo, and thou wilt be the mistress over his empire." "I thank you for the generous invitation," she replied; "I wish I could accept it; but there is a great difficulty in my way. I cannot offer my hands to any until a condition is fulfilled. In the name of Truth, I have sworn to marry him only who would be able to excel me in martial exercises. This is the solemn oath I have taken, and I will observe it as long as I live." It is impossible to describe the surprise of the king's servants, when they heard a young, weak, delicate female challenge the mightiest king of the world. In vain they attempted to convince her that such a daring, foolish oath would bring her to shame, and make her surrender even to a man of common ability; that if this was her condition, one of them could take her in a minute. Finding her firm in her position, they one by one engaged in a duel with the goddess, who killed them all. As the military custom in India is to spare the life of those who bear news, she suffered one to tell his king what had happened. Enraged at the news, the king came out to meet the heroine in the grove, begged her to surrender, promised her his love, but all in vain. She remained where she was. A fearful battle was there fought between them; the king had his troops, horses, and elephants, while the goddess, in a moment, changed her mild appearance, became "Dic-ambonee," naked, and astonishingly fearful. Shiba, her husband, finding the world could not bear her fury, came to pacify her and make her desist. But she was so much excited, that she could not recognize him at all, and mistaking Shiba, who had fallen at her feet, for an enemy, stood right upon his bosom. Hence the image of Kallee is represented as follows: She stands on the bosom of Shiba, has four hands, three eyes, and dark complexion. In her two left hands she holds, triumphantly, a sword and the head of Shombhoo, whom she killed; and by her two right hands she offers relief to her poor children. Her necklace is composed of the heads of her victims who had fallen in the battle.

The intelligent reader can easily find out the meaning of such representations. Taking the fact narrated above to be a true one, we clearly see that Kallee was a great warrior, a woman of unspeakable ability, of generous heart, whom time and ignorance have deified. Again, interpreting it allegorically, we see that the mercy of God unto the helpless, and his wrath unto tyrants, have been beautifully personified. The image of Kallee is a Hindoo illustration of the doctrine of retribution. While two of the hands of the goddess are punishing sin, the other two, at the same time, are offering peace to the deserving.

The worship takes place in the night of Omabushai,—total darkness,—and on the next morning the idol is thrown into water, as usual. The buffaloes and he-goats are cut by the neck as sacrifices.

In the evening of the day on which Kallee is worshipped, the children amuse themselves with torches. The white sticks of flax are tied up into bundles, and each boy takes one in his hand, lights it in the fire, and runs furiously in every direction. Boys strike each other's burning torches, and frequently get burned. This has its origin in a belief that the light of these torches pierces the darkness of hell, and helps its inmates to come out to receive the homage which their descendants on earth pay on that day. "Fourteen lamps are lighted" and put in different places round the house. Some red circular marks, made with Shindoor, a kind of red powder, are made on the head of the outside door.

The image of Kartic is worshipped, also. He is the son of Doorga, very handsome in his appearance, and rides on the back of a peacock. Those who wish to have some children born unto them, offer homage to him; but as they rarely meet with success, they are told that Kartic will bear witness of their religious deeds, and stand in place of their children! However, they do not worship him a great many years,—only four in succession, hoping to have offspring during that period.

CHAPTER VIII.

OG-GROW-HAW-UN, NOVEMBER.

JUGGUR-DHARTREE AND RASH-JATRA.

THE goddess Juggur-dhartree, in the present form, was unknown to the Hindoos who died a few centuries ago. Her name has a fine meaning, — "the nurse or upholder of the universe." She is Doorga in a different form, sitting on the back of a lion, who also rides on an elephant, and tears it to pieces. The chief part of the worship is similar to that of Doorga, in September, but covers only one day. The sacrifices, feasts, and music are alike. There is, however, something peculiar in the mode of killing the beasts for the sacrifice. It is recommended that the victim should be pierced to death by spears, but I never saw it done, anywhere.

In the night of the full moon comes the Rash-jatra. Its origin is as follows. Krishto, the Hindoo god, had some young women for his friends, whom he frequently used to meet in the groves. The sacred poetry of the Brahmuns abound with the details of Krishto's frolics with the women, and the Rash-jatra is one of them. To commemorate these events, they place the idols of Krishto and his female friends in an artificial grove. The opulent Hindoos spend a large amount of money on this occasion. In Calcutta, a rich family is widely known for the display of statuary, pictures, and ornamental works, on the *Rash*. Every American merchant engaged in the Calcutta trade knows that family, of which Baboo Rajendro Narain Dutto is the head. The Rash continues three successive nights, in which the image of Krishto and of his wife Radha are exhibited with great magnificence.

The most celebrated Rash, however, is held in Khor-dah, a place on the Ganges, nearly fourteen miles from Calcutta. But it is not so expensive, so finished, so showy, as that of the Dutto family. They say that the image in Khor-dah was carved out of a piece of marble having miraculous power in it, which circumstance has spread the fame of the idol far and wide. Splendid temples have been built for its abode, and a fund adequate to defray the cost of the service has been invested for its maintenance.

There are other celebrations in the name of Krishto, similar to the Rash-jatra, one of which will be treated by and by.

CHAPTER IX.

POUS, DECEMBER.

This month, from its being very cold, I suppose, has no public worship. Nothing particularly religious attracts the minds of the people, or pleases their eyes. In fact, the artists who make the idols, and the musicians who sing before them, close their business this month. But it ought to be observed that the stage on which the Hindoos exhibit their idols seldom becomes vacant. A worship of some kind, general or occasional, must go on. The prevalence of small-pox demands offerings to Shitola, the goddess of that fatal, contagious disease. A set of men walk round from door to door with small images of the goddess. Coming to the threshold, the idol carrier blows a shell to announce the advent of the goddess, as well as to gather the inmates of the house, and secure a hearing thereby. He sings or recites a false story descriptive of the wrath of the goddess to the scoffers, and her kindness to the believers, etc. I used to ask these men to go somewhere else, and not to trouble us, but my mother would not have me do such things, and asked them to come back, apologized for my rashness, bowed down before their idols, and gave them some money! In the end of this month the farmers particularly worship the barns, rice-stacks, etc., as the representation of Luckhee, — the goddess of harvest, giver of wealth, prosperity, etc. On which occasion the whole of Bengal makes a feast of cakes for three days in succession. In these days some people eat nothing but cakes of various shape, size, and taste.

CHAPTER X.

MAGH, JANUARY.

THE MORNING BATH. — SHORESH-SOTEE, OR MUSE.

THIS month, though third in order, is the first of the three which are held sacred by the Hindoos. On the first day of Magh, at five in the morning, the whole country is up to bathe. The excitement thus created is beyond comparison. Sacred songs, jubilees, exhortations are heard from every quarter. The school-teachers form concerts of their pupils, who sing the praise of the sacred river Ganges, through the streets and before the temple. Men, women, and children crowd in the Ghats, — bathing-places. As they go in they throw some fruits, such as mangoes, bananas, cocoa-nuts, into the water as an offering to the sacred river. Some continue their morning bath through the whole month, others only three days, while a few religious persons continue it through the year.

The Hindoos have no preaching like the Christians, but there is something in that shape which occurs in this month. The religious Hindoo engages a Brahmun to read and expound the sacred books in his house, which is free and open to all hearers. This Brahmun is always well trained, has full knowledge of the Scriptures, a fine, sonorous voice, and is full of fun. In short, he must be learned, a good reader, singer, and actor. An altar is made for him, on which he sits on a cushion. He wears some flower-wreaths round his neck and head, like the Grecian orators with laurels.

In the middle of the month the image of Shoresh-sotee is worshipped. She is the giver of learning, poetical genius, and efficiency in music. Hence the poets, orators, singers, pay her homage and worship. Every family is not required to buy her idol, for the worship of books, writing-desks, ink-stand, pen, musical instruments, do just as well. Even at the foot of the image these things are set in order. The schoolmasters make a grand idol of the goddess, and tax their pupils to meet the expense incurred thereby. There is one thing singular and unpleasant to the children. They are forbidden to eat *Kool,* a kind of plum, until it has been offered to the goddess; and if they do, her wrath will doom them to a life of ignorance. As the Kools grow earlier than the time of the worship of the goddess, they feel very badly seeing the trees smile with red and yellow fruits, while they are not able to touch them. The temptation on the one hand, and the fear of becoming dunces on the other, trouble them. Under such circumstances the cunning boys come to an understanding with the goddess, and promise to present her double or triple the number of kools which they eat before the time. Thus, with care and caution they keep the accurate account of the *kools* they eat, and produce the same before the image, agreeably to the contract made before. The worship occupies one day only, which is spent with music and other amusements.

Besides being the daughter of Doorga, the great goddess, Shoresh-sotte has a legendary tale attached to her person, which is regarded by the Hindoos as a genuine fact. Much as I do doubt its genuineness, I think it is a beautiful story, contrived to show the mercy of the goddess to her children. It is as follows. There was a young princess in India whose youth, personal charms, and mental accomplishments had made her the admiration of the time,

Among other things that brought her notoriety, there was an oath she had taken, to the effect that she would give her hand to a man who would surpass her in power of reasoning, and conquer her in intellectual warfare.* The learned young princes and nobles of literary renown crowded her palace, but success did not smile upon any of them. One after the other they took the field of controversy with the maiden, and were vanquished. Disappointment and shame became their reward. Next to the kings and nobles, the Brahmun sages — whom we might call Depositories of Indian literature — made their appearance, but had to wear crowns of shame. Whether some superhuman intelligence shaped her arguments so as to render them impregnable, or her personal charms, her "lightning-like smiles," or her "voice sweeter than Cuckoo's," threw a net of confusion

---

* This and kindred incidents show the ancient Hindoos did not hold *caste* as favorable, nor regard it as objectionable in affairs of marriage, as they of the present age do. Now, as we have observed in the first part of the volume, wealth, learning, personal accomplishments, bow down to *caste*. A second-caste man *cannot*, on any account whatever, marry his children to those of the first, or to Brahmuns. But in the present case we see the young princess offers her hand to an unrivalled intellect, not caring as to the quarter or caste in which it might be found. There are several instances of this kind, of fathers offering their daughters to a suitable man. Thus Jŏnuk, the father of the goddess Shita, sent a proclamation to the world that "Whoever shall be able to break an arrow in two, shall have Shita for his recompense." (This fatal arrow belonged to Shiba, the Destroyer, and was left in the palace of Jŏnuk.) In the legend we read of King Droupad offering his daughter to any who would pierce the eyes of a gold-fish which had been hung six miles above the ground, not looking at it directly for his aim, but only seeing its shadow in a vessel of water. Doymontie marries a king who, at her wish, boiled rice without fire and water. Bidda took a vow to enter into literary and theological controversy with a man before she would marry him. In the above cases invitations had of course been extended to kings and nobles in general, and not of any particular caste.

over her opponents, I cannot say. While the vanquished party of the Brahmuns was returning home, they determined to know if anything could be done to punish the proud princess. Finding their own literary merits quite inadequate to the purpose, they did not hesitate to resort to stratagem. As the troubled company moved slowly homeward, contriving some way to ruin the learned maiden, it happened that a young man, singular in every way, came before their eyes. He was tall in stature, dark in complexion, unintelligent yet mild in his countenance. To describe his ignorance, which was proverbially great, the story says that the Brahmuns found him sitting on the branch of a lofty tree, and severing the same with an axe from the main trunk, not knowing that his own weight will facilitate the work, and that great will be his fall on the ground below! This ridiculous, yet pitiable scene attracted the attention of the sages, and they halted. This philosopher on the tree would make a good match for the princess, they said, if he could be saved from the ruin which his own hands were bringing upon him. They beckoned him down the tree, hinting that they have something very important to communicate to him, and so he came. In answer to their inquiries he told them his name was Kalidass, a Brahmun by caste, and that he had had no education. They informed him that they knew the latter while he had been on the tree. They asked him to follow them if he wished to marry a rich, noble woman in the country. He begged them not to make fun of him, as he was too unworthy of the bride they spoke of. However, they let him understand that they would do what is necessary, argue with the princess, and arrange the matter prudently, provided he would go with them as their Master, keep himself seated in a dignified look, which they would show him how to assume, and now and then make some gesture during the discussion. He consented to their words, and leaving his axe and anything he had behind him, followed the cunning Brahmuns to catch a woman. The unfortunate damsel fell a victim to the united subtility of the Brahmuns, acknowledged her failure, and, faithful to her vows, married Kalidass, their supposed Master.

At the usual hour a maid-servant showed him his room, and he entered in, tired and excited. Illiterate as he was, he was able to reflect upon the contrasts between his position then and a few hours previous, — a boor in the country, and a master of the sages, — a poor Brahmun in the morning, and the husband of a princess in the evening, — accustomed to lie down on the cottage-floor, now the silvery bosom of a bedstead in the palace is to receive him. There was a mosquito-net round the bed, and he did not know how to get in. The story says, he climbed the bed-post that held the net, to see if there was any opening on the top, and finding none he jumped in, tearing the costly net to pieces. Late in the evening the princess came in, and first of all, wishing to exchange some words, began to look for a topic. In the mean time a camel in the king's stable roared. "The Oostros roar very loud, do they not?" she said. No response came from Kalidass. "Am I wrong? Is it not Oostro which I heard roar just now?" "Yes, you are right," he said; "certainly it is '*Oo'tro*,'" not knowing the true pronunciation of the word. The princess felt quite alarmed at the word "Oo'tro," for a scholar, a man of delicacy would hardly use it. She thought perhaps it was owing to a "*slip* of the tongue," that he said *Oo'tro*, or it might be that he was tired or was making fun.

Venturing again, so as to find out the truth, she begged him to tell her what it was that roared a little while ago. At which he, in his full ignorance of the case, replied, "It was *Ottro*," making it a new term altogether. The literary princess was shocked at it, knowing that the Brahmuns had ruined her; and indignantly striking her husband with her foot, she left the room. I do not believe this part of the story; it is contrary to the Hindoo custom; no insult is so great as to touch a man with the foot. Women, especially delicate and learned ones like the princess, could not do such a deed,—it is not only a great insult to a husband, but a real sin. It may be she had left the room disrespectfully, which, too, was not polite. Whatever was the case, poor Kalidass felt very much mortified, rose from his seat, looked towards heaven, and with tears said, "Mother Shoreh-sotee! the man is a mere animal who does not possess thy blessing in his soul. A woman insulted me! And why? Because of my ignorance of science and literature! To whom shall I go for redress but to thee, O Goddess of Learning? I am too old to begin to study. What shall I do then? I do not wish to live an insulted life without learning, without worth, any longer." He then left the palace and his learned bride, and entered into a desert with a view to put an end to his life there. Finding a lake before him, he went in to drown himself in its water. While on the point of merging into eternity he heard a voice saying, "Do not die, child! here I am, thy Mother, come from heaven; thy tears have fallen at my feet, and thy prayer hath sunk deep into my heart, so I descended on earth to redress thy grief. I am Bak Dabie! Sink thy head into the water of this lake, and when thou hast lifted it up a clearer atmosphere will spread over thy head." At the direction of the goddess, Kalidass immersed his whole body in the water, and lifting up his head, saw the goddess standing in the air. Inspired with a miraculous gift of knowledge, he immediately offered a prayer to the goddess, describing her beauty from head to foot, in language which the Hindoos think very chaste and high. In fact it is a fine specimen of Sanscrith poetry. The Hindoos are taught to repeat it in their schools. Unfortunately the goddess found fault with his description of her face first, and said, "He will be killed by the hands of a vile woman." The sentence has been fulfilled in the life of Kalidass.*

Thus the insulted Brahmun miraculously became the greatest of all the poets whom India ever produced. His writings, still extant, are real treasures, both in regard to their poetical splendor, their sublime depth, and their moral bearings. Such is the legendary manifestation of the goddess to Kalidass, which, although a mere story, has much influence upon pure Hindoo minds.

---

* The circumstances of the death of this noble poet are the following. He was in the habit of visiting a literary public woman, who was widely known for her acquisitions. One evening she was standing near a pond, looking at the lotus-buds, when the king with his nobles was passing by. The royal train halted by the pond to observe the rays of the moon on its placid bosom. The king asked this question of his friends: "Wind bloweth not, the water is calm, why then doth yon lotus tremble?" The woman immediately went to her home and asked Kalidass about it, who said it was for a Vromor, (kind of black wasp,) which had got in to extract honey, but being too much intoxicated as the shades of the eve were closing, the lotus made it a prisoner for the night. As it moved within the lotus, it caused it to tremble. She came and informed the king about the lotus. He was quite surprised, and asked again, "Why the Vromor which gnaws dry woods does not cut through the lotus and go out of it?" She flew to her chamber, and the great poet solved the question. "The Vromor does not use his sharp sting, for two reasons. Having drank too much honey from the lotus he is dissipated now, and unable to use his weapon; secondly, he is too polite to cut the tender lotus, the queen of flowers." The king wanted to know if it were her genius or that of another which solved his questions, and desired to see her more at her home. She wickedly went first and cut the head off Kalidass, who was sleeping then, that he might not be seen by the king at her house.

CHAPTER XI.

FAL-GOON, FEBRUARY.

THE Thole-jatha. This means the amusement of Krishto and his female friends with a swing. In the temple hall, or on some high altar, a throne is set, and the images are placed upon it. This comes in the time of the full moon. A few days previous to this the boys become very troublesome to each other, and to the men in general. They buy small hand-pumps, made of bamboos or tin, fill some jars with colored water, station themselves by the wayside, and seeing men pass by, pump out the water on their clothes. There is no remedy against this plague, for you do not know where they are; they lie in ambuscades, and, to your surprise, wet you with the red or yellow colored water. They will take you unawares, as did the Indians the troops of General Braddock. Sometimes they meet you in the street, four or five at once, and trouble you from every direction. As they seldom attack men with dirty clothes, one might escape the boys by wearing a less showy dress. Again, they make a kind of seal, by cutting an apple into halves, which they dip into ink and stamp on your side, breast, or back. This is worse indeed, for sometimes it is difficult to wipe out the stain-mark by several washings.

In the evening before Thole-jatha, the image of Krishto is conducted to witness *Cha-churr*. A long bamboo, covered with straw, is stuck into the ground by the side of the river or in the field. The Brahmuns who carry the idol and its throne on their shoulders walk round the bamboo post seven times, while the drums, flutes, violins, are playing by hundreds. They then set fire to the post, and fireworks of various descriptions are burned. Early in the next morning the idols are placed on the hanging throne. The people witness the scene with great pleasure, for it is said, "The sight of Krishno will effect salvation."

There is some trouble, again, arising from the chief amusement of the day. Abeer, a kind of red powder which the god is especially fond of, is scattered everywhere. They make balls of it, and hit each other's face and eyes. Fortunately, Abeer does not blind the eyes; for when it falls in, it waters them a little while, and thus makes them brighter than before. In a rich man's house, the guests are almost buried with Abeer, without which the Thole-jatha is nothing.

The feast and music are as usual, for even a poor man must entertain "twelve Brahmuns" on any religious holiday. This is one leading feature in Brahmunism. It distinctly commands its believers to entertain Brahmuns and other castes in the time of the idol-worship. Thus it makes hospitality a part of the ceremony, and upon this the attention of the gods is particularly directed. There is a beautiful story to this effect. A man, according to his promise, offered a thousand mangoes to the sacred Gunga, by emptying the baskets into its waters. A poor man picked up one, and ate it. Now the goddess visited the rich man in a dream, and demanded the full payment of mangoes, acknowledging the receipt of *one*, which the poor man had eaten.

CHAPTER XII.

CHOITHRO, MARCH.

CHURUCK-POOJA.—HOOK SWINGING.

THIS is the last month of the Hindoo year, and witnesses that bloody religious ceremony which is so much talked of in Christian countries. It is Churuck-pooja; or, graphically, the swinging by the hooks. I am aware that the Christian missionaries have taken especial care to describe this fearful institution ably and accurately to their friends at home. But as they write what they see, not what they know of the Hindoos, they often fail to treat of the real state of the thing. However, they are not to blame; for the want of true knowledge of an object makes its description dry and imperfect.

It has been a belief in Hindoo minds from the remote ages, that self-torture is essentially requisite for the propitiation of the gods. The human body being made out of matter which is evil in its nature, and wars against the spirit, it is desirable to macerate it, and give dominion to the spirit thereby. This notion has created various orders of Shunnashi's, Shadhoos, Jog-us, Mohuntros, etc., who are common in India. It did not long remain confined to India, but, crossing its boundaries, reached the people of Persia, Tartary, Arabia, Turkey, etc. Its influence was also felt by the Christian Church in her infancy.

In India it manifests itself in some form or other in all the religious institutions of the people. I have seen a man offer prayer to Shiba, standing on his head; others on one leg for hours under the burning sun. Some would not eat or drink anything unless it should be put in their mouths, while others would not lie down at all for a certain number of years. Nearly three years ago there came a Shadhoo into our village, who spent a whole day and night on foot. His disciples said that many years had seen him eat, drink, and rest in that position, and perhaps his head will not touch the earth until it does forever.

The subject of this chapter traces its origin from that singular belief of which we have spoken. Ban Raja, a king of great religious enthusiasm, is said to have instituted this ceremony in honor of Shiba. From the fifteenth of March the Mool Shun-nashee, with others, walks round the place at the pretended permission of Shiba.* They carry with them a great quantity of Oothuries, or thread, and finding a low-caste man within reach, they put a Oothuries round his neck, crying aloud, "Tarash-orāre nash Shiba!" From that moment the poor man becomes one of the party, forsaking his professional business until the end of Shun-nash. This mode of enlistment seems to command the victim, "Follow me, and let the dead bury their dead." There is no way for his getting out free; he must wear the badge of Oothuries, and walk day and night with the party at the penalty of excommunication or a fine.†

* Mool Shun-nashee is the chief officer of the party called Shun-nash. He is the *elect* of the god, and takes the lead of the party year after year, until he leaves this world for another. After his death his son takes his post, or sometimes another is elected by the priest and the Shun-nashees.

† The punishment by fine is inflicted by the Zamindar, the landholder of the country. The British law does not authorize any private individual to fine another, except the legal officers; but, nevertheless, the poorer classes are in common cases fined and ill treated by their landholders.

It is to be observed here that the Brahmuns do not join the party at all: they put heavy burdens upon others, but do not help them with their fingers. Hence the Shun-nashees are alway from the poor, ignorant, low castes. As there is no fixed limit to the number of Shun-nashees, they enlist hundreds within a few days. However, the number is great or small, according to the popularity of the idol. Though every idol is of Shiba and every temple is his abode, yet some are believed to possess the fulness of the god in greater degree than others, and are revered by the people accordingly. Thus there are three temples of Shiba in one village, and one of them draws crowds of worshippers toward it, which fact increases its income, and its priests receive a great deal. Now Shun-nashees thus gathered together spend the rest of the month in visiting the idols of Shiba and their brethren in different villages, — very like to the custom of the fire-companies in this country, who receive from, and make visits to, their friends of neighboring towns. When two or more parties come in collision, they stand in order, and salute and embrace each other with loud shouts of "Tarash-orare nash Shiba!" Each party has some leading men, who sing a few verses, desiring their friends to expound or solve them as the nature of the question would require. The trumpets are sounded, the bells rung, the flags waved, and the staves carried by hundreds. As they march in procession their music and shouts deafen the ears and make heads ache.

On the day before the Churuck-pooja, the ignorantly mis-

The excommunication from the society as well as from the caste is worse than the punishment by fine; for, over and above the sufferings consequent to an outcasted life, the man is to pay a certain sum of money to regain his lost position. The last state of that man is worse than the first!

taken as well as daring men in the party make *bans*, or pass the thick iron or bamboo sticks through the skin of their arms and tongue. Indeed, it is a fearful sight! Not only do the grown-up men do such things, but boys of thirteen years or more pass sticks through their skin. I have seen men pass four Sholas (bamboo sticks of the thickness of our first finger) through the different parts of their left arm, and binding some extra ones with them, make a little terrace, with a vine creeping over it. Others make a hole in their tongue sideways, and pass through it the tail of Gochora (the flat-headed, venomous snakes). Thus arranged, they go to the houses of the gentlemen and dance there a quarter of an hour, getting a little money for compensation. By a little money, I mean from a quarter to a whole dollar. The money thus realized is disposed of in making some vile shows before the temple, and to buy intoxicating liquors for those who exhibit these bloody feats. A low-caste old man in our village was preparing some fine Sholas, to show a feat altogether new and surprising; but he died before the time came. Among other things his beloved wife remarked, in the course of her lamentation, that "he made grand preparation to excel others in the *ban*, but could not succeed!" Then comes the Churuck the next day, with an aspect more dreadful than the *bans*.

In the morning, the Shun-nashees all go to bathe, and gather a large number of cocoa-nuts, bananas, and other fruits. Before the temple, the *Jhap* is performed. It is a terrace made by sticking some bamboo poles in the ground, and sometimes rises twenty feet high. The Shun-nashees, both young and old, climb up the terrace and stand in two rows, one above the other; the spectators stand all round; some climb up the trees, to get a better view. A few men post themselves near the foot of the terrace, holding a large bag in their hands, by which they receive the men who jump down from the terrace, one after the other. This bag is stuffed with dry leaves, so as to make it soft, and a *Botty* (kind of large knife, not very sharp) is put over it. When everything is ready, then Mool Shun-nashee bends his head to the god, takes leave of the brethren on the terrace, scatters the flower-wreaths, raw rice, bananas, etc., to the crowd below, and, lastly, jumps down on to the bag, or, rather, the mattress. After him, all the Shun-nashees jump down in the same way, one by one, amid the deafening shouts of the crowd and the sound of the trumpets.

In the afternoon, the order of the exercises is as follows. Before going to the Churuck, the Shun-nashees ask the god's permission, which he gives by a nod, seen by the priests only. They put some flowers on the head of the idol, and if one of them, at least, should slip down from it, it is interpreted as the pleasure and permission of Shiba. Sometimes the flowers do not fall easily, being at the centre of the idol's head. This is interpreted as owing to the anger of the god. As the Shun-nashees are to fast certain hours of the day, and live according to the rules appointed by the priests, it is believed that they have violated the rules, by eating or drinking, which circumstance has offended the all-knowing Shiba. Hence, seeing the flowers do not fall from the idol, the priests command the officers to bind the Shun-nashees and beat them with stripes. I have seen the young boys roll round the temples, their hands tied together, in order to appease the enraged god. It is curious that they always suspect the boys of violating the rules of the Shun-nashee's life, even if they observe, with their native earnestness, almost every "jot and tittle" of the regulation. It is the grown-up, old, indifferent men, who privately eat and drink, I believe; and the poor boys suffer for their sin. As the idol delays to give its permission by a nod, and by throwing some flowers from its head thereby, the priests interpret its terrible wrath, and order the town officers to be bound also. It is, however, a beautiful lesson the Brahmuns teach by this; they say, "The sin of the king causeth his subjects to suffer, and brings affliction upon them."

There is a trick which the priests impose upon the people at this time. They contrive every means to open the window of the temple, in order to bring a draught within, that it may blow flowers away from the idol's head. In my village there is a back window in the temple, through which the people on the outside look at the proceedings within. They, of course, prevent the wind from going in, in some degree, and the fanatic priests drive them all away, cursing and rebuking them shamefully. The moment a draught of wind has knocked a flower down, they in ecstasy dance round the temple, clap their hands, embrace each other, and shout, "Tar-āre Shur-are nash Shiba!" etc.

In this state of excitement, they form a procession and march down to the Churuck Tola, which is in some place very near the temple, or but a little way off. The Churuck Garch, or "Swinging Tree," is a heavy, long, wooden pole, set up perpendicularly, with one end on the ground, with *moche* like the main-yard of a ship on its top, and which can be turned round either way. Sometimes the Churuck Garch is nearly twenty feet high. A man — the poor victim to the Churuck — bends down on his knees and hands, while another draws out the skin about his shoulder-blades, and the Cormokar, or the blacksmith, forces two iron hooks (ten inches or more long) into the skin and the muscles. Some daring man will suffer four iron hooks to pass through the different parts of his body, so as to show his proficiency in the affair. There are some strong cords fastened to the hooks, which also are attached to a long, thick cord, and the man is drawn up to one end of the yard. To keep the balance right, a man climbs half way on the rope attached to the other end of the yard. Thus bound and hung, the victim jumps in the air, and turns round the "Swinging Tree" from ten to fifteen minutes.

Once, in my grandmother's village, I witnessed a scene more desperate than the above. A man swung round the pole nearly fifteen minutes in the air, with his head downwards, and four iron hooks catching him by the skin. His long hair began to wave in the air, and his hands beat a drum which was fastened to the same cord. But expert as he seemed to be, he could not as yet make good music. In some places several men hang in this way in succession. I wonder that these men do not seem to feel very much hurt; for I have seen them go to their respective work within a couple of days. Coming down from the Churuck Garch, the victims receive the benediction from the priest, who blesses them with a flower from the altar, as a sacred relic.

The morning after the Churuck, the Shun-nashees gather together before the temple, take off the Oothuries, or the sacred badges, from their necks, return them to the priest, and shave a part of their heads (for during the term of Shun-nash they are forbidden to shave their heads or cut their nails). After this, they bathe in the river or tanks, as the situation of the place will permit, and go to their own homes, eased from the bondage of superstition.

There is one peculiarity, however, in the Churuck-pooja which is worth noticing. During the Shun-nash term, the band is organized somewhat on the principles of brotherhood, each member bearing a kind, brotherly affection toward another, — an affection they do scarcely dream of before. If one of the party dies during these holidays, they all put on mourning according to the custom of the Hindoos. An insult to one is felt by all, for they being different are yet the members of the same body in Shiba. They regard the badge they wear round the neck as binding them together into the sacred bond of fraternity. The ever-vigilant, ever-living caste system interferes, of course, with their manifesting fully the relation they bear towards each other. The Shun-nashess of different castes would not eat at the same table or drink out of the same cup, although in other respects they do not observe all the regulations of the caste.

Thus ends the Hindoo year with so many religious festivals, holidays full of degrading and demoralizing amusements, and ceremonies bloody and mistaken. Though the internal spirit of these hosts of religious institutions tends to devotional and charitable purposes, yet the influence of their outward appearances confounds and corrupts the weak-minded Hindoo. The people in general do not strip them of the veil, in order to find out the real significance within. They hardly understand what those rites and ceremonies do mean, but in their ignorance take them just as they are, and worship all corporeal objects as true gods and goddesses. This feature of the religious belief among the low and ignorant classes is very gloomy, for they are hardly taught to recognize the difference between man and God. The Brahmuns, the priests of these people, do not have a regular mode of religious teaching. In the temples, by the side of the Gunga, under the sacred Burr (banian-tree), or in their houses, very few words are spoken by way of religious instruction. By some fixed mechanical rules they are taught how, what, and when to eat, drink, bathe, walk, speak, and sleep, and in these their religion consists. The language of the prayers, being Sanscrith, is unintelligible to the worshipper himself. Very few attempt to understand the phraseology of the prayer, and think it improper to handle the inspired words. In the prayer to Shuresh-sotte, or the muse, I find the description of almost every inch and each member of her person, with rich, glowing poetical imagery, which a sensible man ought not to apply to her, his mother goddess. So it will be found that most of the Hindoo prayers are immoral, yet beautiful representations of the personal graces of the male and female deities, which simply please our senses and bewilder our reason, instead of creating a deeper sense of reverence in our religious nature. Again, the want of a regular system of religious instruction has brought into the minds of the people all sorts of mistaken, erroneous ideas respecting God, man, and duty; life, death, and immortality. The man on the very verge of his life, standing between the edges of this and the next world, hardly knows where he is bound, whom he is going to, and what will be his true destiny. He, under the burden of superstition, recognizes his god in the person of the Brahmun, standing near his death-bed, or in the sacred Ganges glittering yonder. If he should unfortunately die at home, or on Tuesday or Saturday night, it is believed the gates of heaven will be closed against him, until the Brahmuns, by some peculiar ceremony, should exorcise his spirit, and with mortal hands open the gates of Paradise! This is the substance of modern Brahminism. Its belief is erroneous, its influence pernicious, and the end which it contemplates as destiny is dark. It makes piety to consist in the ordinances, in the law, such as in bathing, fasting, eating certain things, offering worship to some visible objects on some fixed days. Besides what has already been treated as the leading features of the Hindoo religion, there are some additional religious institutions, which I will describe to the reader before the close of the book.

Building temples to the gods, digging tanks, and planting trees on the wayside, are considered very pious. This belief has prompted the Hindoos to spend immense wealth in the erection of temples, which crowd the banks of the Ganges. The number of the temples varies according to the circumstances of the man; either two, twelve, or one hundred and eight are to be erected and dedicated unto the gods. There are very few men who have dedicated one hundred and eight temples at a time. There are some, however, at the expense of the Rajah of Burdwan, which I hear are very costly. On the banks of the Ganges, in lower Bengal, there are several Ghauts (bathing-places) erected with brick or marble. Their stairs are sometimes twenty feet wide and lead into the water several feet deep. On both sides of the Ghaut either two or twelve temples are erected for the abode of the idols. At the time of the dedication, people are entertained at a great feast, money is distributed to the Brahmuns, and the temples are adorned and illuminated.

The digging of tanks, especially where there is a scarcity of water, is commendable, and a part of religion. I can see the necessity of annexing this to the religion, for in a warm climate, were people use water so much, a great many tanks are needed to supply their wants. Hence we see almost every house in Bengal has a small tank, of twenty to fifty yards square, attached to it, and in this they raise fish for the family use. After a tank has been dug, it is filled with water, partly from the sky, and partly from the earth itself. They stick a long wooden pole into the centre. The owner of the tank, at the direction of the officiating priest, crosses it by holding the tail of a cow. This denotes the idea of crossing the river that glides along everlastingly between this life and the next. On this occasion, also, the poor people are entertained; a feast is given to the Brahmuns, etc.

Now the planting trees by the road-side must be noticed. There is, however, a selection of the place where the trees are to be fixed. Always the place where three roads from different directions meet together is preferable. The number and species of the trees are five, — such as Burr, Oshud, Nim, Bāle, and Amlokee. Five young shoots of these trees are planted together, which mode is called "The union of the sacred trees." Scarcely all of them grow together, for, sacred as they are, some of them occupy the places and crush the others to death.

The daily worship. The rich religious people in India have the idols in their houses for the daily worship. There is a room entirely for the accommodation of the idols, like the "baby rooms" in this country. In it there are a throne, bed, seats, furniture, plates, dishes, cups, tumblers, bells, wash-tubs, clothes, and ornaments, of the lifeless gods. In the morning, the family priest comes in, awakes the idols from their sleep, brings them down from the bed, washes and wipes them, repeating some prayers and ringing the bell at the same time. Dressing them according to their shape and size, he worships in the usual way, by strewing flowers over them, offering them something to eat, etc. The head member of the family would not eat his meal until the idols have been cared for. In the evening, the priest comes again, to give the gods their supper. First of all, he lights "punch-prodip," or five lamps, and waves them before the idols. He then puts them in their respective beds, covers them with clothes, or hangs the mosquito net round them, as the nature of the weather would require! Just as the children take care of their dolls, so the Brahmuns serve their idols.

The public worship. In every Hindoo country, a party of young men tax each family once a year and dispose of the money thus realized in the "worship of twelve friends."

They charge also all the bridegrooms who come to marry the girls in their village. A splendid image is erected in the public place of the town, and music and theatrical performances are held before it. This, taken on the whole, is the worst of the Hindoo institutions. It corrupts the young, who, taking this opportunity, do all sorts of immoral acts which they never dreamt of before. You ask the boys when they learned to smoke, steal, or quarrel, and they will point out these holidays to you. I remember distinctly having stolen tobacco and a smoking-pipe (hooka) from my uncle's room, to help the smoking party in the garden. Almost all of us were beginners in this filthy and unhealthy habit. Fearing our parents would know it, we used to chew a piece of green banana-leaf, which in some measure takes away the dirty smell from the mouth.

Again, as the musical performances are performed through the whole night, these boys and young men go round the place, climb up the cocoanut-trees and steal their fruits. As the cocoanut-trees are very tall and the fall of the fruit on the ground makes a loud noise, some seven boys were once climbing up a tree one after the other that they might pass down the fruits noiselessly from hand to hand; the most cunning of them did something to make his successor laugh, and he doing the same, there wont a peal of laughter from the head to the foot of the tree, which apprised the owner of his loss. One of the boys attempting to come down quickly, fell upon some broken glass and was badly injured. Fortunately I was not with them. To enumerate the evils that rise from the Hindoo worship and holidays would occupy a book. Coming out disfigured and bruised from the dark caves of Brahminism, I hoped the British government would stretch forth its hand at least against the most immoral, and ruinous institutions of the

Hindoos, because their own eyes are not bright enough yet to notice the defects thereof. But my

> "Hopes that were angels in their birth,
> Perished young, like things on earth."

The late Sepoy mutiny has, as I see, given a lesson which the government must mind. However there is yet a hope of India's regeneration. The influence of the Missionary as well as the government schools will open the eyes of the rising generation, and thus bring the matter to a slow but happy close. Father of lights! let Thy knowledge shine in every creek and corner of the world; and bring it to the recognition of Thee, who art its Creator, and loving Father! Let India worship Thee as her God and Father!

MISCELLANEOUS.

India is inhabited by a people of various colors, customs, and languages; and consequently affords a picturesque scene to the traveller. As the climate varies in different parts of the country, the color of the inhabitants changes likewise; although they are one and the same people, and their origin is the same,—the Indo-Caucasian Stock. And what is more striking is the difference in the color in one family. Thus, a mother is dark, the father olive, and the children are yellow, of different shades,—one is as burning gold, while the other is as gilded brass.

The people speak different languages in various parts of the country, but all trace their origin to the great source,—the Mother Sanscrith. The Bengalee, which has much resemblance to the Sanscrith, is spoken in Bengal; the Orria in the Orissa, the seat of the celebrated Jogger-nauth; Tamul in Madras, by the Moharashtros, and the Hindoosthanee in its various forms in the regions of the northwestern provinces, and in Nepaul. Besides, there are several wild tribes, such as Naug-poorias, and the Saun-tals, who speak tongues of their own. The Brahmuns, in their religious services, and sometimes in their conversation, speak Sanscrith, but the other castes use Bengalee. For illustration I will give specimens of the same thing in different languages of the country,—*I will go*, is in Sanscrith, "Jochamee;" in Bengalee, "Amee Jabow;" in Orria, "Mo-ja-bow;" and in Hindoosth-anee, "Haum gaga." In their characteristics the

Bengalees are mild, peaceable, intelligent, speculative, and subtle, and those of Upper India are brave, haughty, warlike, but kind. The Bengalees in their bodily structure are delicate, while others are robust, and well built. In the late Sepoy mutiny, the Sepoys — the people of the northwestern provinces — took the lead, and the Bengalees did not help them by their fingers. The latter hardly use warlike instruments, while the former make them their companions. A gentleman in Upper India carries his sword or a club, wherever he goes; but a Bengalee thinks it savage to equip in this way.

I have been often asked whether my people smoke and drink or not. The Bengalees do not smoke cigars, they think it mean, and ungentlemanly; they use the Hooka in smoking.

The *tamack*, or tobacco, needs much care, and is composed of a great many ingredients, such as thocta, or tobacco leaves, dry roses, and banana shells, molasses, cinnamon, etc. These being chopped and mixed together, are put under the earth for several days. When a person smokes, the vapor does not come right into the mouth, but, passing through a long pipe, comes into the bottom of the Hooka, which is full of cold water, and making its way through another pipe, reaches the mouth of the smoker. The people of Orissa smoke cigars as in this country. Drinking spirituous liquors is very common with the young men in the cities and mercantile places, where the Europeans import a good supply of wines of various names and natures, and set the natives the example. The Hindoo religion condemns a man who touches wine, except in case of alarming sickness, which nothing but spirituous liquors can cure. "As medicine, *Soora* is to be used," is the doctrine of the Brahmuns. Some people carry it so far that after having recovered from their sickness, they make *Praosh-chitro*, or atonement, for using English medicine, which they believe is always prepared with spirit. Others will not apply to a foreign physician at all, fearing that his medicine, while it saves the animal man, may strike a death-blow to the soul. Hence "it is preferable to die by the hand of Boitho, a physician by caste."

Tarie, or the juice of the palm or date tree, is used by low-caste people generally. It has intoxicating influences, and is to be had at a low price. The juice of the palm-tree is taken by squeezing the stalks, which will fill a large pitcher with *tarie* in a few hours. It is used as yeast by the bakers in India. The Hindoos do not eat meat; they have a great aversion to beef, ham, pork, etc. In their villages a single cow is not killed in many centuries. The man who whips his cattle so severely as to make them bleed, is out-casted, ridiculed, and hated by the public as a *Koshie*, or a butcher. The Hindoo law regulating the treatment of cattle is very kind to the beasts and severe to their masters. If a cow, calf, or bull should die with the rope round its neck, that is, through the master's carelessness, the law holds him guilty, and prescribes penances for him to observe. He is required to walk from door to door, with a piece of rope round his own neck, a straw in his mouth, and making imperfect sounds like the cows. After three days of humiliation in this way, he abstains from food and drink a whole day, shaves his head, offers money to the Brahmuns, and redeems his sin thereby. Again, if a calf or cow should fall into a pond and die, both the owner of the pond and that of the beast, are regarded as sinners. The rational intention of all these prescriptions is to inculcate the law of care and kindness towards dumb beasts, especially the useful ones.

The Knowledge of Art and Science.—The Hindoos from a remote antiquity cherished the knowledge of the heavenly bodies, reckoned eclipses, and watched the motion of the stars. These they did and do by means of their fixed system of astronomy; they have no scientific apparatus at all. European astronomers calculate the day of the eclipse, using several instruments, but the Brahmuns do the same thing without such aid. Architecture was known to them also from a distant period. The remains of the old temples and ghauts in various parts of India distinctly speak of their proficiency in architecture. On the temple walls you will see the representation of the heavenly bodies, the signs of the Zodiac, and the images of their gods, carved by men who had lived, so to speak, in the very infancy of the world. The knowledge of minerals was found among them also, for the universal use of gold and silver ornaments, and metallic household utensils, is evidence of the fact. They are unrivalled in the skill of working in gold and precious stones. The manufacture of fine cotton cloth, such as Dacai, and of shawls (the Cashmere), has obtained the undisputed applause of the world.

In fact, the Hindoos did and do largely cultivate all the appliances of civilized life. Only their knowledge of art, science, and civilization is not progressive, but limited. They feel satisfied to live, move, and die within the boundaries of their own acquirements, and hardly desire to add to or vary from the prescribed institutions of their forefathers. While the countries beyond Hindostan are making astonishing advances towards enlightenment, discovering new inventions for promoting temporal comforts, and introducing the best and choicest things of the world among themselves, the Hindoos dig trenches round their borders, and nourish their old national institutions in good earnest. But there is a strong possibility that a mighty revolution will take place in the social and spiritual condition of the country. The introduction of European civilization has dazzled the eyes of the young, some of whom, (though few,) are now eagerly co-operating with their friends for the welfare of the country. The School of Industrial Art, the Civil Engraving College, the Medical College, etc., are blessings coming from the British Government, and to these the young men from the high classes resort for instruction and improvement.

The Hindoos possess remarkable genius in imitating almost everything put before them, provided their caste and religion do not interfere. The low-caste people who work in the English factories, warehouses, steamboats, etc., display a ready and admirable talent for the business. On the Ganges, the uneducated, low castes manage steamboats. They serve in various capacities in the dockyards, founderies, factories, etc.

The Hindoos have their own system of agriculture, and raise fruits, flowers, and grain, of various kinds. The chief productions of their husbandry are rice, flax, sugar, indigo, cotton, potatoes, peas, beans of different species, and fruits too numerous to name. India has no winter; her rivers do not freeze, her high trees stand clothed with leaves and decked with flowers all the year round; her birds are merry, her sky fair, her sun bright and warm, her rivers grand, her mountains high, her children numerous, intelligent, and philosophical, her religion superstitious, her gods many, and her age old. May she thrive and grow upward, high as her Himaloy, giving her light to, and receiving that from others, — this is the heart-felt prayer of her absent son.

APPENDIX.

Ever since my arrival in America I have heard with great surprise the statement, received on the authority of missionaries, that the Hindoo mothers throw their infants into the river Ganges. Almost every man, woman, boy, or girl in these United States knows it, and has seen the illustration of it in various books. During my tour over some sixteen States and the Canadas, I noticed that the Hindoo mother, her baby, and the alligator, were the subjects of constant inquiry. The story of the infants being thrown into the Ganges by their heartless mistaken mothers, is believed by the people of this country to be either a custom or a religious institution of the Hindoos.

I am aware that to speak against this prevalent belief is to falsify the reports of travellers and to criticise the statements of foreign writers who have disseminated this report throughout the whole length and breadth of the land. On the other hand, I cannot suffer a groundless and strange story to run so freely through the Christian community, and bring upon the poor innocent women of India such undeserved reproach. I do not wish to cover the really defective institutions of my country. Her religion, rather than custom, sanctions suicide in different ways, as manifested in the voluntary offering of the widows upon the funeral fire of their husbands. The throwing of babies into the Ganges or to the alligators, then, I would say never was in the customs or religious ordinances of India. I never heard of it even as a grandmother's story; while, on the other hand, my mother and other friends often spoke of the widows who burned themselves alive with their dead husbands, of their preparation, their bidding farewell to their children, committing them to the care of some kind relative, etc. It seems strange to me, that, being a native of India, a Hindoo, yea, a Brahmun, by birth, I did not know nor hear of this custom of my own country, which is known to the people who live nearly eighteen thousand miles from the same. What did not come to my knowledge during my twenty-one years of life in India, came to my ear on the day I reached America. "What is this?" they ask me. "What do they mean? Hindoo mothers throw their babies into the Ganges to be devoured by the alligators! Horrible!! Hindoo mothers do such things!! The same mothers that sit with malshas (earthen pans) with fire burning upon them, on their heads, shoulders, hands, laps, before the goddess Doorga, and solicit the health and life of their children! The same that lie down (hothea) without food and drink before the temple, in case of the severe illness of their children, and who vow to appear before the goddess with an axe tied round their necks, or to shed blood by voluntarily tearing the flesh from their own breasts as an expression of gratitude for the recovery of their children!"

The Hindoo parents love their children as well as do any parents in Christendom; or perhaps I should say more, for some reasons of which Christians are ignorant. The redemption of the Hindoo parents depends in a great measure upon the lives of the children who send their spirits to their destination by a peculiar ceremony.* They believe the

* It might perhaps be said by some, that, as the Hindoos do not regard the female child worthy to redeem the soul of her parent by Shrautho

childless person has no heaven to inherit, no celestial pleasures to enjoy. The Hindoo religion commands a man to marry several wives, in order to raise up seed needed for his spiritual welfare, to say nothing of his temporal. In case of failure, he secures the birthright of a male child by adoption.

Now the question comes, Did these honest travellers and the reverend missionaries report a falsehood? In reply, I would say, I have no right to answer for them. They know themselves the grounds of their assertion, whether it is based upon their personal knowledge of the case, or upon the story of some tale-teller, who often takes advantage of our ignorance and deceives us accordingly. To speak for myself, I will confess that, although a Brahmun, a native of India, I never saw a child thrown alive into the Ganges, nor heard of such stories until I came to America. I have shown, by reasons drawn from the Hindoo scripture, as well as from custom, that the sacrifice of an infant is as monstrous in the sight of a woman in India as in America. I will allege further, that the maternal affection is everywhere the same, implanted in the human breast by the Creator. I thought perhaps some traveller might have seen the deed done in certain wild portions of India, away from the civilized and learned communities. In fact, several of my friends here said, perhaps I do not know this. I was in Bengal; it might have taken place among the ignorant people in the wild regions. To my great surprise I met the following in a large pictorial work on India, pub-

(as I have myself observed in the first part of this book), they might throw her into the water. To this I reply, that the male child of a daughter has the same privilege with the sons of the father, to make the Shrautho. Hence, in India, the daughter cannot inherit her parents' property, but her son is the heir of the same.

lished in Boston. "Here (from the Saugor island) thousands of mothers have thrown their children into the Ganges to be devoured by alligators; not because they were destitute of maternal affection, but because a mother's love was overpowered by her fears of the wrath of some offended deity." Those who have ever visited Calcutta, know that the Saugor island is at the mouth of the Ganges, and only a few hundred miles from the city, the seat of wealth, learning, and refinement. To present this matter in its true light, I will describe this island and the sanctity attached to it. It is less settled by men than by wild beasts. It has a population of tigers, monkeys, and wolves. Very few children of Adam dare to dwell among these disagreeable inmates of the isle. There is a light-house, however, built by the British. The men who take care of the light, and a few solitary monks who live there, are considered the destined prey of the tigers, who are ready, whenever an opportunity occurs, to make their meal of them, or, to use a Hindoo expression, "if not a breakfast, a dinner, or a supper." This place being near the confluence of the river Ganges with the sea, is regarded as sacred by the Hindoos, who resort there in the month of January to bathe, and spend three days in tents pitched on the sandy banks of the river. Its sanctity draws immense crowds only once a year, when hardly any mother carries her child with her, for the place, as well as the river, is very dreadful. The efficacy consists in the bathing in this place, not in throwing children into the river. Those who go there go for the purpose of purifying themselves with the sacred water, and not to commit so cruel a murder as throwing children into the river.

So much for the Saugor island. I have sometimes looked at this matter in a different way; that a traveller had seen perhaps an insane woman throw her child into the water, which he interpreted as the institution of the "heathen." But it seems to me an unjust inference, to name the fruit of insanity as the custom of a people, to stigmatize a whole people for the folly of one, or a few even. I read in a Boston paper, that the average number of suicides in the United States is nine per week. Will it be proper for me to report in India that suicide is the custom of the American people? No, I cannot tell such a story. When I am asked about it, I will ascribe it to insanity or drunkenness. Once more, I will say, then, as a Brahmun I never knew nor heard of the story of children thrown by their mothers into the Ganges. If a Hindoo mother hears this story she will press her babe close to her heart and say, "Sweet treasure, I have drained the ocean for you. My tender kiss is more genial to you than the sharp lips of the alligator. My loving lap is a better place for you than the unconscious bed of the Ganges!"

A SKETCH

OF

MY LIFE AND EXPERIENCE.

DEDICATION.

THOMAS GAFFIELD, ESQUIRE.

THAT you may know the personal and religious experiences of one in whom you have taken so much interest, and as a token of gratitude for all you have done for me during my stay in this country, this imperfect sketch is respectfully dedicated to you by

Your friend and brother,

JOGUTH CHUNDER GANGOOLY,
Of Calcutta, India.

PREFACE.

To speak of one's self is not an easy matter. There are two things to be avoided, — vanity, which would cause one to put on what he never possessed, to say what he never was, and thereby to exaggerate the whole matter; second, cowardly humiliation, which would lead him to hide what he really has, and not to say what he has a right to say, lest the world should call him an egotist. It is better to take the middle ground, and proceed with prayer and watchfulness, keeping in mind "Thou God seest me."

Since my arrival in this country, my friends have expressed a great desire to know my personal history, — how I was educated, what led me to change my former religious views, etc. This brief sketch, which I leave to my friends as a "parting gift," will answer all these inquiries in a measure. This has been written in great haste. I have not had time to revise this sketch. Whenever the reader finds a point not clearly explained, he will please remember the circumstances under which this has been written. Only a few weeks before my departure for home I commenced writing it; and at the same time I had to attend to all other duties, and to make preparation for the voyage.

J. C. G.

SKETCH OF MY LIFE.

CHAPTER I.

My Childhood and Education.—My Mother.

I was born of a Brahmun family, in a place called Balie. It is nearly seven miles from Calcutta, the metropolis of British India, and is beautifully situated on the river Ganges, the sacred river of the Hindoos. Balie, for its numerous population, especially the Brahmun, and its learning, is universally regarded as one of the large and renowned places of Bengal. It has several districts, in which the people are settled according to their castes; thus, in our part—the Southern District—the Brahmuns live in one district. The physicians, the astrologers, the barbers, the farmers, the goldsmiths, the blacksmiths, the washermen, the dairymen, the fish-men, the shoemakers, the hog-keepers, etc. have distinct quarters of their own. When you come to a Brahmun, he can introduce you to twenty, more or less, of his fellow Brahmun neighbors; and such is the case with almost all other castes. The Brahmun population of my birthplace numbers more than two thousand. There are several temples in this place; the chief of which is one belonging to the god Shibā. There is a large market, perhaps the largest, where people from the neighboring towns and villages daily buy and sell their merchandise. There are two rum distilleries, owned by two French gentlemen, a large sugar factory, established by an Englishman, I presume; besides several castor-oil, gunny-bag, brick, and rope manufactories. A canal, passing through it, has made its north district a separate town, called Ootterparah, or north village; the other, however, is connected with the main village by two iron suspension bridges, one built by the East India Railway Company, and the other by the Government. The Government bridge is long, and handsomely constructed. As you sail up the Ganges from Calcutta, you see it distinctly on your left, hanging in the air.

There are three or four English schools, and one of them, standing on the Ootterparah side of the canal, belongs to the Government, to which the high castes send their sons for an English education. To come to Balie from Calcutta, the shortest way would be by railroad, which makes its *first* station here. There are also hundreds of small sailing Dingees, which carry passengers to and from Calcutta several times a day.

My father was a new settler in Balie; his native place is Vimpoor, of which I have no knowledge. While a young boy he was left an orphan, and with the care of a brother younger than himself. The only near relation he had was his aunt, the wife of a celebrated priest in Balie, who kindly invited the two orphan brothers to live with her. I cannot help speaking, if but a word, in this connection, of his uncle, as he seems to have been a very good and righteous man. The simplicity of his character, his devotion to good causes, his love for his fellow-creatures, were purely Christian. Among all his noble acts of charity, the most prominent was his taking care of the orphans, houseless, friendless, and helpless ones. He himself did not, as we hear, have a large family of his own, — not numbering more than eight members; still every day the floor of his dining-room had been overspread with twenty plates or more. His guests were not from his own caste exclusively; any child of God coming to his door for food or drink, would meet a loving welcome. Indeed, to love God through love toward man, was his darling motto. He manifested his love towards the low castes as much as his office and his religion allowed him. His door was open to all, — his house was the home for those who had "no place where to lay their heads." Like other priests, he used to bathe in the Ganges early in the morning throughout the year, but excelled them in his prayer and worship to the idols, which occupied daily nearly four hours on the stretch. By two in the afternoon he would come into the inner department of the house, and speak words of love to all around, inquiring of one after his health, congratulating another on his success, lamenting with a third his sorrows, etc. Entering into the kitchen, the first question to his wife would be, "Has every one got something to eat?" And receiving a satisfactory answer, he would put his hand on her head, with the benediction, "Yes! God has answered my prayer then!"

As this good old man had no time to inspect, nor inclination to interfere with, the private proceedings of his guests, there arose a universal outbreak of looseness and corruption of manners to which my uncle fell a victim. But fortunately, my father, conscious of his own responsibility as a moral agent, and desirous of becoming independent, escaped the general contagion which was then making dreadful havoc among his friends. But he could not save his younger brother, who chose his own course, and ran headlong to destruction. Applying himself diligently to the pursuit of theology, my father soon was able to take care of the temple services, and to help his uncle in the discharge of his priestly functions. By and by, serving as an assistant to a Brahmun, — the priest over a wealthy family in Calcutta, — he stood on a firm footing, married a wife, and determined to build a house and remove his family into it. There was a piece of land close by his aunt's, which he bought with a small sum for the following reason. There were some cocoanut, mango, and other wild trees on that lot which were, as they believed, the homės of demons, so hardly anybody dared to go to gather fruits thereon. It happened that my father, being a young man of courage and good common sense, fearlessly used to go there after the fruits which otherwise would have been left on the ground untouched by human hands. The owner of the lot, finding that my father enjoyed all the fruits of his trees which he had given up for fear of demons, thought it prudent to sell it to him for a reasonable sum. My father availed himself of the opportunity, and secured the lot with all its trees, and speedily built a house on it. He often used to say, he had driven all the demons from his place with "prayer and fasting" unto the god Rama. It would have been difficult for him to have moved to his new house, had it not been that my mother's courage was strong as his. For this new place had so bad a reputation that her female neighbors did not dare to call on her in the evening, for fear of the demons. She believed in their existence, but feared them not, saying, that if we behave well and do not offend them, no demon would trouble us in the least. I used to hear from her the stories of the demons coming invisibly near the house in the shades of midnight, and filling the place with the fragrance of some exquisite flowers. Such fragrant flowers she knew did not grow in the neighborhood. Four or five years after my father had removed to his new house a misfortune happened to the family. He was on a visit to a friend in a neighboring town, and my mother was left in care of a female servant. It was dark midnight when "the object on the lap could not be recognized;" she was sleeping in a room with her infant Joguth, — myself, — and the favorite domestic was in her own bed close by. Some burglars, taking advantage of my father's absence, broke through the house, and robbed it almost of its last penny. With a view of taking off the ornaments from the ankles of the sleeping women, one of the burglars touched the feet of my mother and thereby awoke her. She thought perhaps the servant had in her sleep touched her feet with hers, and spoke to her to the following effect: "Your limbs are pretty long, I see, On-nō!" "What made you think so, madam?" "Why, from there you could reach my ankle." "*Your* ankles? did I touch them with my feet? I am sure I shall die pretty soon. That's the reason why I do not wish to lie down close to the Brahmuns, lest I should kick them while sleeping. Sleeping and dining are just the same, you know," etc. She rises from her bed, puts her hand reverently to my mother's feet, salutes her, and stretches herself on the bed again. It can only be imagined with what deathlike silence the sons of sin heard the conversation, and, waiting a little while, took off the ornaments from my mother's body by force, and in a few minutes went on their way with a rich spoil. The cries of the women and the child gathered a crowd from the neighborhood. Some Brahmuns examined the house and found it rifled; boxes and chests were empty of their contents, as if they were just brought from the carpenter's. In fact, such was the entire loss of property, that my mother did not have a second suit of clothing left, and the family had to eat their dinner the next day on banana-leaves, on account of the plates, cups, etc., being all taken away. With a manly resignation my father bore his misfortune; and to add more to his discouragement, the next year his house was broken into and robbed by the same burglars a second time. The chief of these was a man belonging to a respectable family, now living, I presume, who with his son has thrown several families into poverty by robbing them in the midnight gloom! My uncle, being invited to his house, a few years afterwards, recognized the very tumbler he used to drink from at his own house. As the Brahmuns deem it a great sin to swear by the Ganges, no matter under what circumstances, my father did not raise any complaint against the man. He would rather go poor and suffer loss than regain his property, if possible, by swearing before a magistrate. His family grew larger, and what he subsequently earned was consumed for their support; so he never could gain a comfortable position again, in regard to pecuniary prospects.

Nine children were born unto him, of whom five are living. Of the living, the first is my brother, the second and the third are sisters, the fourth is the writer, and the fifth is my youngest sister. Our names, although not in essence, are, in significance, pretty. My oldest brother is named after the god "Krishto and the moon;" the oldest sister is "Drop of Honey;" the second is "Young Beauty;" the meaning of my name is "The Moon of the World;" and our youngest brother, who died at seven, was "The Summer Moon."

There being no system of female education in Bengal, my father applied all his energies for my training, and being a religious man himself, cared more for the right development of my heart than for my head. I remember distinctly sitting in his lap every evening and committing the prayers, proverbs, etc., to memory.

He had a remarkable faculty of cultivating, improving, and enriching another's memory. Every evening I had to learn either a part or the whole of a prayer or moral precept, in the Sanscrith poetry, and to recite to him *all* the old ones beside. Thus, while other Brahmun boys of my own age or older knew nothing about proverbs and parables, my memory was amply supplied with the same. With such care he had taught me these things, that what I learned while a boy, perhaps nine or ten years old, I can repeat today, word by word, most of it being prayers to nearly twelve deities, such as the Sun, the River Ganges, Doorga, Shibă, Rama, Krishto, etc., and "an hundred and eight proverbs," besides select pieces from old Sanscrith poems, etc.

He did not aim at crowding my youthful mind with dry, unintelligible precepts, but bathed it with their sweet juice. Indeed, ere I was made Thejo, or Second Born, I could almost draw pleasure from those Sanscrith proverbs, and recognize their applicability to the internal phenomena of the world. My fondness for poetry — which afterwards grew so strong that, though a renouncer of the Hindoo gods, I took much pains to compose several pieces of drama from the legends — was implanted in these younger days. And, as the result of learning the stories and legends of the gods, a deep reverence for them filled my heart. My childhood's devotion to the idols was exemplary. My dear mother told me several anecdotes of my early days, about my offering or rather reciting prayers to the deities. During the great worship of a goddess in our neighborhood, my father was going to see the theatrical shows late in the evening. He awoke me from my sleep, and gladly I started with him. It was my habit to thank the gods, each by its respective name, before going out of doors. There was an idol of Shawlgram in our house, and as I passed through a narrow entry, I bent my head against the wall of the room in which the image was, and offered prayers. One by one my favorite gods all came into my mind; of course it took a longer time than usual to ask blessings from them all. My father walked almost to the place of worship and turned back to speak to me, but I was not there. Fearing some accident might have happened, or that I was taken aloft by Neeshie, he hastened toward home,* and found his little boy slowly striking his head against the wall. He felt doubly happy in learning that nothing unpleasant had happened, and that his boy was growing religious. How little did he know then that a Spirit more hurtful than Neeshie had already taken possession of the tender heart of his son. It was superstition that caused him to "bow down to wood and stone."

Through his precious help and guidance I early learned to read distinctly and understandingly almost all the Bengalee books containing the lives of the gods. The legends of Ramà, Krishto, the Ganges, etc., were my favorite studies. To do justice to his noble discretion, I should say that he never put any reading of a light character within my reach. I read over and over those religious books, which after a while grew so familiar that I could read the most of them merely by glancing at the page. The fact, that nearly half of my time was occupied in reading became known to the

---

* Neeshie, or Night, is the name of a species of evil spirits who are believed by the Hindoos to walk invisibly on the earth in the shades of night, and to entice young children to go with them. It is a dangerous thing to be under their control, as the children cannot speak a word or call for help when they are carried aloft on the trees. The testimony of those who had been taken away by Neeshie is thus: "While our friends were crying for and searching after us we saw them, and wished to speak but could not." The spirit, however, does not detain its victims long, but brings them to their home invisibly.

people, who would come to my house or invite me to theirs for the purpose. On holidays, I had to edify them by reading or reciting the sacred things.

Some elderly woman would conduct me to the inner department of a Hindoo house to read to the young women who are inaccessible to young men, and not being themselves taught to read or write are strangers to intellectual pleasures. My age and ability were remarkably adapted to the case, because though a little boy I could accomplish a great deal. I distinctly remember the congregation of women; one fanning me, a second holding a plate full of confectioneries, a third, an old woman, congratulating my mother for her having had such a child, etc. My father would occasionally let me accompany him in his official visits, that the religious zeal of his people might be quickened in hearing the voice of truth "revealed unto the babe."

I was sent to a Patshala, or house of instruction, at the age of five; but I acquired more at home than anywhere else. Mental arithmetic, letter-writing, composition, etc. I learned from my father. Such was his untiring zeal to load my mind with all possible useful information, that my first acquaintance with a few English words was made through him. His priestly mouth, after imparting instruction in the Sanscrith, would teach me a few words in English, such as the pronouns of different persons and numbers; the word for God, man, hand, dog, etc., which he had picked up in some way, from those who studied English. But I am sorry to see now that the good man taught me two or three phrases in English with which the vulgar people swear. He of course did not know the evil; he thought what the Englishmen use must be delicate, proper, and useful.

Although not educated herself, my mother could teach me a great many things in the absence of my father. She knew the multiplication table up to how much eighteen times nineteen would be; also parables and proverbs, all by heart. She would comment upon and furnish hints on reading, explain difficult passages, and use the best materials in her conversation. She too, like my father, valued more our spiritual than intellectual accomplishments. Respect to age, love and devotion to the idols, honor to parents, faithfulness to conviction, strict observance of the customs of the country, were the themes she dwelt upon. These she would require obstinately, not willing to take off the veil and examine the substance within. How much I had to struggle against from her displeasure when the free tone of my thought and desires after reformation came into collision with her conservatism and adherence to superstitious institutions, I cannot tell. My position, in after years, proved diametrically opposite to her wishes in a great many respects, and she persistently labors, even up to to-day, to reconcile them, not making in the least any surrender on her part though. She exhorted me all the time to observe "every jot and tittle" pertaining to Hindooism, and would apply reason, persuasion, entreaty, and finally threats for the purpose. My oldest brother had not the chance of being under her care, nor of hearing her advice, — being absent from her most of the time, — and he has grown a self-willed, immoral young man. She laments very much over him, and says, "she would take twofold care over Joguth," lest he too should slip away from the path of right, and disappoint her accordingly. Always she used to say, "He who comes last runs towards the direction in which the first has gone." That she might not have occasion to suffer again on my account she built some walls around me.

I know no mother in our neighborhood who watched the steps of her sons so vigilantly as mine did. In fact the women of the adjacent houses often said that "they never dreamed of or prescribed such regulations for their children, and that they did not watch their *babies* so closely as my mother did her adults." When anything unpleasant, wicked, or vicious happened in the place, she would take the opportunity to warn me, saying, "I hope, Joguth, you would die before you would become guilty of such things. I should feel anxious to leave you alone in this world, in case I should die first, much as it will be a happiness to me. Remember the saying, 'Let go your life, but retain your honor.'" Her favorite mottoes were the following, which she would always hold before me. When we complained of any one, she would say, "If I am good, the world is good unto me." In time of temptation, "Conquer within first, and you will conquer without." When any one is discontented, and cannot live in peace with his brethren, her motto is, "Peace accommodates nine persons in one room, but discord puts them in nine separate ones." Speaking of quarrelsome persons, her saying was, "She who is naturally quarrelsome would quarrel with her work-basket." Of those who bring discord, "Wicked man and mouse break; good man and needle connect." Beside these she had other sayings: "Where there is right, there is victory." "Walk in the way of righteousness, and you will receive your meal even in the midnight." "If you want to be the greatest, be the lowest."

I have observed before that she would watch me on every side. She did not feel satisfied with merely prescribing regulations for me, but with strictness would see them carried out. Sometimes she would put some false charge upon me, in order to teach me a lesson. "Joguth, were you quarreling with the boy?" so saying, she would paint the evil of fighting in dark colors. I was not allowed to dress gay like other young men of my age, nor even to part my hair: "Comb your hair simply; look *clean* but not *foppish.*" She would comment upon my mode of walking, smiling, and talking, and give some sharp rebukes if there was any fault in them.

One evening I came very near the kitchen where the women were, walking so slow that none could hear sounds of my steps. To my utter confusion she said, "I am afraid of you, Joguth; what kind of walking was that? You came in, giving no warning with your steps, so slow they were! O Joguth, gentlemen do not do so; *thieves* do. Were you practising how the thieves walk?" When at home I was not allowed to talk to my aunt, or brother's wife even. My mother had great fear of young women, saying that man could not corrupt them unless they yield; so more than a dozen times she begged them not to speak to her Joguth.

She does not find any pleasure in gossip and slander, and avoids the place where such are indulged. Her counsel is, "Speak good of others, and bring their evil before you simply for the purpose of deriving admonition from them. We are all liable to make blunders. 'The saints may err,' is the Sanscrith saying. Our talking of the imperfections and immoralities of others is just as ridiculous as the censure of the sieve, which cried out, 'Brother needle, why, there is a hole in your body.'"

In her daily occupation and habits she is worthy of our imitation. She is the last to go to bed and the first to leave it. You awake in the midnight and you will find her at work or whispering hymns; rise early, and you will see she has gone to the Ganges to bathe. Inaction is an abomination to her: she would urge all to do something innocently profitable. She hates debt, and fears it as death itself. At the first call she would pay her debts, even if her children should suffer for it. She believes that he who dies a debtor will have to settle his dues after death; and to confirm this doctrine she points out the trees that grow one upon the other, such as a banian tree upon the trunk of a palm; explaining, thus, that the latter did not pay his debts, so after death he has become a tree, and his creditor grows on his head in the form of a banian. Such is an imperfect sketch of my dear mother, under whose care and supervision my early days were directed. Any good thing I have in me was the gift of this noble woman; she laid it in my heart in its rude state, and a Teacher wiser and more unerring than she has polished it afterwards. May God judge and reward her according to the light she has. To whom much is given of them much shall be required. God grant that before she breathes her last breath, she may know that in deserting the idol gods her son has not committed an unpardonable sin!

CHAPTER II.

My "Second Birth." — Consecration for the Priesthood. — Religious Training. — Death of my Father. — English Schools. — Zeal for Idolatry.

The Brahmun boys are not permitted to touch idols or to perform any religious services until they are become "Second born." Accordingly at the age of thirteen, I believe, I was consecrated to Brahmun life.

On a bright summer day the friends from far and near assembled together at our house, having been previously invited to attend the ceremony. In the course of the services the officiating priest cut three locks of my hair in the name of the three principal Hindoo deities, Brahma, Vishnu, and Shiba; then the barber shaved my head and put two small ear-rings in my ears according to the religious law. After invoking the presence, approbation, and blessing of hundreds of gods, the priest put a thread round my neck. It is a sacred badge of the Brahmuns, made of cotton, and not worn by the low castes. A yellow robe was thrown over me, and a veil round my face, and I was conducted into my room. The period of staying in this room without seeing any low-caste man is either of three, five, or seven days, during which the Second born learns his Shundhas — the especial forms of prayer. These are long, philosophically constructed, and regarded *very* sacred. The low castes dare not hear of nor utter a word of them. My term in this secluded room was very short, — only three days, — because my good, thoughtful father had taught me those things beforehand, charging me not to tell them to any low castes. I found them very useful now as I was to repeat them three times a day.

Now begins a new scene in life in regard to religious affairs. We had an image of Krishto at our house, and I had to worship it twice every day, besides the idols of other families occasionally. Early in the morning I would go after flowers for the worship. The rules for gathering flowers are numerous, yet beautiful when understood. First, wash your hands; do not put your dirty fingers upon the delicate, clean person of the flowers; be very careful not to break a branch or to pluck a bud; do not smell of any flower before you have offered it to the gods; keep the basket with its treasures in your hand, and place it not on the ground. Leaving the flowers at home, I would go to the school for instruction, where again my discipline was novel. I must not put anything into my mouth, nor sit on the same seat with boys of other castes, etc. In the street the young as well as the grown-up low castes would salute me, and I had to raise my little hands to bless them, saying, "Be victorious!" or "Live forever!"

Some would bring a little water in the palm of their hands, desiring me to touch it by the end of my first toe of the right foot, that they might drink it. The form of words used by all the Brahmuns for this purpose means something like this: "The sanctity of the right foot of the Second Born is equal to the sanctity of the world and sea combined together." Heretofore I had no especial rules to observe in time of eating, but now I must bathe first, then offer my prayer, worship the idols, and afterward take luncheon. Again, keep silent while eating; I must not leave my seat on *any* account, unless I choose to forfeit my meal; I must spare something on the plate for the creeping things, etc.

I would speak of my daily idol worship. After washing myself, either in the river Ganges or in some tank (in the latter case the Hindoos sprinkle a few drops of the sacred water on the head), I would go into the room where the image was kept on a small wooden throne, elegantly furnished with cushions, pillows, curtains, etc. On the floor there was a carpet-seat for me, some copper and brazen vessels, a hand-bell, a large plate, with a good display of flowers, perfumatory powder, and some edibles. Bringing down the idol from its throne, I would put it into a vessel and pour water on its head by the right hand and ring the bell by the other, uttering some words at the same time. Wiping it with small towels, I would put it on a seat and scatter flowers, powder, etc., on its head with much ceremony, offering prayer and praise to it, ask its glance at the edibles, etc., and finally prostrate myself on the ground in humiliation, and partake of the "food offered to the idol." By and by, when the dinner had been cooked and set in order, I would carry the idol into the dining-room and offer the food to it the second time.

While I was thus worshipping the idol, and forming plans for a higher grade of devotion, my father was removed from this to the world above. I was then fourteen years old, I think. He suffered a fortnight from a fever, which finally brought an end to his existence. He retained his consciousness, yea, even his literary priestly sensibilities, unto the very last. It is customary in our country to read, from Hindoo sacred books, to the sick. A priest was called upon to do this service to my father. When he had finished his reading, my father remarked: "Friend, to sell needles to a blacksmith is not an easy matter; what you read to me has been *particularly* meant for a case different from mine." I was not at home when he died, having gone to Calcutta to a

Brahmun woman who had taken much interest in my father. While I was returning home in the afternoon a neighbor inquired of me "if I knew how my father was," and receiving a negative answer said, "Go home and you will see." Drawing myself nearer home the cries from my friends told me my dear father was dead. His body was then on the funeral pile on the bank of the Ganges, but I could not see it. They would not let me go there. He did not leave any fortune for us. While breathing his last, he said to my mother that the richest thing he left for her was Ish-ur, or God; and, next to him, the "three diamonds," his three sons. "These three," he said, "duly and rightly used, will meet all your wants." My uncle, the younger brother of my father, stretched forth his kind hands over us. Not being a religious man himself, and inclined to follow the fashion of the community, he desired me to study English part of the time, and requested a fine Hindoo young man, a student of the "Hindoo College," to give me instruction. Accordingly I began to study what is called "the language of the Jobuns," and the first English book I had was Murray's Spelling-Book. Some four or five boys came in, and we formed a class. Our teacher had only half an hour to give to us, and after he had gone to his own school we used to talk foolishly, play tricks, tear each others' books, and thereby used to enjoy *good* but frequently *bad* times. Finding me little promising, our teacher advised my uncle to send me to a good English school, which he accordingly did. It was a government school, at the distance of a mile and a half from our house. I was admitted into the third class, and our studies were The First Reader, Elements of the English Grammar, and Geography. There being no especial teacher over our class, the second teacher had the charge of the two, consequently he held to the one, and took little care of the other. Not being able to hear each boy read and recite, he would ask every second or fourth boy to read a paragraph. We could know at once if anything would fall to our lot, and could prepare that particularly. In the course of four months a Bengalee gentleman, fresh from college, became appointed as the third teacher, and we followed him to his forms. He was a very irritable man, and would use his whip quite smartly and frequently too. Among ten or twelve unfortunate boys who were the favored recipients of his whip and blows I was one. Receiving some stripes for a couple of days, I determined to get rid of them, because I had never met with these disagreeable things before. The trouble was, I did not know how to prepare my lesson; I wanted some help, but could not get it. He, seeing me tolerably good in other studies, found out that I was not "totally depraved." So one day he asked me when I studied my lesson at home. I told him I did not understand what study at home was; for I open my books at school and nowhere else, as my friends do not know English to guide me. He kindly suggested to me what to do. I followed the advice, and in a week became one of the leading boys in the class. One thing is worth observing, as far as modesty will permit, that whoever was acquainted with me, admired my faculty of retaining things in the memory. Those who know me can testify well to this point, but for my part I can simply say this, that if I had anything in me which drew the attention of a large circle, it was my memory. To-day I can repeat word by word the chief part of the books which I had read ten years ago. Whatever prizes I acquired in the schools were rather due to my memory than anything else. When I had made some progress in English studies, and my uncle refused to supply me with all the books I needed, to the surprise of the school, I retained my honorable position in the class, although I did not have more than four or five books out of eight or nine, — the studies for the time. At this time my uncle, who was a widower, married a young girl whose mother came to live with her. She is a remarkable woman. Not having a good time with her husband, as he had several wives at the same time, she fled from home with her daughter of seven or eight years old, and some money, came to our place and married her infant child to my uncle without the knowledge of her nearest relatives, who made violent struggles for her afterward; but it was too late. After staying a year or more at our house, the woman managed to poison my uncle's mind and destroy the peace of the family forever. Quarrels, misunderstandings, rash and unkind remarks, often marred the domestic happiness. In order to vex my mother, she would, before her presence, speak slander of others; ridicule the words of the Brahmuns, teach villanous stories to the children, sing audibly nonsensical, comic pieces, and make rude remarks, etc. My mother used to send me away with my books to some neighbor's house, and would keep herself in her own room. By day and night my mother's prayer became at this period, "Gods, remove me and my children to a wilderness, among the wild beasts and the fowls who do not know slander, neither do what they ought not." For fear of the odium which would naturally fall upon him, my uncle could not withdraw his help at once, but gradually effected the object under various pretences. We could hear distinctly in the evening the mother-in-law of my uncle entreat him to stop the expense of my studies. In justice to him I should say, that a great many times he rebuked her, saying, "His father has committed Joguth to my care; it would n't look well to neglect him. If he grows a man, he will doubtless be a help to me." But though "he feared not God, nor cared for man," her importunity wrought a revolution in his feelings. The regulation of the school required the pupils to bring their school-fee on the first day of the month in advance, and in default thereof they would be sent home. My uncle would not give the money in season; he would make excuses, and I had to stay at home. Thus in the early part of every month I was compelled to be absent, and of course lose my high place in the class. My teacher once opened the register to show Mr. R. Hand, the head teacher, how my rank miserably suffered for my absence during the time of delayed payment for the schooling. Finally my uncle said he was in debt, and it cost him a great deal to support us, so he could not pay the expenses of my studies any longer. It was a dreadful calamity to me, which will be ever remembered.

The very boys who were juniors to me, and whom I used to help in various ways, made astonishing progress in a few years, while I remained almost where I was. The idea of taking instruction privately from one who knew more than I did, did not satisfy me, for I had tasted the pleasures of the school, deriving much from maps, globes, library, and competition too.

There were free schools in Calcutta, founded by the missionaries, but the expenses of attending them from Balie would be treble what it cost me in the Ooterparah, Government School. For a year I remained at home, making little progress in the English studies, and performing the priestly functions as well as I could. Afterwards I was admitted to several schools, but in none could I prosecute my course for more than five or six months. Although busy in my scholastic duties, I did not give up the habit of observing the fasts, worship, etc., of my country. Yea, these troubles and misfortunes fixed my eyes steadfastly upon the idols, and happily brought me to the arms of the "King eternal, immortal, the only-wise God," — the loving Father of the universe!

With a double zeal and devotion I pursued the course laid out by my father; the love for the gods grew stronger, and their lives, as displayed in our sacred books, seemed sweeter. Desiring to live and move within a broad sphere of piety, — to observe the rituals and fasts with the enthusiasm of grown-up persons, I made a new routine for the exercises. The daily "morning bath" in the sacred river Ganges is held by the Hindoos as a great religious act, productive of spiriual excellence. I took a vow to do this regularly. At this period a peculiar feeling, which is almost foreign to most of the Hindoos, seemed to dawn its splendor upon me; it was an earnest desire to see my gods respected, feared, and worshipped by all, and to bring all men under their allegiance. This very desire, when reawakened by Christ, and I forsook the idols, gave a sincere response to that soul-stirring sentiment —

"Be thou, O God, exalted high;
And as thy glory fills the sky,
So let it be on earth displayed,
Till thou art here, as there obeyed."

I summoned all my energies to serve the gods and goddesses according to the rules laid down in the Hindoo Scriptures. In the morning I would go after the choice flowers, that I might satisfy the idols with just what they are fond of; for some Hindoo gods are fond of a certain kind of flower or leaf which the others do not care for. It pained me exceedingly to see the young men, my neighbors, go without prayer, worship, or fast. I persuaded them to follow my standard, — assured them if they would only come to the

10

gods, their imperfections, wants, sorrows, would be removed by the celestial grace. My exhortation found immediate response from them. Among them two were shamefully lazy, — could not prepare their lessons at all, — were the worst boys of every school they went to. These finding me in a better and more honorable position, begged me to show to them the source whence flows "all good and perfect gifts." As I had myself strong faith in the benevolent disposition of the gods I urged my friends to come to them for help. Accordingly a party of young devotees was formed under my guidance, of whom all were Brahmuns. Being large in number, and having among us daring elements, we could gather the best flowers from distant parts of our village for the worship. While other Brahmuns had hardly left their beds we were on the tops of large trees, and there filled our baskets with varieties of flowers. We would then move towards the Ganges, where, performing our ablutions according to the prescribed rules, we visited the principal temple to worship the image of Shiba. As my friends did not know how to worship it, and what form of prayer to use in the different parts of the service, I had to do the business of the priest, uttering audibly the sacred words learned of my father, and making them recite after me. Before leaving the temple I would decorate the altar and the image with the flowers, using all my skill and earnestness. So regular were our visits to the temple, so many flowers were carried there, that other Brahmuns coming in earlier would say, "Joguth has not been here yet, we see." The Hindoos fast a great many days during the year, so I wished to do; but my mother interposed, as it would have destroyed my health to abstain from food and drink entirely for twenty-four hours. I used to observe one fast only, — in the month of February, I believe. It is called Shiba

Rattree, or the Night of Shiba. The first part of the day was less trying, but in the afternoon and night the face would turn pale, the eyes sink, the body become weak, etc. Still, hoping to receive a blessed seat in the heaven of Shiba, I would bear all these, and go through abstinence with a cheerful heart. Once, while quite a number of us fasted, the forenoon passed along nicely with fun, plays, and walks. A friend older than I left us, and after an hour returned again. I noticed his face looked easy, entirely different from that of an hour ago, and suspected he had, perhaps, taken some food, and asked him about it. Before he had time to say yea or nay, I saw something yellow on his lip which proved to be the remainder of a fruit he had eaten. At this one felt indignant, a second laughed out, a third said he would not fast longer. I was left with one more to satisfy Shiba, by passing the whole day and night without food or drink. My belief in the gods was so strong, my faith in their protecting power was so unwavering, that I thought I could hold close communion with them, see their smiles beaming forth out of the eyes and mouth of the images. To Shiba I prayed for learning; to Luckhy for wealth; to Doorga for relief from dangers; to Krishto for heaven, — and I was pretty sure of getting them. Little did I dream then that these deities are mere ideals, whom I worshipped, loved, and feared, and for whose grace I fasted so hopefully. During the time of evening worship, when hundreds of lights were burned, the band played, the incense filled the place with sweet perfume, and joy shed its charms over all, I would stand reverently before the image, look earnestly at its face, repeat silent prayers, and thereby feel myself happy. At the close, I would kneel down, or sometimes prostrate myself on the ground with humiliation.

The Brahmuns desired my mother to commit me to their

charge, which she did not, for various reasons. One of them, who had a large parish, would send a substitute round quite often to the houses of his people to worship the idols for them. I had to go, too, to a town across the river Ganges to attend to the images. So strong was my affection for the idols, so earnest was I to see all people worship unceasingly, that while playing cards with my friends one day, I proposed an extra worship of the goddess. The little band approved it; the cost was counted and found too large for our private pocket to afford. I encouraged them with a promise to construct the image with my own hand. They considered the possibility of the enterprise, and we at once set out to work. Accordingly, bamboo was brought, a piece of board, nails, straw, string, etc., were secured. Fearing our parents would interfere with this, we carried the materials to the top of a house, which in our country is flat. One day a respectable Brahmun, looking at the parapet, saw the hands of the image and came upstairs to see what we had done. The neighbors flocked in to see, admire, and help at our work, and a universal enthusiasm prevailed. A great many doubted my ability to finish the idol, but I think I did it nicely. My oldest brother painted it, and we received the praise of the people. To commemorate this event we worshipped the idol annually, defraying the expenses by subscription. It makes me smile to think that, when my friends invited me to take the lead, as usual, in things in subsequent years, I pointed out to them the error of idol worship. Of course they did not feel like myself, so they came to a conclusion that I had grown crazy, and would certainly become Christian very soon!

CHAPTER III.

First Views of Christianity. — Prejudices. — Sermon on the Mount. — New Testament. — Efforts and Struggles. — Comparison of Hindoo and Christian Doctrines. — Conversion. — First Zeal. — Perplexed by the Trinity. — Visit to a Missionary. — Trinitarianism. — My Difficulties. — Deistical Companions. — Arrival of Mr. Dall.

Now begins an important stage in my life. The dawn of a bright future breaks upon me with a serenity never before dreamed of. My Heavenly Father, not willing that his child should go away from him and remain ignorant of his gracious majesty, turned my course slowly toward his infinite goodness. He could no longer suffer his child to prostrate himself before "wood and stone," and He sent His "Beloved Son" to teach him and bring him to his "Father's Home." While much occupied in observing the religious ordinances of my people, while summoning all my energies for the cause of the idols, and offering all the treasures of my heart and head at their feet, I heard of the celebrated Christian Missionary, Rev. Dr. Duff of Calcutta, and his colleagues, making converts of the Hindoo boys. My animosity towards Christianity rose with all its fury, and I wished to see it die out, that it might not rob the peace and prosperity of the Hindoo families, by stealing away the young boys and leading them headlong into vice, immorality, and misery. For the Hindoo's impression of

Christianity is this: That in order to become a Christian it is essentially necessary that a young man should treat his parents unkindly, eat animal food, such as beef, pork, ham, etc., which the Hindoos detest very much, drink wine, not wash his mouth after the meal, as the animals do, and forsake all things which bear the name of Hindoo, no matter how beautiful they are. Now, if these are the essential features of Christianity, why should I have wondered that the Hindoos fear it? But thanks be to God that *these are not* parts of the religion of Christ; these have little or nothing to do with it. Again, the Hindoo hatred towards Christianity arises from another important cause; viz., that the lives of most of its nominal advocates contradict its spirit. No nation is so furious, proud, bloodthirsty as a Christian one. No country, I presume, is flooded so often with human blood, as that which is studded with "meeting-houses," which publish the Gospel of Peace by myriads, annually, of different editions, versions, and illustrations. The gentlemen, the senators of Christian countries, impelled by animal passions, fight duels, and thereby abuse the precious gift of God, the life. These are the men who declare themselves disciples of Christ, who own pews in the church, whose wives and daughters are Sunday-school teachers. "But whosoever shall smite thee on thy right cheek, turn to him the other also," is a precept of their Teacher. My dear mother would point me out the ambitious deeds of the English people, saying, "There, Joguth, do not you speak of the religion of Shahebs to me; put it on the shelf yonder; they have no religion at all! What! what did you say, 'And if any man will sue thee at the law, and take away thy coat, let him have thy cloak also!' Very beautiful words, indeed! O Joguth, what do the Shahebs do? Do they care a fig for them? No!

Their religion is 'to rob those who have nothing to do with them.' Poor Runjit Serigh, the Queen of Nagpoor! I pity them; they fell victims to the ambition of your Christian Shahebs. How I should like to see their Queen, and tell her, 'Shame to your subjects! They fight, they quarrel, they rob our country. You do not know what they do out of your sight. When they go abroad they forget the instruction of home,'" etc.

Having had a fear, and hatred, too, towards Christianity, I determined to investigate its true peculiarities,—which I felt quite sure must be childish and fallacious,—that I might be qualified to argue with the Christians and triumphantly expose their errors. Some Christian books were necessary, but how should I get them? I was too timid to go to the missionaries; first, I could not speak English; and, secondly, I feared them to be the "boy thieves," as the Hindoos designate them. On a holiday I saw low castes carrying home a quantity of "*Tracts*" given to them by the servants of Christ. I managed to secure a copy which contained that portion of Christ's teaching known by the name of the "Sermon on the Mount." Need I tell to a Christian reader the sublime beauty of these words of *Life?* I should say, however, that I was quite disappointed in not finding fallacious, weak, foolish doctrines in it as I anticipated. Its pages opened heaven before me, and I could see distinctly its joys, its angels, and its blessedness. I could see also the *earth*, not like one around us, in which the life and its attendant functions have been manufactured by our own hands, but one fresh from the hand of the Most High,—a pure, simple, loving world! Over and over I read the tract, and wished to get some more. A few tracts which I subsequently received contained a great deal of the teaching of men, and less of His who had studied his theology in the bosom of the Father, and who said, "My words are not my own; what I have heard of my Father, that speak I to you."

Reading the first tract, containing the "Sermon on the Mount," carefully, I became so familiar with Christ's voice, that I could recognize him from out the crowd. "Sheep know the voice of their shepherd," he says. I was told that a book called "Holy Bible" contains the life of Jesus in full, and I longed to have a copy of it. As there was no Bible in the house, I had some difficulty in procuring a copy for some time. Providentially a Brahmun boy had brought some pamphlets and a book to me, and begged me to make some kites for him with their leaves. To my unspeakable joy the book proved to be the long-sought one,—the life of Christ, by four evangelists,—the New Testament! I made some kites with my own writing-paper, and the lad gave me his blue book in turn. Now begins a period of investigation, study, contemplation, of the teaching of Christ. Among others, his kind words, inviting the poor, the suffering, the despised, to come unto him,—"Come unto me all ye that labor, and are heavy laden, and I will give you rest,"—struck me very much. I was the worshipper of several male and female deities, and some of them were my beloved ones; but none called me in such a loving, affectionate way. His saying, "Take my yoke upon you, and learn of me, for I am meek and lowly of heart, and ye shall find rest unto your souls; for my yoke is easy, and my burden is light," furnished me with ample materials for meditation. Who is this, I asked, that promises us "*rest*," without demanding any compensation, as the Hindoo gods do? Carefully I followed Christ in all his walks, listened to him while he was on the mountain, saw him cure sickness and cast out devils, heard him bid the rough sea "be still," watched him at his table in the upper chamber, witnessed his arrest, trial, and crucifixion, and his victory over death. With a view of comparing Christianity with the modern Hindooism I took some leading points of each. First, the Creator of the universe, who is he? what relation is there between him and his creatures? where can he be found, and how worshipped? etc. The belief of the Hindoos in regard to these subjects differs in accordance with their caste, culture, and opportunities. The learned Brahmuns derive their belief from the Sacred Vedas; others from tradition; and the low castes have no knowledge of them, perhaps, or the little they have is ridiculous. Christ tells us our Creator is a Great Being, — God, — and that he is One. I received the doctrine, as it confirmed beautifully my impression of a Creator. I had this consciousness from my early years, but did not know who that Being was, for Bromho is said to be the Maker of all, but he too rises from the Bishto. Leaving aside the speculative theory of my country, I found relief in the simple yet truthful words of Christ.

The Hindoos bear different relations to their gods. This seemed to me absurd. For instance, Shiba is called "*Father*," his wife Doorga, mother, his two daughters are our mother too, who, according to the common rules, ought to be our sisters. Krishto is addressed by the term *Father* also. Now the great Teacher says we have only one Father in heaven, even God. When I learned of Christ that my Creator is *one* great Being, and though his majesty is infinite, his wisdom unfathomable, his power unbounded, his position high, he is our Father still, my joy knew no bounds. I became aware that my recognition of a creator in the Bromho, Bishto, etc., was just as bewildering as to seek an object in the gloomy chambers of Mammoth Cave. But Christ stood by my side as a blazing light, and pointed out the shortest, easiest way to my God, saying, "I am the light" and "I am the way." I used to think we could come to God through different routes, but now felt convinced of the great advantage of entering in by the strait gate, treading the steps of Christ, and following the guidance of the celestial Guide. When I want to visit the city of New York, the prudent course will be to take the express train at the Worcester Depot, and not step into the Boston, Concord, and Montreal cars which will surely take me far, far away from my destination; it will cost more money and longer time into the bargain! *

Where our Creator is to be found and how worshipped became the subject of my inquiry. Hindoo gods have their respective heavens, some particular places for their abodes, which they do not wish to be away from. Thus Krishto reigns in his Goluck, Shiba in Koylas, etc. The latter is said to have wept on leaving Kashie for a season at the solicitation of Debodass, a worshipper.

But turning to Christ, I heard him say, our Father is everywhere, — fills immensity with his presence; that there is no place so high, so happy as to monopolize his presence, to confine him within its enclosure; there is no place, on the other hand, so low that does not contain him. The Mighty Omnipresent sits on high, the great King of all, controlling the affairs of the universe with his powerful, yet loving

* When I speak of our coming to God through Christ I do not mean anything dogmatic in it. My ideas in relation to this point are practical, — I mean an approach unto the throne of the Most High with the *spirit* of Christ, acting as he did, living as he lived. Put on Christ around you; let his spirit approve your acts, guide your thoughts, and sanctify your affections, and you will find yourself not far from your Heavenly Father. This is the rational way of knowing him as "the only true God, and Jesus Christ" whom he has sent.

sway, — receiving homage from the Seraphim and Cherubim, and the "just made perfect;" yet, at the same time, noticing the fall of the sparrows.

In regard to worship, I was taught to worship the images of the gods, to offer food and clothing to them, and occasionally to visit the sacred cities, such as Orissa,* or Benares, etc. But Christ taught me otherwise. He says, "neither this mountain, nor Jerusalem," is to be the favored place for worshipping God; "Worship him in the Spirit, for he is a Spirit." This seemed to me a beautiful idea, for it enables high as well as low to worship the Creator, — to hold communion with him, — to lay before him all their joys, sorrows, and disappointments, instead of going after him in Jerusalem or Benares. Again, what a great consolation it is to know that a pure and contrite heart, with all its poverty and meekness, is more acceptable to God than the richest offering, than temples of gold? How many thousands of the Hindoos live and die in despair of that degree of spiritual perfection, that peculiar blessing of the gods, which a few hundred dollars would have secured for them! The poor man, notwithstanding all his righteousness, the purity of his heart, and his love for holy things, is not entitled to share the joys of heaven with the rich wicked man, who has spent enormous sums of money in visiting temples, in pilgrimages, or in worshipping costly images. This is the absurd belief I had in regard to the worship of the gods, and I thanked God heartily when I got rid of it. Secondly, I wished to know about *man:* my relation and duties towards other men, etc. The theory that man is our brother, being the child of a common Father, has been falsified by the sys-

* I did not live a Hindoo long enough to perform any pilgrimage, but used to hear the stories from those who had been to the holy cities.

tem of the *castes*, and by the power and sanctity of the priesthood. A low-caste man is no more a brother to a Brahmun than are the inferior animals. If a shoemaker accidentally should touch the plate of a Brahmun, he would not use its contents; it is as if a dog should touch it. I know that in this world we must have, of necessity, differences in position, culture, accomplishments, etc., that one demands respect of another; but do we stand high or low agreeably to our caste, wealth, intelligence, before Him who is "no respecter of persons"? When a Brahmun, I felt it was my duty — making a right use of my position and its attendant prerogatives — to look at the low castes with indifference. I did not touch them if I could possibly help it. I put my foot on their prostrate heads, I gave the dust of my foot to them to eat, and I promised them earthly and heavenly blessings. But the moment I learned from the lips of Jesus what my relation is to my fellow-man, and what duty I owe towards him, I clearly saw the low castes are just as high as myself. Hearing that "God maketh his sun to rise on the good and evil," that the harlots, the despised, would enter into blessedness before the proud Pharisee, I cheerfully abdicated the honors, the prerogatives of my high position as a Brahmun, and wished to jump down upon the level where the despised low castes stood. Indeed, who but God knows the magnitude of the delight I enjoyed in standing by the side of the low castes! While in the street I would walk close to them, and thereby get an opportunity to touch them. Of course the grown-up low castes would not come in close contact with me, fearing it would be a dangerous thing for them. So I used to hide my sacred or priestly badge under my clothes, which, if kept in its proper place would have testified of my caste, and to speak kind words to the despised sons of humanity.

After reading the life of Christ carefully, I came to the following conclusions: — That our Creator is one God, who is not only the highest, greatest, and most powerful of all, but at the same time a Father, — a loving Father, with a heart more tender than that of any earthly friends. Indeed, I love to dwell upon this latter conception of God alway. In hours of joy or in hours of sorrow I seem to forget that he is a Lord, and I lean against his bosom with filial confidence. I had to *fear* the gods of my fathers, but when I sat at the feet of the Divine Wisdom which presented to me one God, a Father, I wished to *love* him.

Secondly, that man is my brother, no matter whatever be his caste, creed, color, or country, because the same Father has given us life; we are alike the recipients of his blessing, and have equal claims upon his unbounded love. I learned that the best and truest way to love God is to love man; for what kind of love is that, if I bear it toward a father, and hate his children whom he dearly loves?

Thirdly, that man is a free moral agent, subject, however, to the moral laws of his Maker, the ultimate end of whose whole counsel is the welfare of his children. It came to me that when we love each other, live in peace, "bear each other's burden," and guide each other in the path of righteousness, we are "co-workers with God;" and when we do otherwise we bring misery and wretchedness upon ourselves, for which we suffer and stand responsible to God. Although I had believed in a future life long before I came to Christ, yet I did not possess a rational idea of it, — it was wrapped up with a garment of mystery. The worshippers of Shiba will be received in his Koylas; — those of Krishto in his Goluck, etc., where they will breathe the breezes of different Paradises. I often thought these must be narrow heavens indeed that do not admit all. Again, how could the joys of heaven be perfect if we do not meet with those dearest relations who died a long time ago, and the objects of our love and affection taken away from us at different times? My mother worships Krishto, and Shiba was my god, so of course we both will be received by our respective gods. Would not the pangs of separation attend us wherever we go? and even, taking for granted that we are to see each other occasionally, it must be something like visiting! But the future state which Christ promises us is where not only our kindred might be admitted, but where those from east and west, north and south would "meet to part no more." "In my Father's house are many mansions," he says, which "he goes to prepare for us." What a blessed hope it is for one who loves all the children of God, and likes to see them, to live with them, and pray with them! In regard to Christ, my impression became that he is the *Sent* of God, his "beloved Son" indeed. He was raised especially by our Father to regenerate the world, to proclaim peace and good will unto men,—to bring the wanderers back, to uplift degraded humanity, and break the sting of death, and "bring Immortality to light." He was a true model of Humanity,—a perfect man. He was what man ought to be. Whatever attributes of the Most High could be grasped by a finite nature were fully given to him; so it is no wonder when we call him Immanuel or the "express image of God." We are all made in the image of God; but it is a pity that we do not long stand in the state of purity, do not retain our original stamp; the world paints us over, and thereby disfigures us. But the plane where Christ stood was very high,—far beyond the reach of the world; so that while on earth, he lived and moved with celestial graces, and enjoyed sweet communion with his God always, and died as a resigned Son indeed.

He was entirely different from all other religious teachers who have ever blessed the earth with their instructions. There was one peculiarity in him which had not attained its perfection in other religious teachers. Whatever this divine Teacher taught he exhibited in his own life, showing thereby to the world the practicability of his doctrines. A geographer informs us of the position and the height of a mountain, the rise, course, and fall of a river, and draws a map for illustration, that he may convey the truth distinctly unto us. In like manner Christ performed his mission. He teaches us humility, — behold the Saviour of the world washes the feet of the low castes of Judea! He speaks love, — lo! he breathes love from the cross, when the cruel and wicked sons of man were driving nails through his innocent limbs! "Father, forgive them, for they know not what they do!"

Desiring to be profited by Christ and to throw off the burden of superstition, and to put on the yoke of Christ instead, I secretly yielded to the longing for a new life. The old habits, religious ordinances, the once beloved idols, seemed dry, unimportant things. I could no longer hide myself within the "veil of taciturnity." Now and then I dared to speak to my friends new things, to breathe unto them new affections, and to surprise them with new deeds. I would detail as well as I can remember the trials, misunderstandings, and ridicule that crowned my brow subsequently. The life of Christ proved so sweet to me that I felt quite sure others would like it, so in the afternoon I would go to some friend to read from it. Some liked it as a story; others felt quite amused hearing of the miracles of Christ, as they see most of them attempted by their countrymen, and their legendary books too abound with such things. Even the raising of Lazarus from the grave and the resurrection of Christ did not surprise them because there was no novelty in them. I must confess, however, the miracles of Christ did not strike me very much. Having witnessed some like them done before me, and having read of such in our religious books, I did not "seek after a sign," but perceived wonderful miracles performed by Jesus spiritually in my own case. These very hands of mine which did not touch the low caste before, now stretched forth to embrace them. Having eyes, I could not before see my path clearly; but Jesus made and put clay on them, and told me to wash them in the pool of the Gospel, which I did, and now I begin to see. I was deaf to the cry of duty; but the gentle voice of the Teacher entered in, and I now hear it without prejudice. I was possessed with "*devils*," — the "*legions*," for they were many, — such as caste feeling, hatred towards low castes, prejudices, etc.; but they all fled before the divine presence of Christ, saying, "What have we to do with thee, thou Son of God." Thus I cared more for these spiritual miracles which helped me to begin a new life and understand the worth of Jesus and his mission more vividly than anything else could have done. I am aware that Christ himself appealed to his miracles to prove to the Jews the divine sanction of his mission. "If ye believe not me, believe my works." But it was to the simple yet weak-minded people that he spoke in that way. To some he refused any miracle, — declined to do anything surprising, but spake with authority as no man did before. I do not disbelieve the miracles performed by Christ, as he says whatever he does he does by the power of God, to whom everything is possible; as our poets say, that "He can cause a pigmy to reach the moon, and a lame man to jump over a mountain." So is the belief with almost all of the intelligent Hindoos.

The Raja Rammohun Roy, too, cared more for "the precepts of Jesus" than for his miracles. In his compilation of the words of Christ, he begins with his words in the Sermon on the Mount, I think. He wanted to have his countrymen know and value and follow what Christ said, more emphatically, than rest upon what he did miraculously. Therefore, believing as I did, in the miracles of Jesus, and knowing what would be the feeling of my friends, I did not hold them as the foremost part of Christianity, but presented to them the wise yet intelligible, the rich yet simple, counsels of our Master.

While I was proceeding in this way to read and speak from the New Testament, some Hindoo friends rose against me and reported to the village and to my mother that I was soon going to be a "*Beef-eater*" or Christian. This, of course, alarmed my mother exceedingly, and she aroused all her energies to save me from the impending ruin. Where shall I hide the New Testament? was the anxious question that troubled me. She herself cannot read, so that was some relief on that score. But the boys would come in my absence and take any Christian book from my room and show it to my mother, making her miserable thereby. Her fear of losing me grew so great, and also of the disgrace that would surely fall upon the family in case I became an apostate, or, worse than that, a "beef-eater," that I had to feel anxious about my other books while away, lest she should throw them all into the water. Being acquainted with Rev. Mr. Dall, who kindly gave me Unitarian tracts, I found great relief afterwards, because the tracts being small, not handsomely bound, and not having the "Holy Bible" written on them, my mother did not care about them. A large book, handsomely bound, often creates suspicion among the Hindoos, especially if the bearer be known to be an Anti-Hindoo in the least. Once I was coming home with a large volume of the Bengalee translation of "Lamb's Tales of Shakespeare," which I had borrowed from a rich Brahmun friend in a neighboring town. Some men, pretending to hold a friendly talk with me, made me stop. One said, "You have read a great many books, I presume more than G——, P——, and M——, etc., have done. That's a pretty large book in your hand; did you get it from a Missionary?" I gave the book to the speaker, who curiously opened it and read, "Romeo and Juliet," "Tempest," "Macbeth," &c., as its contents.

Christ says the tree will be known by its fruits. And again, if ye love one another the people will know that ye belong to Christ. Seeing our Master visit frequently the low, the despised, and the publicans in their humble homes, my affection turned toward the publicans in India. An angelic love hitherto unknown, which is "not a respecter of persons," sat in my eyes, and before them all the castes of the Hindoos, from the Brahmun down to the hog-keeper, looked alike. I could no longer accept their salutation without returning the same, and this brought upon me the indignation of the Brahmuns and the terror of other castes. With much fervor and perhaps with less prudence, I went to the extreme at first, in returning the low caste the very *kind* of salutation he made; thus, when he bent his head to me I did likewise to him; when he touched my foot, I wished to do the same. Of course this was too much condescension on my part, which my friends could not bear for a moment. They feared that my teaching them that way would offend the gods, and consequently that something dangerous would happen to them from their wrath! In order to make the matter sure and expose me to the public hatred, some Brahmun boys would engage a low caste to salute me reverently,— to take the dust of my feet and see what

I did. If I returned the honor thus offered me, the whole company would clap their hands, ridicule me, and report it to my mother and other high-caste relations. I realized in a measure how our Master had been troubled by the cunning Jews who now came to gainsay his words; then rebuked him for eating with the low castes, &c. One night while we were discussing religious topics, (as they were wont to do, in order to get from me my free thought that they might accuse me of infidelity,) one asked, "Joguth, suppose you wanted some advice in relation to religious matters, and the son of the washerman, B——, was fully able to give it to you, would you go to him or to a priest?" Although I knew the craft underlying the question, still I answered that, "If I can find pure gold in a ditch close by my house, I would not go to Australia for it." The curious brother sprung up from his seat and hurled anathemas on my head, saying I was the ruin of our family, a shame to my caste, and an unworthy son to my father; that I would soon wear a coat and hat, eat cows and hogs, and drink wine, etc. Such disagreeable experiences, frequently visited upon me with ridicule and contempt, gave me courage and wisdom. I applied the wisdom of serpents and the innocence of a dove, as far as I possibly could, in my encounters with those fault-seeking brethren. Under such circumstances *peace* seemed as if it would desert me; but I retained its sacred influence in my heart, and longed for that peace which the world cannot give nor take away. Notwithstanding all these discouraging surroundings I determined to be "about my Father's business," to go to the people and speak to them kindly what I believed would promote their happiness in life here and hereafter. Besides speaking to those within my reach in my daily walks in life, I sought as places of my resort, the workshops of some goldsmiths and weavers.

These men I found very pleasant, possessed of little education, but with a great deal of intelligence, able to conduct a discussion upon high themes, and to comprehend the best writings of the country. I found them, too, very familiar with the Hindoo legendary works. Every afternoon and evening almost, half a dozen men would assemble there, and one of the party would read aloud from a religious book. But their attachment to the gods and their legends did not hinder my going to them; on the contrary they always used to talk with me upon religious and moral topics. By and by I sought acquaintance with a party of young rowdies belonging to several castes. Almost all of them drank wine, and frequented disreputable places for pleasure and music. Nowhere did I enter with such an earnestness to do good as here. I thought this was the true harvest to be gathered, and I must work in it. Modesty stops my pen in writing about the character I exhibited among them, but it is enough to say that love and perseverance characterized my labor here. The young men belonging to my own caste remonstrated with me, protesting that instead of doing any good among these corrupted low castes, I should surely bring ruin upon myself, and that my course was foolish. To these I did not hesitate to repeat distinctly the words of Christ, to the effect, that the sick people want medicine, but the healthy ones do not.

In course of time I found myself entirely deserted by my former associates, — the friends who lived in the same quarter with me. In fact, their animosity, arising from my not joining them in their excursions for pleasure and sporting, grew so great that very few would favor me with a smile or a word. One afternoon, as I was coming home from Hourah, I met a dozen of them playing Mou machie, or beehive. One of them inquired of me where I had been, and I answered in a low voice and slowly, for I was very tired then, having had to walk home seven miles without dinner. This amused them exceedingly, and each of them attempted to surpass his comrades in imitating my voice.

These brethren reported to my mother all about my visits to the low castes, my teaching them Christian doctrines, etc., and thereby made her doubly miserable. Sometimes she would not eat anything, would weep for hours, and throw away my books. "Joguth, I cannot bear all these jokes and hard words; they complain of your teaching their children not to fear gods, respect Brahmuns, etc. Being a Brahmun, you mix with low castes. I am afraid you will sit at dinner with them some time, as you say 'caste is nothing.' O Joguth, has Jom (or death) forgotten your house?"

Although I felt quite sure that the gods of my country are mere imaginary deities, or some ancient heroes deified after death, still I could not readily free my mind from the fear and respect I bore for them from my infancy. But something must be done, some measure must be taken to make an experiment of their power, so that I need bend before their images no longer. An old anecdote coming vividly to my mind, seemed to discourage me for a while. It was this. Nearly a couple of years before I had been to worship the idols belonging to a widow. It was a winter evening, and carelessly I had forgotten to cover them with their warm clothes. Next day I was told by that widow of the great crime I had done, and I felt much frightened to see the images suffering in cold. She said she retired late, as usual, and notwithstanding a quantity of clothes on her back she felt chilly. Not knowing the reason of such an unusual experience, she came to the closet and found the idols laying unprotected in the cold! Now a great fear filled my heart at the thought that, if owing to my carelessness, the innocent woman suffered, how much more will I have to suffer if I neglect the gods forever. But upon consideration that God is mightier than all, that if we come unto him for protection, no god, no spirit, can hurt us in the least, I grew strong. I would not have gone so far as to touch irreverently the idols, had it not been to see whether there is any consciousness in them; because I had been taught to believe that they are living beings. So, one by one, I tried the strength of the idols that fell within my reach, in treating them with less care. Thus, one day while I was bringing down the idols from a high place, like a mantlepiece, the heaviest of them fell down on the floor, making a loud noise thereby. Hastily I picked it up, examined whether any damage had been done or not, and washed it as usual. At first, I thought I would not worship it in the prescribed ways; but, fearing it would be too much for the first time, I thought it prudent to worship it as usual. Thus privately taking steps too bold, too improper for a Hindoo to venture, I determined to see the end. During the time of Shundhas I would not repeat the creed-like formula, but simply say Gayothrie several times, because the latter is a prayer to an invisible, immortal Creator. My mother watched my movements for a while, and inquired whether I had forgotten my Shundhas, saying that I used to repeat them in an hour, but that I now finished in ten minutes! I told her I remembered them all. But she would not believe it, and called my older brother to examine me, which he did to his entire satisfaction. He told her I knew them so well that it did not take me a long time to repeat them.

To a town on the other side of the Ganges I had to go

occasionally to worship idols. During the holidays I was sent by my mother there to worship the goddess of Learning. I did not repeat any prayer. I sat down before the idol, and scattered flowers in the usual way. The matron said, "I wonder how you could perform this worship in so short time!" I felt embarrassed, and sitting before the idol in the next house, spent more time in reciting slowly my English lessons learned long ago, — such as "The English Grammar is the art of speaking and writing the English language correctly." "The Caspian sea or lake is surrounded by Russia, Tartary, and Persia." "A straight line that divides a circle in two equal parts is called its diameter," etc., and no complaint was made then. I am fully aware I did a great many things at this stage of my experience which certainly wore a double aspect, — not daring to let these changes in my faith be known to my friends, and at the same time not wishing to follow what I conceived to be superstition. Finding me going daily toward the wrong way, as it seemed to my dear mother, she determined to commit me to the charge of our family Gooroo, or spiritual guide, and to put his yoke on my neck! This I resisted with my indifference, argument, and obstinacy, because the life under Gooroo is indeed a life of foolishness. The Gooroo selects from the hosts of gods a certain one for his disciple, — the name and the nature of which he is to hide from the world and worship it as his own. Again, what is worse still, he is to regard the Gooroo as identical with his god, to worship him and do homage unto him, just as he would to his God himself! When he visits the family every member prostrates before him, and worships him. I hated to do that for three reasons, — first, that since I had lost my faith and loyalty to the very gods, I could not have any regard for a man whose only office was to bind me into slavery unto him and the gods; secondly, I felt satisfied with that unerring, unselfish Teacher who said, "Call no man thy master," etc., "I seek not mine own glory," "Why callest thou me good?" etc.; and hence, thirdly, I believed that the Gooroo and myself were walking on the same road, side by side, so that neither ought to gain a mastery over the other. But my good mother, like all other Hindoos, felt otherwise. She sincerely believed that the influence of Oopodesh, or regeneration by the hands of the Gooroo, would fill my heart with new grace from *Istdele* (the god selected by the Gooroo).

She sent for him, and he came to our house to convert me, not by reasoning to the truth, but by the pretended majesty of his rank,—by his appeals to the Hindoo customs,—unto gross superstition, which, with prayers and tears I was trying to get rid of. At first I made excuses, saying, "Let him give 'montra' (sacred words) to my oldest brother; I am young, so there is no hurry about it now," etc. But I knew full well the purpose of my mother,—that she was anxious to chain *me*, who was about to fly away from the gods! She said it would look well to have the two brothers take *montra* together—that it would cost less, etc. More than six times the day for our "Oopodesh" had been fixed, but I was where I was, or perhaps a little "higher." Sometimes, seeing that man coming to our house, from a distance, I would immediately go to some friends and remain there until he had gone home. My mother would follow my track now and then and bring me to him, and plead for my indifference! One afternoon I was sleeping in my room, and he came and began to talk to my mother. I determined not to see him (as the rule would require me to prostrate myself before him, which I hated to do). I thought I would go out by the back door, and thereby escape the degradation of worshipping a man for the present, if not the rebukes of my mother. But she came into my room ere I had time to put my theory into practice, saying, "Joguth! Joguth! there is Gooroo, who wants to see you." I tried vainly to keep still and pay no heed to her, as if I was in a profound sleep! She whispered into my ear, "Do not insult the Gooroo — it is an unpardonable sin on your part, Joguth. His look of displeasure will surely burn you to death," etc. At last, finding her too urgent, I declared openly that I had got the "montras" from a Teacher, and that I did not want any other than these, "The Lord our God is one Lord," or "Om aka meb 'ŏ the ti-ung," "There is *one* God without a second." This did not satisfy her; although my constant indifference to the Gooroo frightened him so he never dared to raise the question again, yet my mother, perhaps, still hopes that I might yield, for she *cannot* conceive how I could do otherwise.

Thus troubled at home and ridiculed abroad, I longed for a free, genial atmosphere. The very gentleness I wished to display at home, the kindness to the low castes, brought ridicule upon me, and many times I went to secluded places to cry to my Father and my God. Providentially I had been acquainted with Baboo C. C. S., a native convert to Christianity, and an energetic, highly-educated young man; but the community hated me *more* for this reason. As, owing to the opposition and vigilance of my friends, I could not find a chance to study the New Testament, I resorted to the memoirs of noble men and women for Christianity. The life of Mrs. Mundey, the missionary to India, interested me very much; the "Pilgrim's Progress," "Chambers's Biographies," etc., gave me ample instruction. Indeed, I seemed to find Christian truth almost everywhere, — in grammars, geographies, histories, in the world around, and in the heaven above.

Through an earnest search I gathered a few friends who, though they did not quite dare to forsake the gods and to reject the caste prejudices, still promised a happy result in future. But none of these were my nearest neighbors, so that I could go to them and spend a little time in a pleasant way.

To see whether our caste feelings were gone or not we proposed an experiment — and as it would not be possible to take a meal in a low caste's house because of the household, we resolved to cook some food privately, and see what we could do. Accordingly, on a rainy evening, we three, one a young farmer, a physician, and myself a Brahmun, cooked some Khichwry (rice and a kind of peas highly seasoned with spice). I could not help in the cooking, being entirely unacquainted with the process, but our farmer friend, I think, was a "pretty good cook." To rise to the climax of the freedom so privately sought, I consulted with some trustworthy and religious brethren, who hailed the enterprise with joyous hearts. We used to meet in a field, and, on account of the ground being wet, to spread some leaves over it, and thereby made quite soft, comfortable seats. We did not know then what particular form of prayer to offer to God, so I suggested to our brethren that we would offer child's prayers — bring all our wants, both temporal and spiritual, before the throne of grace in perfect trust, and let Him give or deny unto us whatever he pleased. So we prayed that the good Father would cure our headaches, fevers, etc., that he would make us good, honest, learned men.

This novel gathering in the field aroused the curiosity of the people, who feared we should some day become very troublesome to the community. The report reached almost every ear, and we were taken for adulterers, or what is worse still, "*Kistans*" (Christians). This latter charge was brought especially on account of *my* being connected with the party. But we did not feel discouraged, for we believed that to make our thanks and wants known to our good Father, we need not go here or there, close our eyes or open them, kneel down or stand on our feet, utter words or observe silence, for the Object of our worship is a Spirit, that fills the universe with his presence, and who knows all, inspects all, loves all his creatures. Still man is a social creature, — he wants advice, guidance, and help from others, — he improves himself by others' example. This change of my religious ideas gave me one singular feeling: love for man in general, or in other words, love for the low castes wherever they could be found.

Nothing pleased me more than a crowd of men in whose faces, eyes, and movements we distinctly read the wisdom, love, and spirit of God. So I wished very much to be with them, especially for religious purposes; but my singular views of religion drove them away. In Calcutta there are Christian churches where I could not attend, much as I desired to do so. On Sunday, on my way to or from my friends in the city, I would stand in a street on which a church is placed, watch the people as they entered in, and eagerly lend my ears to the voices that were sending up to the throne of grace the praises and songs. Of course I could not stand long there, the bustling noise of the carriage-wheels would drown the joyous voices, and so I reluctantly would direct my steps homeward, uttering, "Blessed is the place where God is worshipped in spirit!" O Father! though my countrymen worship thee through idols and pictures, through forms and ceremonies, I rejoice to think that others adore thee in spirit! A young Brahmun sold me six English books which he had bought at a public auction in Calcutta. One was the "Memoir of Mrs. Mundey," two were books of

Common Prayer, and the rest were novels. My soul swam in ecstacy when I found that almost on every page the prayers begin with "Our Father," "Most Gracious God," "O God, our Father!" etc. Reading them earnestly, reflecting on the sweet, fervent, childlike expression of the heart therein, my joy knew no bounds. I made a present of one Prayer-Book to a Brahmun friend, and reserved the other for my own edification. I must confess, however, that the closing lines of the prayers, such as "in the name of our Saviour," "through Jesus Christ our Lord," etc., filled my heart with confusion. I believed God is unbounded love in his very nature,—gives his blessings to his children before they know to ask for them. Why then should I implore his mercy in the name of Christ? In the Hindoo prayers I had found such conditions. I had been taught to expect blessings from a deity through a second or third hand, so I feared these expressions in the Prayer-Books might have the same meaning. In the heat of enthusiasm at my freedom from superstition — with a desire to come to God directly, I took my pencil and cancelled these lines. By and by I came to the Litanies, where I met with "Glory to God the Son, and to God the Holy Ghost," etc, Who can these Gods be? inquired I of myself. What book is this that teaches us to worship them? Let me see; is it a Christian Prayer-Book that I have bought, or what? Spending a few days in doubt and confusion I sought my friend to whom I had given a Common Prayer-Book, and to my utter surprise found him troubled likewise. He had marked out several passages in that book which ascribe glory and worship to God the Son, and God the Holy Ghost, etc., which he declared foreign to the New Testament doctrine. We examined carefully some of the leading places in the New Testament the second time, and found no such thing as glory to the Son there. The Son says he did not come to seek his "own glory." When the disciples desired him to teach them to pray, he said, "After this manner pray ye, Our Father which art in heaven," etc. Again, the very idea of worshipping "God the Son," and "God the Spirit," seemed to us quite amusing if not quite *new*, for we were accustomed to worship god the son, god the nephew, goddess the niece, etc., while Hindoos in faith. So we thought we would not worship these extra gods of the Prayer-Book, however moderate their number is. It seemed absurd to us to offer supreme homage to a person subject to hunger, thirst, weakness, sorrows, death, etc., and who worshipped the same God with his disciples, and who craved for sweet communion with his God,—to lay before him all his soul's deepest longings. Christ, I read in the Gospels, often sought mountain-tops, or river-sides, away from the little band, to spend hours in prayer.

Not being able to remain in this state of suspense any longer, I went to a clergyman and informed him of my sincere desire to know the God of whom Christ is the "Beloved Son." Very kindly he offered me his cordial hands, introduced me to his library, and promised me his blessing every way. At his request that I would attend the morning services in his church, which were held at seven, I rose early and walked six miles so as to get there in season. The services were conducted in Hindoo fashion in some respect, as he did not read the Scripture himself: there was another present to take that part. Prayers were offered in behalf of the queen, the council, etc., which I liked very much, because in seeking good for others we show our love for them. But alas! the old trouble again! Again I heard of "God the Son, and God the Holy Ghost" there!

Learning my troubles, and with a view to alleviate them,

the minister gave me a book called "Catechism," but unfortunately, owing to the peculiar state of my mind, it made the matter worse still. In it for the first time I read expressions like the following, "As the very God of very God," "begotten, but not made," "one in three, three in one," "yet distinct," which to me sounded anything but rational. I begged the minister to explain these things to me as they appeared contradictory among themselves. I believed the very God is always very God, and the very man is always very man, — they cannot be otherwise; that humanity and Deity are two distinct things, so that they cannot be made identical. Again, the word *Trinity* was something new, which, in my study of the New Testament I did not meet with. I was told that these things lie beyond the reach of human conception; that our best effort to understand or to explain them would be fruitless; that although they seem contradictory and absurd to us, in reality they are not so, because they are unfathomable truths, — the children of the Revelations. This did not satisfy me, for I could not believe that our reason would contradict what the Revelation has to say. In looking at the matter with a simple and earnest mind, we see that Revelation brings us new and important truths and is not afraid of the close inspection of reason. Revelation owes much to reason, without which it cannot perform its mission. God gave Revelation unto *us*, who are endowed with reasoning faculties, that we might examine, reflect upon, and receive its contents. Reason, then, is the key to open Revelation.

Again, there is *no failure* in God; whatever he wishes to do is done in the best manner possible. So if he wished to bless his children with new truth in relation to his own nature, under the new dispensation, he could do it distinctly, intelligibly, and to their satisfaction. Our reasoning faculties do not object to the sublime truths like these, " Behold, Israel, the Lord our God is one Lord," " Love thy neighbor as thyself," etc., because these and their kindred ones are substantial truths that men can live and die by. Men of different religions, culture, age, and accomplishment almost unanimously regard the above-mentioned precepts with reverence. There is no controversy about them. Thus truth stands on its own ground, self-existent, self-supporting forever.

" A thousand honest doubts are more manly than a single cowardly assent to a proposition," are the words of a Boston clergyman. I realized the beauty of his doctrine in this stage of my inquiry. As I had got over the fear of being damned, for not believing what my reasoning powers bore testimony against, and what *my Teacher* does not speak of, I bade *farewell* to the Christian minister with reluctance, and directed my steps towards home.

My disappointment in seeing Christianity set before me in so many unintelligible, mysterious doctrines, reminds me of a curious anecdote. A man, poor from his early years, accustomed to live upon all sorts of coarse food, became the guest of a very opulent man. He anticipated a great treat there: he thought he would get some luxurious food, but to his great surprise he found nearly the very coarse things he used to eat at home, ready for his disposal. Astonished, he stood before the table and began to give vent to his disappointment. " Friends! I left you all in my broken cottage; here I am in a princely mansion, how did you manage to come here? I did not think of meeting you so soon, and in such a place!"

My disappointment was strong when I was greeted by so many absurd doctrines, that pass under the name of Christian. I left Brahmunism on account of these same obscure, dry, unintelligible precepts with which it is crowded, and approached unto the handsome edifice of Christianity with the hope of finding something better. But lo, the very absurdity again! In Christian countries the people open their Bibles, not so much to derive a certain belief from the pages as to find support for an already acquired one. They go already prepared to find this or that view. Thus a Unitarian child meets the doctrines on the Unity of God throughout the Bible; and on the other hand, a Trinitarian child finds hints and supports for his Trinity almost on every page within its covers. My case was quite different; when I came to Christ I did not anticipate much save that whatever he would utter unto me must be sublime, redeeming, vital truths.

"What shall I do now?" became an important inquiry; go back to the gods and goddesses of my fathers, or what? I felt ashamed of that *catechism*, so I hid it under my books, that no opponents might see it and ridicule Christianity before my face. Christianity is not at all responsible for the hosts of dry, strange, unintelligible dogmas that claim our assent. Some time afterwards my nephew, a boy of thirteen, happened to open this old catechism of mine and to read the "creeds." He smiled a little, and said, "Uncle, what book is this?" "That 's a catechism; don't you see? It contains the Articles of Faith!" "Of what faith, uncle?" "Of the Christian faith," said I. "Don't say so! I declare! Is n't the New Testament sufficient for that purpose? Here, you see, I read Christ was both God and man. God is one, yet has three distinct persons. Do the English people believe in these things?" "Certainly they do," I rejoined. The little boy closed the book, saying, "Uncle, it makes me smile to think that the English people who drive railroad engines, build steamboats, and send messages through electric wires, should not know the difference between man and God, — one and three," etc.

After a short season of the "Suspense of Faith," — not knowing where to go, I met a young friend from Calcutta who is a member of the "Brahmo Somaj," founded by the celebrated Raja Ram mohun Roy himself, or by his followers, I am not sure which. He brought me a large sheet of partly printed paper in which I entered my name, residence, date of subscription, etc., and thus took the name of "Brahmo," or deist, as far as the *unity* of God is concerned. But as we wished to make our religion depend more upon our *works*, our affections, our love toward men in general, than upon a certain belief, I did not find much satisfaction in my deist life. The Bengalee deists are men of admirable character, of great intelligence, and of mild disposition, but the majority of them lack the spirit of freedom. They do not have much faith in the idols I think, but they have idols *at their houses*, which are worshipped and taken care of at their expense. How far they repudiate the caste system I am not sure, for I have not seen nor heard of high-caste deists dining with low-caste brethren publicly, nor have I known a Brahmun deist to marry the daughter of other castes. I do not mean that *these*, i. e. eating, drinking, and marrying with different castes are the essential parts of religion, and that as such the Calcutta deists do not observe them. No; the caste system, notwithstanding all its policy and the good it pretends to do, is obviously detrimental to the progress of the masses in India. It lies like the heavy Hymaloy over the heads of the low castes: they cannot rise upward intellectually, socially, or spiritually. Hence the first religious, philanthropic act of those who see the defects of the caste system, ought to be to help its removal and to inaugurate a state of equality among the people. My deistical brethren hardly take that step, although they eat and drink forbidden food and liquor with rich low castes, or with

Christian people even privately. They have some saintly men among them. I admire their precepts, honor their private lives, and deem them noble. But they do not come like Jesus of Nazareth unto the publicans and sinners, or to those with unwashen hands.

I became acquainted with a young Brahmun deist, — Baboo Raj-kifsen Bannerjea, of Mahessolla, whom I found the embodiment of truth, love, and piety. Indeed, the first *angel* I met in this world was he. His very mild appearance, his soft eyes, shedding forth love from them, his tender voice, are the index of his inward accomplishments. He is a man of considerable learning, and of wealth and high standing in the community. Would I knew what first led him to reject the idol gods! It would make a volume to write all about his life, which, though short, is full of noble, philanthropic acts. His charity is broad, yet discriminating; his dealings with others are frank and kind, yet impartial; his manners are prudent, yet childlike. He observes Christ's rule as far as it is possible in regard to giving alms, — not letting the left hand know what the right hand doeth. For the benefit of the children of high and low castes he established a school at his own expense chiefly; for the little help which he received from a few individuals was frequently withdrawn on account of his anti-heathen principles.

He has a large landed property which he manages with great caution, as well as to the entire satisfaction of his subjects. I was present one day at his office when a Mohammedan man was brought in on the charge of robbing the garden of our Brahmun friend, his landlord. While he was swearing vehemently in the name of his Allah, to convince the officers of his innocence, our friend had been working an algebraic sum. Having finished his work, he looked at him pityingly and with a tender voice, said, "Friend, swear not! Think how much wrong you have done unto us! You know all! you owe some money to us, — you are my subject. These two obligations bind you to our family, as you say; you ought to protect my property against the usurper, — lo! you are a usurper yourself! I wonder you do not feel sorry for your conduct!"

Noble as this brother is, admirable as his deeds are, he lacks, as I have observed before, that degree of moral courage which none but the "Sent" of God could give. While enjoying the pleasure and privilege of being with these brethren, and deriving much edification from their amiable lives, the under-current of my soul was constantly flowing toward Christ. I could not go away from him, nor forget his loving, precious words that brought me out of superstition. Are not there men who believe as I do, — that God is *strictly* one, — that Christ is the best of all religious teachers whom the world ever had or will have, that he is the Sent and oldest Son of our common Parent? If there are not any found professing such belief, — no matter; I shall stand alone, and offer my help unto the world as far as I am able. Theological differences would not stop my hand and heart from serving and loving others, and this is the best religion indeed! While thus defining my position and receiving instruction from Jesus secretly, my esteemed friend, Baboo C. C. Singha, a convert to Christianity, and who has been a preacher for three years, I should think, told me me that he had been told by Hodgson Pratt, Esq., of the arrival of a Unitarian missionary in Calcutta, under the auspices of the American Unitarian Association, and whose views of Christianity are different from those of other missionaries. I could not understand the term *Unitarian Christian*, because I was told if I did not believe in the Trinity I was not a Christian, but a deist. We went to hear the missionary, Rev. C. H. A. Dall, but not being accustomed to hear or talk English, I did not gain much at first. He gave us his printed sermons, and the writings of Channing, Burnap, Elliot, Cordner, Bartol, etc., which, as I read them, not only confirmed what my belief had been, but whispered to me, saying, "Friend, there are thousands on the other side of the Atlantic who hold the same views of God as you do, so you are not alone. Our fellowship and sympathy are yours." Being made acquainted with and interested in this missionary, I began to attend his religious services on Sunday; but I could not do it regularly for several reasons. Mr. Dall's place is nearly seven miles from my house; besides, there is the majestic Gunga to be crossed, which "alone is twenty miles," as the Hindoo saying is.* I had to take my breakfast very early and to walk to and fro all the way, crossing the river by steamboat either at Shal-kea, or Howrah. My dear mother was told by my Hindoo brethren that I attended the religious services in a Christian church, with Baboo C. C. Singha. She felt very much frightened at this, and took measures to stop my going to Calcutta on Sunday. "If you will not hear me, but will go to Calcutta on Sunday, go Joguth. The people tell me, and I can presage too, what a disgrace and ruin you will bring upon the family. They say you are almost a '*Kistan*' now. You eat *beef* with the Yobuns; or, if you do not, they are quite sure you will soon! I am afraid they will turn you out of the feast sometimes, and I don't blame them for it.

---

* The river Gunga is not twenty miles wide. This saying of the Hindoos is applicable to any large river in the world, on account of the inconvenience and delay, and perhaps danger, of crossing it. We can walk or run on land according to our strength, but while on water we are dependent upon the element.

Joguth, have you forgotten the proverbs your father taught you? Remember that one member of the family destroys its peace as one tree burns the whole forest, in creating fire by conflagration. You will be the ruin of the family! You would not hear the advice of those who are older and wiser than yourself; nor would you heed my words. And why should you? The young bird, the moment its wings are covered with down, leaves its mother's nest to look out for itself; so you, Joguth, you are grown up now; my advice, my guidance would not be of any service to you (at least you think so). I do not blame nor hate the Christians. Let them follow their own customs faithfully. Jesu Kisto is their God; let them worship him; I have no objection to that. As Brahmuns, we ought not to hate the gods of other nations. Still we cannot worship them, for they are not ours; we have gods over us. O what a pleasant sight it is to see the young Brahmuns going to the sacred river, to the temples, etc. My heart is delighted to see them! And you, mistaken child, hardly go to the temples or to the Ganges! What business have you in Calcutta? If you will go there on Sunday, go without breakfast; I shall not have it ready for you so early," etc.

Now, under these circumstances, I could not attend Mr. Dall's services on every Sunday, much as I wished to do so, and whenever I went, I went without breakfast, and to the utter displeasure of my mother. On my return, at four or five o'clock in the afternoon, she would not set the plate before me, nor help me while I ate my dinner, but would go out of the room to weep over the loss of her child.*

* If such were not the difficulties to be struggled with, how many good Hindoo young men would come to hear Mr. Dall's preaching. There are additional troubles: the neighbors watch their steps closely. This is *one* principal reason why Mr. Dall's hall is not crowded on Sunday. Judging

I grew so unpopular and the people began to dread me so much that they would not let their boys visit Calcutta with me, lest I should make them "Kistan." But "where is will there is way," is a true saying. Notwithstanding all vigilance, ridicule, many from "north and south, the east and west" of Calcutta would be glad to meet in Mr. Dall's room. Not fearing the difficulties, but rather rejoicing in them, with an inward consciousness that we are not doing wrong before God, — that to seek after the spiritual welfare of man in love, is the best service humanity could render unto God and man, — some of us determined to form a band of believers in and seekers after Truth. The Sunday-school cards, containing beautiful verses, and the Sunday-School Gazette, which Mr. Dall gave us, suggested the plan, and we succeeded in gathering twenty-one high-caste boys, all of whom knew English more or less. Not finding a convenient place for our purpose, we would meet in some garden, away from the Brahmuns, and there read, sing, and speak of God as set forth in the publications of the American Unitarian Association, and of the Sunday-School Society. Again I was connected with the school of Baboo C. C. Singha, a noble, energetic gentleman, and this gave me a good opportunity to be known to many and to disseminate the seeds of truth in their youthful hearts. But "a man's foes will be of his own household." The brother of Baboo C. C. Singha, a Trinitarian in his belief, having been converted to that faith in his early years, began to trouble us in various ways, and not unfrequently to take unfair measures and to use unkind words. From an American book, called "Sargent's Reader,"

---

the hearts of the brethren by my own, I feel quite sure that the Unitarian rooms in Calcutta are crowded by them in the spirit. While at home on Sunday, I used to reflect on the services and the Bible class of Mr. Dall, and the elementary class of R. Counsel, Esq.

No. 3, I believe, I had selected a beautiful piece, "Prayer for a Pure Heart," and asked my young friends to write it down and commit it to memory, which they did cheerfully. This gentleman, while examining their writing-books, saw it, read it, and liked it I am sure, and asked them who gave it to them. Of course they told him that I had given it to them. He uncharitably made some unkind remarks which surprised us all, — saying, in effect, "Joguth is a hypocrite. Let him first be baptized, and then teach these things to others," etc. I smiled at this, and realized then the truth of Dr. Channing's discourse on the Church.

In the next chapter I shall attempt to give some reasons in relation to my faith, and to state in what respects I differ from the brethren of other denominations, and why.

CHAPTER IV.

Why I became a Unitarian. — My own Reading and Study of the Bible. — The Missionaries' Doctrines.

Before I begin to give my reasons in regard to my taking the Unitarian name, I should say that these reasons are my own. They are the fruits of a mind uninfluenced by Unitarian, or Trinitarian theology. Beside the New Testament, and the Author who studied his theology "in the bosom of the Father," I had no missionary to influence me at first. So that what I say I utter from my own heart, and on my own responsibility. Let not the Trinitarian condemn, nor the Unitarian triumph on account of my views and interpretations of some of the leading dogmas, which have split the Church of God into fragments. But let them both charitably hear my free thoughts and testimony. I do not attack nor flatter any particular dogmas, through force of sectarian feeling.

My object is to seek truth with an unprejudiced mind, and to speak it faithfully when found. I would observe perfect frankness in my statements; and if I use any word, or expression, that sounds irreverent to the reader, I would beg him to regard it as unintentional, for I mean nothing irreverent, nothing hostile to true piety. Moreover, I should say that I did not resort to Neander, Clarke, Livermore, or other writers and commentators for help, not because I should not value them, but because they are almost strangers to me. I did not know that they were to be had, and so could not go to any such commentary on the Life of Christ. I believe that the best and most infallible commentary a man can write, is to explain Christ, by his life, by his actions; thereby exhibiting him in vivid, living illustrations. The blessed Teacher did not come to puzzle us with intricate enigmas, nor to bind us under the heavy burden of mystery. Nor did he come with imperfect knowledge of things, to favor us with half of the necessary information, and leave us to guess out the other half. Whatever he deemed necessary to the life, comfort, and salvation of man, he taught distinctly, intelligibly, though often in parables. He did not even resort, like the modern preachers, to those truths in nature which lie beyond the conception of the masses; such as the solar system, or the attraction of gravitation. But, that we all might understand, and be profited by him, he alluded to the fowls in the air, the lilies of the field, the fall of the sparrow, and the hair of our heads. He prayed, and thanked his Father that through him He had revealed truth unto babes, or simple-hearted men.

But I do not undervalue the earnest labors of those good Christian men, who have written and who will write, commentaries upon the Gospels. I honor every honest effort to edify man. But, as I said before, I put more stress upon, and can understand more distinctly and profitably, the commentaries written in actions, than those drawn out by pen and ink.

The following are the points which I did not dream of, while studying the New Testament, — which, when stated to me, I could not look at without surprise, and could not believe. They are the doctrines of the Trinity, — the total depravity of the human race, or human nature, — and endless punishment in hell. Now as I hear of these, and their kindred doctrines, I do not believe them, nor think they have anything to do with true religion, because they seem to me irrational and unscriptural.

The Trinity. — In giving my reasons for not believing this doctrine of the church, I shall be as brief as possible. It is a self-contradictory, and unintelligible riddle — a production of the fancy wrapped up with a sense of piety. They say the Trinity is a sublime union of the Three in One, — the Father, the Son, and the Holy Ghost. Common sense teaches us that one is always one, and three are always three. We distinguish persons by their respective individualities. So the Father, the Son, and the Holy Ghost, must each have a distinct individuality, otherwise they could not be persons; and if so, then they have their wills and affections separate from each other. Under such circumstances, it is as absurd to receive the Father, Son, and Holy Ghost as one, as it is to say, James, Mary, and Ellen are one.

The religion of my country has a Trinity which I find far more rational, more logically and philosophically consistent than the Christian Trinity. And I do not think it a prudent choice to reject the former, and accept the latter. Here is the Hindoo trinity, and the relation — the equality between its three persons. "In the beginning, there was Shuck-tie, or Power." It is somewhat parallel with St. John's "In the beginning was the Word." This "Power" was like the "Word" of the Evangelist, a term of broadest import, including power in all its elements, creative, sustaining, redeeming, sanctifying, destroying, — in short denoting the whole substance of God, or it *was* God.

Power manifested itself in three leading ways, — creative, sustaining, and destroying. First of all, we need creation; so that power of God (Bromho) which creates, becomes the first. Then, when something has been created, we need support. The power or providence of God, that supports the creation becomes the second. Finally, the economy of nature requires destruction, so the power that destroys is the third. These three are called a Triad. But it is obvious, that far from their being the trinity of persons, they are the trinity of the attributes of the same, one, great Being. These have been personified, and are worshipped by the philosophical Hindoos, as the three deities.

One remarkable fact worth noticing is, the perfect equality between the persons of the Hindoo Trinity.

We read in our sacred books, of Bromho (first) offering prayer to Bishto (second); Bishto paying homage to Shiba (third). Sometimes Bromho and Shiba worship Bishto, etc.

Compare the Christian Trinity with the Hindoo, with an unprejudiced mind, and you will recognize a great difference between them. The former would show its unsoundness when placed in contrast with the latter. The Father, the Son, and the Holy Ghost. The first two are Beings, and the third, which is essentially God himself, is not a Being, for the spirit of a being cannot be a separate individual. In Oriental countries, we address one man in various ways; taking one of his peculiarities, and personifying it in rich allegories. The three persons of the Godhead must be equal in power, glory, and substance. There is no equality between the three in the Christian Trinity; at least, this does not appear satisfactory to one who is unacquainted with the system. There are numerous indisputable places in the New Testament, where the subordination of the Son, is set forth in a clear manner.

The very passages, which are produced to prove the equality of the Son with the Father, speak in connection of his subordination unto Him. "All power is given unto me in heaven and earth," is a passage put forth, by intelligent men and women, to show that Christ is God. They put much stress on "*all power*," while a simple, uninfluenced mind would put it upon "*is given;*" for whatever is given unto us does not make us equal to the giver.

The more we receive from him, the more subordinate are we, and the more thankful ought we to be unto him. The world might call us great, and be dazzled with our splendor, which is given to us; still the sense of obligation demands our respect, our thanks, our worship for the Giver. But Christ did acknowledge his Father as the giver of his wisdom, power, and honor, and never said that these belonged to himself. Before or after performing some miracles, when the weak-minded spectators were liable to have taken him for God, he was particularly careful to destroy that impression about himself; saying, that he himself could do nothing; and thanked God for the power which enabled him to perform wonderful things. He would offer prayer to his Father, soliciting his smile upon his works. Thus, standing by the grave of Lazarus, he lifted up his eyes to heaven, and said, "Father, I thank Thee that thou hast heard me. And I knew that Thou hearest me always: but because of the people which stand by I said it, that they may believe that Thou hast sent me."

Frequently, in view of his mightiest works, he tells us that his Father is greater than himself. Now, he, who is greater than another, cannot be equal to him, at the same time. Two and two are always greater than one and one. With us it might be possible to compete with, and surpass one who was greater than ourselves, in wealth, learning, and popularity; but God's glory is unchangeable. If the Father, who is distinct from Christ, — being one of the three persons who form the Trinity, — be greater than Christ, he is forever so. I know there are some passages, in which Christ identifies himself with God; such as "I and my

Father are one." "He who hath seen me hath seen the Father." Let me give my experience as these passages fixed my attention. It is an undeniable fact that both the Old and New Testament were written in Oriental languages, which abound in allegorical idioms.

My own thoughts very readily suggested to me the meaning of such passages. When a plenipotentiary goes out to a foreign people, to adjust or secure political or mercantile interests for the people or king who sends him, he might very properly say that he and his king or people are one. For he speaks and acts agreeably to the instructions given him by the king or people he represents, and whatever he says and does has been put into his power.

So Christ says he and his Father who sent him are one. He never did or said anything against his Father's will, and so he convinced the world that he was the Sent — the especial viceroy of "the King eternal, immortal, and only wise," on the earth.

It is affirmed by Unitarian divines that, in order that the disciples might not misunderstand Christ, when he said he and his Father are one, he explained to them the nature of that oneness or union, by saying, that the very disciples about him were one with him and with God. "That they all may be one; as thou, Father, art in me, and I in thee, that they also may be one in us." Still it seems to me that the disciples did not have any difficulty in understanding what he meant by, "I and my Father are one;" for this is a common expression — a prevailing phrase — of Oriental lands, and they were familiar with it. When two or more persons are said to be one, it is obviously meant that they are of the same spirit, profession, culture, or will. We see in the New Testament, that simple, unadorned words of

Christ puzzled the Jews more than his figures and allegories. For instance, when Christ told the sick man, "Son, be of good cheer; thy sins be forgiven thee," behold, certain of the scribes said within themselves, "This man blasphemeth."

The expression, "I and my Father are one," does not strike an Oriental as having some unfathomable, mystic meaning; nor does it convince him of Christ's being equal to his Father in glory, essence, and existence. "He who hath seen me, hath seen the Father." These words, I am told, are regarded as the strongest support of Trinitarian doctrine; "Christ in them declaring most distinctly his identity with God, in every respect."

But this is a simple thing again. Ask a Hindoo child of seven or eight years old, to show you his father's house. He will direct you to go straight ahead a few rods till you come to a store, and leaving the store on your right, to go a little way and you will presently see a palm-tree; and if you see the palm-tree you see his father's house. Does this imply that the palm-tree is his father's house? No. So the passage, "He who hath seen me hath seen the Father," does not convey, to any one accustomed to the Eastern mode of expressing thoughts, the idea that Christ is God. The palm-tree of the Hindoo child is so *near* to his father's house that if you see the one you cannot help seeing the other. Our dear Master exhibited such divine graces in his life, that it is not blasphemous for him to say, "If ye have seen me ye have seen the Father."

I did not dream of a triune God as I studied the New Testament, and when it was presented to me in the creeds I found no support for that dogma in the Scriptures. It seems to me that the doctrine of a triune God, is not able to give "life, comfort, and salvation to the world." It is neither essential to, nor a part of, the religion of Christ. It is the production of Oriental philosophers. In the course of time, it migrated from the East to the West. As it passed from hand to hand, and country to country, it lost much of its peculiar beauty. In conclusion, I should say that an intelligent Oriental finds nothing rational in the doctrine of the Trinity as it exists among Christians, because he has seen a better one in his own country. Indeed, to receive this doctrine, so absurd, so unintelligible, would be as ridiculous for him, as for a Bostonian to sail to Calcutta for a piece of ice.

The Total Depravity of Human Nature. — As my time would not permit me to consider this subject in a way I would like, and thereby show my reasons for not believing it, I would simply resort to common sense and the Scriptures to expose the awkwardness of this doctrine. I fully believe that such enormous doctrine as that of calling a child of the Most High a totally depraved creature — having nothing good in him, *is* not, and ought not to be a part of any man's creed.

It discourages man. It puts a mountain in his way. It weakens his faith in a loving Father, when he is told that impartial justice will hold him responsible for all the iniquities which he was created to commit. I am aware that believers in this doctrine would say that the atonement, made by Christ for our sins, has satisfied eternal justice, — that "the blood of the Lamb has washed our sins."

"Bad leads to worse, and better tends to best."

Admit one absurd theory, and it will bring others of the same nature to its support.

The doctrine of the vicarious atonement is the centre of gravity which supports the theory that man is a totally depraved creature. Without the former, the latter will fall down on the ground, and break to pieces, and no one would dare regard himself a wholly depraved being. If I hear that a certain man in my city is an infallible physician to cure consumption, I would not feel afraid to call my slight cough by that fatal name — consumption. It troubles me to know what became of the millions of souls born totally sinners, and who died before the blood of the Lamb had been shed. Is it possible that our good Father filled hell with human creatures, who bloomed in their infancy in the garden of creation, — those simple, pure-minded ones, whom "no murder clothed and no murder fed," — who spent their lives in doing good?

Perhaps some will tell me that Christ died for all; both those who lived before his appearance on earth, and those who lived after. Here is some trouble again.

If I understand rightly, it is said that the mere fact of Christ's offering himself, would not wash away our sins. We must believe in him in order to receive the benefit of his dying. If so, then, even to-day, there are millions who have no opportunity to hear of Christ; consequently they cannot believe in him and his gracious atonement. St. Paul writes, "How then shall they call on him in whom they have not believed? and how shall they believe in him of whom they have not heard?"

The idea of one man's suffering, or making atonement for the guilt of others, is a strange one. In the world we do not see examples of it. The man who is guilty before the court suffers. His weeping wife, loving children, and kind parents are not called upon to take his punishment, much as they might wish to do it. I am reminded of a poem in the Rama ona. When the god Rama was coming home, the sea stood before his car, in a human form and thus addressed him:

"The ten-headed, — Rabona, the great tyrant King of Sunka, or Ceylon, stole away thy wife, and thou didst erect a bridge over, and chain the sea, to reach his kingdom. O Son of Rhaga, nowhere do I hear of such a strange decision, — that one commits a crime, and another suffers for it."

The total depravity of man's nature is a doctrine that is not recognized by Scripture. Of course, there are many places in the Bible where the sins of man have been set forth in dark colors; but that does not imply that he is wholly a sinful creature, — born to be so. There are instances too numerous to mention, both in the Bible and in the annals of the world's history, of men and women living a life of purity and love.

Let us see what the Scripture says, — that God created man in his own image, is an undeniable fact. "So God created man in his own image, in the image of God created he him; male and female created he them." In what sense is man the image of God? Is he the image of God's person? No, it cannot be so. If we say that, we become pagans, and give a physical form to God. Now, the safest and most rational way to answer is, to say that he is the image of God's nature, spirit, and love; because we recognize glimpses of these Godly graces in man, more or less. Here comes a proposition that the image of anything must contain the peculiarity, or some likeness of the original, otherwise it would not be an image. If I wish to draw a picture or make an image of the sun, I cannot make it an oblong, triangular, or square figure, I must make it a circular one; otherwise, people would call me a poor artist, and the image a wretched one, — the image of some fanciful object, but not the Sun. God is infinitely pure, holy, perfect in his nature. How, then, could his image be totally depraved?

Again, if man be truly a depraved creature in his very nature, our Master, then, must have uttered some sentimental words when he said, "Be ye perfect even as your Father in heaven is perfect."

It is hard for us to understand that the image of unbounded Holiness is totally depraved, and that totally depraved creatures should become perfect as their "Father in heaven." Let theologians call man a born sinner, yet he is not so. The Great Theologian, who knew human nature well, its capacity, its excellence, bade it "come up higher," and "be perfect."

The Doctrine of an Everlasting Hell. — I cannot conceive of anything as everlasting but God. Everything has its end at some time, or in some way; but God is without end. All but God is subject to change. He, our good Father, is unchangeable and everlasting. The Great King is the Sovereign over all, — heaven, and earth, and all the hosts thereof. If there is a place called hell, it must be before His omnipresence; for there is nothing that is not known, and seen, and made by God. He could not create an everlasting hell to torture his weak, frail children. Whatever He has created is for their good.

Heaven and earth, with all their wonders, unite to contribute to the welfare of God's creatures.

Everything that lies within, without, around, or above us, speaks of God's unfailing love towards his children. He has placed us under his moral government, the violation of whose laws brings suffering. The same is true also in our relation to the laws of Nature. When we break them we suffer for it; and the suffering is conditional.

I put my hand into a blazing fire, and immediately I feel the effect of my imprudence. I then take my hand back from the fire, and resolve not to put it there again. If I try the experiment again, the same suffering is inevitable.

The All-wise Father has so ordered, that the violation of his laws, physical or moral, will bring suffering; — suffering produces repentance; — repentance will beget reformation; and reformation will meet the approbation and smile of God. Such are his laws, and they must do their mission. He punishes to cure, and not to kill. "He wounds for his mercy's sake, — He wounds to heal."

"The parable of the Prodigal Son," verifies this truth. When the son wanted to have his portion given to him, the good father knew well what would be his lot, by and by. Yet he did not interfere with his wish, for he had made him a free moral agent. The child leaves his paternal abode, and spends his portion, his energies, in riotous living. He becomes poor, has nothing to eat, and takes care of swine; — the *very* menial business in Oriental countries. His sufferings create repentance in his bosom, and he starts for his father's home. What did the father do? Did he say, "Go from me forever, and live in everlasting misery?" No. He is too good, too loving to say that. He comes out of the house, welcomes the wanderer back, clothes him with the best robe, and makes a feast. In the Bible there is mention of everlasting fire; but the words are not in meaning according to what they sound. If they were literally true, they would falsify Christ's "parable of the prodigal son." It is a common Oriental way of describing the state of unhappiness. When a boy I read these things in Hindoo books. "It is said, Jom, or Death, has his angels, who dip sinners in boiling oil. They fix large hooks in their throats and drag them on some high places. They cause them to embrace pillars of fire, and finally thrust them in 'Nonuck Coondoo,' or pit of dirt, in which 'kit' (a worm) dieth not."

I am told that, taking the words of the Bible in a literal sense, the Christian people believe in many absurd things, and teach them. For instance, in a Sunday-school book, there is a question like the following: "Where do the wicked go?" "To hell," is the answer. All right. "What kind of a place is hell?" "It is dark, and there the worm dieth not, and there is fire unquenchable." Now our common sense springs up to protest against this unfortunate statement; declaring that where there is fire unquenchable there cannot be dark at all. Such a fire would light hell so splendidly as to enable its inmates to pick up the very sand off its floor, — of course, if there be any.

Heaven and hell are within our own breasts. We experience the joys of one and the pangs of the other. When we perform our duties faithfully, and "love our neighbor as ourselves," we then commune with God and his angels; and that is what constitutes the joy of heaven. On the other hand, when we neglect our duty, — seek after carnal lust, — defy God and man by our thoughts and actions, and thereby bring sorrows, the hatred of the world, and remorse of conscience — we make hell within us. A pure and contrite heart is heaven, and a heart that loves self exclusively, is hell.

Thus I have, very poorly but sincerely, attempted to give my reasons for not believing in the Trinity, — the total depravity of human nature, and everlasting torture in hell. To me they are unscriptural and absurd doctrines. I do not trouble myself with mysteries, but receive the simple words of Christ as my all-sufficient law, of which, "love to God, and love to man," is the essential part.

My Christianity begins where Christ opens his life, and ends where he closes it. In his words I find my duty towards, and my relation to, God, clearly defined. In Christ, I find a perfect humanity, and a safe Guide to liberty holiness, and love. Skilful orthodox ministers, who are used to teaching those who are willing to hold their doctrines, may pick apart these simple things which I have said. It will give them no pleasure that I, a young man, have come out of the dark ways of my people, and have found what rejoices my heart in Christ and in his God, because I do not and cannot take with my blessed Christian faith the opinions of the orthodox. I know what those opinions are; I knew them before I gave up Hindooism, and they prevented me for some time from finding light and joy in the Gospel. I know, too, what many of my own countrymen, who have the best minds and who have outgrown Hindooism, think of the views offered them by orthodox missionaries. Intelligent Hindoos think that what these missionaries wish them to believe, as a part of the doctrine of Jesus Christ, is very like some of the worst things in their own religion, which made them doubt it and throw it off. I know my countrymen will never be converted to these orthodox views, though some of the missionaries are good men and work hard. Their doctrines, which we do not find when we read the Bible ourselves, stand badly in the way of their success. Intelligent Hindoos who throw off their religion, generally become what are called here, "Infidels," or "Deists." When a Hindoo gives up the superstitious practices of my country, all the religion which he keeps is by clinging to, and loving and trying to obey, some beautiful lessons of piety and morality scattered over his sacred books, which are just like the best things in the Old Testament. The orthodox missionary tells these Hindoos that their sacred books are all "humbug." The missionary is ignorant what is in those books. At the same time he tells my countrymen that all the Old Testament was written by God. My countrymen will never change their religion for "orthodoxy."

CHAPTER V.

Interest in America. — Desire and Purpose to go. — My Friend agrees to accompany me. — Ill reports of America. — Horror of Slavery. — My Friend fails me. — Will go alone. — Arrangements. — My Mother. — Last Days at Home. — Voyage. — Arrival in America. — My Experiences here.

As I was studying that phase of the American mind so richly exhibited in the Unitarian tracts and books, — the sweet eloquence of Channing, the astonishing clearness of the arguments of Burnap, the spiritual insight of Bartol, etc., — I was drawn very close to America. I thought these people must be wonders, who have been able to sift out substantial grains from a mass of chaff. Often with an exulting heart, I have thanked God that the simplicity of the gospel is not lost, — that the Christianity of the Apostles did not die under the sentence of the Nicene Council, but is still alive, in good health, and *ever* will be, until our Master has brought the whole world to subjection unto his Father and our Father, and the creation bends its knee before the throne of his God and our God, in the *name*, or more distinctly, in the *Spirit* of Christ.

My interest was not confined to the Unitarians of America, but it extended to the country itself. I wanted to know about the people, the customs, government, and prosperity of the country as much as possible. The *very* few books which I could get hold of, containing accounts of America, were eagerly perused; and that portion of the history of England which speaks of the American Revolution, was read over and over with a throbbing heart. I felt indignant at the proceedings of England against America, and in my sympathy suffered with the American people, who I thought were better Christians than the English. I prayed for and rejoiced at their prosperity, and determined to visit them some time. Such was my habit of looking at the map of North America, that the boys at our school used to joke me, saying, "There, there is your America!" In our family circle every opportunity was availed of to speak of the United States. My dear mother, who rejoices at the prosperity of others, and hates tyranny and injustice, heard with great pleasure of the American Independence. But hearing me speak so much and so often of America, the younger portion of the family, such as my sisters, aunt, etc., would joke me whenever an opportunity was offered. For instance, if I said, "This cloth is not good," "You will find a better one in Amārică," was their joke.

One bright Sunday forenoon, three of us were coming from Bali to worship at Mr. Dall's chapel, and a conversation took place upon the future welfare of Unitarian missions in India. Our valued friend, Baboo C. C. Singha, suggested that it would be a grand thing for the mission if some of us who are so closely connected with the mission would go to visit the brethren in America, tell them of our needs, offer thanks in our behalf for the blessing they have sent in the person of Mr. Dall, and bring home their help and sympathy. As for himself, he said he could do this errand elegantly, were it not for his wife and children and his school. I responded to his suggestion, and informed him of my desire, — that this very thing had been the all-engrossing subject in my mind. There was a young man, a native Christian, who wished to join me, and thus we reached the chapel, making suggestions, discussions, and resolutions on our way.

After the service, Chundy Baboo spoke to Mr. Dall about our wish to visit the American brethren. He approved of it, looked at us with a kind heart, and gave us encouragement. There was present with us a gentleman, Mr. J. M. Hurd, of Clinton, Mass., who promised to report us to the brethren at home, and to ask the American Unitarian Association to respond to our wishes.

A few months passed away. Advices from Mr. Dall came to our friend C. C. Singha, Esq., and he asked us if we were ready, and firm in our position. I told him that I was firm but not quite ready to take a decided step, as the circumstances under which I lived were against my plan. The love for my mother was the crowning obstacle. In India I never could spend three nights without my mother. From the houses of my sisters I would come home not caring for rain or storm. Again, I was very particular about taking my meals among strangers: hardly could I make my dinner unless my mother was sitting by me. I was shy, homesick, and unhealthy. One thing frightened me more than others, — it was the food of the American people. They eat animal food, for which I was not prepared, although I had no prejudice against it. My taste is peculiar and sensitive. To eat "rare" beef (which in fact is raw) is out of the question. I could not bear the flavor of duck's eggs, which some Hindoos use. Indeed, the charge which the Hindoos bring against the native Christians, to the effect that they become Christians for the purpose of eating beef and drinking wine, would not be justly applicable in my case. For owing to my peculiar taste and fastidiousness about food and drink, I can say, that during my two years' stay in Amèrica, I have not eaten as much animal food as the Calcutta deists use in a fortnight. I have always been unable to eat custard, which I am fond of, and plum-pudding, if they are mixed with wine, — not for any superstitious hatred against it, but I could not bear its smell. which, however concealed under other ingredients, is sure to encounter the acuteness of my senses. Hence, the good lady whom I boarded with the most of the time in this country, would not use wine in her cooking, even at the risk of spoiling things for an American mouth.

Our friend, the young native convert, said he would come to America, as he was outcasted and had no parents living, and no new sacrifice to make. He wrote a beautiful letter to the Secretary of the American Unitarian Association. He was older than I, and had a considerable knowledge of English literature and life, having been a great deal with the missionaries. In his character there is a mixture of childlike simplicity with matured experience; he is a good-hearted young man. I rejoiced at his earnestness, and hoped some one would join him in the undertaking. He was speaking of his intended visit to the United States to a deistical gentleman who is a great English scholar, the head teacher of a government school, and well informed about European, but less so, as it appeared, about American communities. My friend heard him say that the Americans are a rough people, that most of them are wild, and walk about with bowie-knives, pistols, and other deadly weapons, — that their government tramples upon the rights and lives of millions whom it holds in absolute bondage; and, what is more wicked, that if a man should dare to speak a word against this unjust, inhuman, and wicked institution, he would be insulted by the community, tried and imprisoned, or hung by the law.*

* He did not exaggerate all the particulars of this matter. During my two years' stay in the United States, I have seen, and read, and heard enough of these things. For trifles men quarrel, fight, and stab each

At this time I saw a book called Uncle Tom's Cabin, in the parlor of a rich native merchant in Calcutta. Not knowing the nature and contents of the book, I opened it and read the letter which a negro woman wrote to her mistress before her flight with her child towards Canada, — the Egypt of the slaves. I read of the pursuit of the master, — her crossing the river Ohio, the hospitality of the Quaker, etc. I, of course, took the story as fictitious, — something like the Arabian Nights' Entertainments, for I *could* not believe that a man could buy or sell a human being, whatever might be his color, intelligence, or position. My friends told me that this book gives a true sketch of American Slavery. I would not at first believe it, and, calling up all my good feelings towards the American people, came to the following decision. Slavery might be existing in America, — it is a large country, and perhaps among the aborigines, who are wild savages, this system is prevalent. I hoped, also, to hear that the people of the United States are diligently engaged in driving away the men-sellers. Sad logic! I saw the picture of the *master*, — a white man, with coat, hat, and watch-guard. Even then I could not persuade myself to believe that this man was a citizen of the United States. I thought it was not necessary to believe that all the white people are good, — these man, woman, and baby-sellers are heartless ruffians, whom the laws of the Christian United States cannot always reach. No! I was mistaken still! They are the Americans, — the descendants of those who had come over from England. Finally, I concluded that these slaveholders have no *women* among them, as the ten-

---

other, and these are gentlemen too. On Sunday they hear their pastors exhort, in the words of Christ, to "turn the other cheek also," when any man smote on the one cheek, and on Monday they fight duels for words. Orations and Eulogies are delivered to their memory!

der, kind-hearted women would have put the abominable trade to destruction. To my utter surprise, I was told by my friends that the slaveholders have their families, churches, pastors, etc.! God only knows with what a sad shock my heart sank down. I could not but think that in no portion of the globe had the blessed religion of Christ been made into a machine to work for the selfish man, to satisfy his cupidity, as it had been in the United States of America. These men support, by Christianity, that very system of bondage which Christianity came to destroy. The parable of the master releasing his servant from his debt, and of that servant tormenting his fellow-servant for a small sum he had owed him, came into my mind, and I realized the truth uttered by those wise lips of Jesus twenty centuries ago. Mr. Dall told me that there are free States in the Union. This puzzled me again. Union of *free* and *slave* States! It must be a queer Union! No! it cannot be so. St. Paul could not very well understand the communion of things of contrary nature: "And what communion hath light with darkness?" etc. (2 Cor. vi. 14–16). The union of fire and water, light and darkness, freedom and slavery is impossible. So I concluded that there are good antislavery men and women in America, as it cannot be that human nature there is totally depraved; but these States must be pro-slavery, since

> "He who friendship with knave hath made,
> Is judged a partner in the trade."

Reading in a small book something like —

> "The British flag floats over land and sea,
> And beneath it the slave is *free*,"

my joy knew no bounds. Hardly could I read the lines; the tears dimmed my eyes, and I cried, "Father of the poor, bless the flag of England! Wave, wave thou mighty flag with the cross on thy bosom, and draw the low, despised children of God to come under thy protection. Thy charms melt the iron that binds the feet of slaves! Wave majestically and on high, that the bond may see thee through the wide country stretching from Maine to Florida, and from Massachusetts to California!"

After a few months had passed, instructions from the American Unitarian Association reached Mr. Dall, authorizing him to send a couple of young men to America, that they might prepare themselves for the ministry under its care. Mr. Dall asked the young man who had written to the Association to get ready, and hearing that he could not sail alone, found another to join him. By and by the first of these began to make excuses, saying, he would be ready within a year or two, etc., while the second stood alone, ready to come provided he could find a companion. Mr. Dall came to me and laid the affair before me. He did not urge me, but he reminded me of my promise and inclination to come to America. I regarded this as an especial call from God, and thus I prayed: "Father, wilt thou indeed have thy child, who *first* proposed going to America, carry out the undertaking? I see the cost of the project: it will deprive me of my mother, sisters, brother, home, and kindred during my lifetime; yet, if Thou wilt have me make these sacrifices for the benefit of thy other children, thy will be done. Enable me, then, to let the dead bury their dead, and to follow the call of Duty!"

I gave my word to God, through Mr. Dall, and began at once to get ready, because the call was so sudden that there were only six or seven days for making the necessary preparations.

I had then been suffering from the effects of a violent

sickness, which had confined me to my bed for twenty-one days, a little while before. My body was so weak that I could hardly stand long without holding to something. But this did not frighten me. Within the weak, unhealthy frame, my moral courage began to move as usual, with vigorous throbbings, and I determined to sail on the day fixed by my friends. It required great caution to arrange my things, as it would have been impossible for me to leave home had any of my nearest relatives known my purpose. I wrote some letters for my mother, uncle, brother, and other friends, and hid them under the papers. The contents of these letters differed according to the person I wrote to; but to no one did I tell where, why, and how long I should be gone. I begged in my letters to six different persons that they would take care of my dear mother, — asking one to visit her occasionally, the second to attend to her shopping (as the Hindoo high-caste females do not go to stores or market), a third to read my letters to her, etc.

Three days, I believe, before I left India, my companion and I were walking on the "*Strand*," looking at the ships and talking the matter over. He said the Americans are not trustworthy people, — that perhaps the captain would take us to some island and sell us to the savages, etc.

Once more we talked upon the American Slave-Trade. I hear in this country the pro-slavery people call the Abolitionists fanatics, affirming that they misrepresent the system, that they exaggerate the cruelties practised on the slaves by their masters. But the world beyond the United States does not blame the slaveholders merely for the true or supposed cruelties practised by them. I hate the system itself; the very name is a terror to me. As a pea has two pods which enclose the seeds arranged in order in its womb, so slavery has two pods, buying and selling human beings, and these enclose in them vices of all descriptions. They say the slaveholders feed and clothe their slaves comfortably. This does not justify the system. They do not deserve our thanks for their kindness to the slaves. Slavery will be profitable in proportion to the good treatment the *masters* extend towards the slaves; so that kindness to the slaves is generally based upon the self-interest of their masters, for which no thanks are due to them. "If ye love your brethren only what thank have ye? do not even the publicans so?" Who would thank a farmer that feeds and fattens his turkeys to make money out of them at the thanksgiving market?

My young friend, with an astonishing forethought, sketched out the dismal days which would inevitably be our portion if we visited Christian countries. He informed me of a fact which the Trinitarians had told him, — that the Unitarians in America are very few in number — a set of fanatic, daring men, who have no truth, no church, no fixed organization, etc. This did not frighten me, for I believed that it is not always the case that truth dwells with the majority. When God destroyed the world by a deluge, the faith of Noah and his small household was entirely different from that of the overwhelming majority, but this made no difference. God approved the truth of this little band, and rejected others. In regard to the outcast life and its attendant sorrows, insults, and helplessness, I looked on them with indifference, believing that there is a Being who knows what I need, and will provide for me accordingly. In days of sorrows I will lean towards Him, and be comforted. My good Father is the richest, highest, wisest, and most merciful Being, so if I trust in him, I shall have no occasion to regret it. I would not let my heart be troubled with these things, — with "what shall I eat? what shall I drink? and where withal shall I be clothed?" and with whom shall I live? "The laborer is worthy of his hire." My own dear friends would not keep any social intercourse with me I know; but God will bring others to me, he will raise kind hearts to bless and sympathize with me. "When one door is closed against, hundreds are open to you," is the Hindoo saying, so I would follow the call of duty, in hope, courage, and patience; believing that all things work for the good of him who loves God.

My friend fell back, and I stood alone. Mr. Dall seemed to give up all hope of sending young men to America, and asked me if I would act like others. "I have put my hands to the plough and I shall not take them back," was my reply.

A rich native merchant of Calcutta had told Mr. Dall that he would give the passage-money of two young men if they came to America; but as my young friend fell back, he paid the passage money and other expenses of one.

The day before my departure I had to go to Calcutta to do some shopping with Mr. Dall. My dear mother inquired of me the reason of my going to Calcutta so early in the morning, as I had to go to the school by nine A. M. I simply said I should probably return in time! but I did not get home till nine in the evening. Mr. Dall rather injudiciously detained me in Calcutta, carrying me here and there to see that everything I needed had been bought. I begged him to dismiss me,—told him to attend to, and arrange all that was necessary, and it would be agreeable to me. But he would not. This detention had caused such an alarm in my house that were it not a true purpose in me to go, I could not have left home the next morning. I fully realized what the phrase, "wise like a serpent," means. As I was passing by the house of a gentleman, my steps drew the attention of a boy, who cried, "Who are you?" "It is I, Prosono," I answered. "Where have you been, uncle? Your mother has been crying the whole afternoon for you." With slow steps and anxious heart, I entered into my mother's house. "Is it Joguth?" "Yes, mother, it is I." I walked into the dining-room to eat my supper, with a heart full of fear and anxiety. She did not speak a word, but sat by me and bathed the floor with her tears. I looked towards heaven, and my spirit whispered, "Father, this is the beginning of the tears that must flow from those loving eyes of my mother! Kind, loving, affectionate as she is, I must leave her and follow the call of Him who said, "Who is my mother?" I desire to be "about my Father's business," so strengthen me to bear this separation. In Thee I recognize a heart more tender than that of earthly mother. Most High, I would not look *around* me in this juncture, but *above*, for all the help I need." After I had finished my supper, she spoke, "Child, I heard that you had gone to America." This information was given to her by a friend whom I had told that I should go to America very soon.

I leave the reader to imagine what kind of a night I had. Early in the morning my dear mother, as usual, went to bathe in the Ganges. A young lady had given me her ornament to carry to a goldsmith to have it mended, as I was a friend to the low castes in general. I felt that I ought to bring the ornament from the goldsmith and return it to her, because if I did not, the lady would not know whom to ask for it, and neither would the artist know to whom to return it, as it was given to him in private. I went to that man, but he was not at home. In vain I searched for him in several places where he was supposed to be, and I could not wait any longer, because my mother would expect me to breakfast. I returned home by half past eight, I believe, took my bath as usual, and entered into the dining-room for breakfast. The day before was the fast day of the Brahmun widows. So when my dear mother sat down to help me she looked very tired, after twenty-four hours' entire abstinence from food and drink. I put the things into my mouth but had no strength to chew them. A deep anxiety, love for my mother, the thought of separation, seemed to fill my heart, and I cast side glances at her face, for I knew that if I lived a hundred years as a Christian, after my return from America, I should not be allowed to sit at meal on this floor and near my dear mother. She noticed the uneasy feelings, and asked, "Joguth, what is that cloud on your face? You look very pale. Are you unwell, child? Tell me what ails you, — I am your mother. Can't you confide in me?" etc. I knew not what to say at first, and answered, "Mother, a young man has a great many things to think about." After breakfast I entered into my bedroom and she followed me there. Not knowing what to take and what to leave, I walked from one end of the room to the other, putting my hand upon my clothes, books, pictures, etc. I sat on my bed, and whispered, "No more will my tired, sleepy, or sick body lie on thy bosom; no more from thee my voice will rise, in midnight gloom, to the throne of grace; no more shall I bathe thee with tears, which are counted and known by Him only who knows no sleep." My mother said it was almost time for me to go to school. So I got up and thought I would not loiter about the room as it would create suspicion in my mother, and perhaps all my cherished plans and precaution would be crushed and frustrated. I must go without scrip — without a second suit of clothes — just as I am. The celestial voice bids me to "let the dead bury their dead;" and so I must not look at these things, my books, clothing, etc., useful as they are. God will provide me with all I need; I would "come and see," with a filial confidence, how good my Father is. Just as I was, with one shirt and one mantle on my body, I went out of the room. My mother came after me, and said, "Child, how long it will take you to learn to wear your own clothes properly," and began to button my shirt or outer garment. I saddened at the thought that on my return from a Christian country, those fingers that fix my shirt now would not touch *me*. The last words I heard from her mouth were these, "Joguth, do not eat confectionaries on the way: you are sick, and can't digest those rich things, child. Come right home after the school, and you will find your supper ready." "Mother," thought I, "the supper which you so kindly wish to prepare for me will be, I am afraid, a two-edged sword for you. I do not know where I shall take my supper to-night," etc.

Thus equipped with moral courage, taking no money, nor clothing, but a trusting heart, I left home and its inmates never to enter therein again, as my own. I commended my kind mother and other dear friends to the care of Him, the good Father of all.

In order to make another effort in relation to that young lady's ornament, I called at the goldsmith's house, but with no better success. A dear young Brahmun friend, who is a hearer of Mr. Dall, and to whom I had confided my secrets, informed me that if I would go with him to a public woman's house, I might possibly find the artist there. As there was no time to lose, and the ornament must be obtained and returned to the owner, I agreed to his suggestion. There, on the Ganges, stood the cottage of sin, and as we knocked at its outer door, a female voice inquired, "Who are you?" "Please let us go in," said my friend. "No," she said, "first tell me what you want, and then I'll see whether I can let you in or not." "I want to see Ombika for a minute, and that is all." "Ombika is not here," she said, and we heard her voice no more. "What is to be done?" I said. "You come with me," my gallant friend replied; "there is a large opening on the wall which would be a capital approach for us to get into the house." I hesitated a little, but he said I must do it, under the necessity, — that these cunning girls must be intruded upon that way. Slowly we walked to the opening, which was large enough to admit us both into the house. We found the artist there, and I asked him to return the ornament to me. He began to make excuses, said it was not quite ready, but would take a couple of days to finish it. "Friend," said I, "I cannot wait a couple of hours for it. I am going to a distant place, so please return it to me just as it is." He talked and argued about the matter, and wanted to know how long I would be gone. Of course, I could not tell him directly about my plans. He returned the ornament partly done. It would not have been safe *at all* for me to have returned it to the owner for two reasons: first, that she lives so near my mother that if I went to her my mother would the first person to see me, and her fears and surmises would be doubly confirmed by my untimely return from the school; secondly, the young lady would feel surprised to find her jewelry half finished, and suspect my proceedings, and inform my mother accordingly. "Be wise as serpents and harmless as doves," is a saying full of wisdom. I called a boy, whom I knew to be very good and reliable, and said, "Will you take this package, to P——, to-morrow, and tell him that I desire him to give it to T——?" I charged him to see P—— the next day, because if the young lady received her ornament the same day the matter would be worse, — my mother would know it, and my friends would at once start in pursuit of me.

The good boy performed his mission satisfactorily I heard. I begged my friend, who helped me to find the goldsmith, to go to my mother two days after I had left, and tell her about the letters I had written and hidden in my desk. While passing by an apothecary's I remembered that I owed him a little money, and paid him with the small silver pieces I had in my pocket.

Much as I wished to reach Calcutta before the high tide, I could not. I asked the boatmen to land me at Bag-bazzar, at the lower part of the city, whence I proceeded to Mr. Dall in a covered Palkee, or Palanquin, as foreigners call it.

Desiring to get a musical instrument (a flute), that I might practise with it on board the ship, and thereby cheer up the lonely hours, I tried hard, but could not succeed. Mr. Dall said he would bring me one, but, whether for want of money or of time, I do not know, he failed to do it. As I must embark right off before my friends could arrest me, Mr. Dall took me to his room and asked me to wear pants, cap, etc. O, I *hated* to do it, fearing the people, even the low-caste boatmen would laugh at me. I told him that there was no necessity for my wearing this strange costume here in Calcutta, that if I had got to do it, I would do it at sea. He would not hear my reasons. I told him again that the English dress would not help me to become a good Christian, — it would only make me look like the strangest and ugliest creature in the world. Fortunately my logic prevailed, and we got in a carriage with our respective dresses.

The ship Sabine, that brought me to this country, belongs to Mr. Tredick, of Portsmouth, N. H. Not knowing where she was lying at anchor, we came down the river as far as Bishops' College and had to go back again. She was near Baboo ghaut. Leaving me on board the ship, Mr. Dall returned to the city with a view to bring the necessary things for the voyage. After dark, our party of four sat at the table, and another, the cabin boy, waited upon us. They all drank wine and ate smoked fish. The smell of these two things was so disagreeable that I thought that they were fit only for savages. One of the party, a young man with a large round face (the second mate), began to sing comic songs and make music with his feet, striking them on the cabin floor. The words of one of his songs were like these —

> "I love her, but she does n't love me!
> She loves another. O dear, who can that be?"

By and by the captain, Mr. Hendee, came on board with a few friends, and they all entered into an adjoining cabin. I retired to sleep, but these gentlemen made such a noise the most part of the night that I doubt whether the people within half a mile had any rest at at all. The corks coming out of the wine-bottles with loud reports, the gentlemen knocking on the floor, their songs and imperfect utterance of "Fa-re-well," all these filled my heart with new and various thoughts. I feared if these men were to be on board all the way, I had better learn Christianity in Calcutta, and not take the voyage to America. The first part of their singing was very good I enjoyed one song especially, —

> "I am bound for the land of Canaan," etc.;

but as they got under the influence of new or old wine, their songs changed into —

> "For to-night we will merry, merry be."

The knocking on the floor grew so violent that I feared they would either hurt their feet or break the boards; and a

Sanscrith saying came into my mind: "The animal with long, pointed horns and sharp teeth, and a man with wine in his stomach are to be avoided alike." By midnight I heard some one vomiting, and remembered the saying that the pleasures arising from dissipation and sensuality very soon bring sickness and misery.

Early on the next morning, Wednesday, January 27, 1858, Mr. Dall came on board with all the necessaries for a four months' voyage, and went down as far as the mouth of the Ganges, returning to Calcutta on Friday by the steam propeller that brought our ship down. Among various kind, useful, and fatherly counsels, he warned me not to learn the profane language that is freely used on board the ship, and wanted to know if I had any farewell words to say to him. "Take care of my dear mother," was my charge to him, which he has carried out in Christian ways. He also made a little blank-book for me which he called my "Journal," with the following advice and instructions:—

JOURNAL.

"I left Calcutta on Wednesday, January 27th, 1858, for Boston, United States of America.

Resolves.

"(1.) I will read the Bible as often as I can, and stay my lonely heart on God by faith, prayer, and trust in Jesus Christ.

"(2.) I will daily pray the Lord's Prayer, and rest all my anxieties on 'Give us THIS DAY our daily bread,' and on 'THY WILL, not mine, BE DONE.'

"(3.) I will try to read the Bible *through*, from Genesis to Revelation, on this voyage, and will make a record, if possible, of the best thoughts as they suggest themselves to me.

"(4.) In the Bible I shall look for my comfort; in the history and devout trust of the patriarchs, prophets, and apostles, from Abraham (Genesis, 12th chapter), — 'The Lord said to Abraham, Get thee out of thy country, from thy kindred and from thy father's house, and thou shalt be a blessing,' — through the Psalms of David, not forgetting the 25th and 26th. 'The Lord is my Shepherd, I shall not want,' and 'They that sow in tears shall reap in joy. He that goeth forth and weepeth, bearing precious seed (i. e. of faith, hope, and holy purposes), shall doubtless come again with rejoicing, bringing his sheaves (fruits of his toil) with him.' God grant it may be so with you, Philip, my son, my first-born in India. God help you! Do you struggle, with God's help, to be an honor and praise to your family, your city, your country, and your friends, both in India and America, more and more as long as you live, and when called to depart out of this world, may it be to dwell with pure-minded spirits, — with the holy angels, and with the just made perfect in heaven. Read the *Old* Testament, but make the *New* your refuge and your rest. Trust in Jesus's call, 'Come unto me all ye that labor and are heavy laden and I will give you rest;' 'Take my yoke upon you and learn of me, for I am meek and lowly in heart, and you shall find rest unto your souls.' Matt. x. 29. And again, I will have perfect faith in Jesus's saying (as in Matt. x. 29), 'Verily I say unto you, There is no man that hath left house or brethren, or sisters, or father, or mother, or lands for my sake and the Gospel's, but he shall receive a hundred fold now in this present time, houses, and brethren, and sisters, and mothers, and lands, with persecution, and in the world to come eternal life. But many that are first shall be last and the last first.'

"Often say, —

"'Jesus, I my cross have taken,
All to leave and follow thee;
Naked, poor, despised, forsaken,
Thou from hence, my all shalt be.

"'Perish every fond ambition —
All I've gained, hoped, or known,
Yet how rich is my condition,
God and heaven are still my own!'

"*A True Christian.*

"Let me strive to be a student and educator; a worthy representative of my country; an ambassador from Asia to America; a mediator between the East and the West; the bearer of pure and precious hopes between two opposite sides of the world; a man of faith and love; a student of human life; a seeker of knowledge in distant lands; a follower in the steps of prophets and apostles, of Abraham and St. Paul; a practical believer in human brotherhood; a pilgrim on the face of the world, seeking pearls of knowledge; a servant, minister, and angel of God; a man whose name is written in heaven; a man appointed by God to bring together the ends of the earth; a leader and a pioneer to begin the great work of union between the sincere and devout spirits of America and Bengal.

"*Things to be done if possible while at Sea.*

"(1.) Get the list of the Books of the Bible by heart so as to facilitate reference to them.

"(2.) Make all the progress I can in my Greek Grammar, that I may thus come into nearer contact with Jesus's words of everlasting life.

"(3.) Translate into Bengalee (prose or verse) those great thoughts of the Bible which move me most deeply. Above all, put them into Bengalee hymns, and so prepare in due time an original Bengal Hymn-Book.

"*Direction of Letters.*

"To the care of the Rev. C. H. A. Dall, Calcutta, India, Overland Mail, via Southampton.

"When you reach Boston, you will find letters from Calcutta waiting you at the office of Dr. Miles, which is No. 21 Bromfield Street, Boston.

"Ask any Boston friend to forward your letters, enclosed in his, and he will do it. Mrs. Dall will do it once a month, if you wish.

"*I will remember daily,*

"(1.) To *speak out* clearly every word I wish to say, and look straight in the face of the person I speak to.

"(2.) To say promptly, 'Yes, sir,' 'No, sir,' to every question.

"(3.) To walk my full number (200, 300, 400,) of rounds on deck; exercise essential.

"(4.) When any one speaks to me my first duty is to *look at him* with respectful attention.

"(5.) To practise writing my name after a good copy."

In regard to carrying out the above rules successfully, the reader will understand it perfectly, when I say that as to the *first*, the ship rode on the blue waves of the Bay of Bengal, I felt sea-sick, and got rid of it only on the day when I arrived in Boston. Nearly *four months*, this great monarch, the most disagreeable of all diseases, had an undisputed sway over me. Occasionally, in very mild weather, I could walk a little and move about on the deck. My constitution is very peculiar, — I shall never get used to the sea. It seems to me that if I were forced to spend my life on the sea, it would be under constant sea-sickness. A trifling motion makes me sea-sick. I have frequently been made sick in riding in stages. On my way from Fitchburg to Templeton, by stage, I felt so miserable, that a good lady, Mrs. J——, kindly invited me to come to and spend the night at her house.

It is customary in this country to offer the "rocking-chair" to a guest. I always refuse it with thanks, for fear of its making me sea-sick. On board the ship I could sit at the table at regular hours most of the time. Knowing that nothing but *land* would cure this ugly feeling, I hoped that some provision, or water would be used up, and thus compel the captain to touch at some place for fresh supplies. But he had enough of everything.

While we were in the river our table was furnished with fresh vegetables and fish, but as we launched forth into the ocean, we had almost everything salted. Never accustomed to eat meat I found it difficult to get along, as most of the edibles on board consisted of salt meat of various kinds. Two days in the week we used to have pea-soup and rice and curry. To be true and just to the Sabine, I should say she had a large supply of provisions of various kinds, which an American would regard as "real *treats*." But I could not relish most of them, being a stranger to their name and nature. Mr. Dall had a large bunch of bananas, some tamarinds, etc., for me, which became very serviceable to me for a fortnight. As the Hindoos are taught to share eatable things with their friends, I gave some fine bananas to the mates, the boy, etc. After a week I offered them some again; but one partook of them, and the other refused them with thanks.

Now once, at midnight, a large, dirty hand was thrust into my state-room and pulled some bananas from the branch; I did not know who that hand belonged to. The same hand helped itself with my fruits again the next day, and I could not help smiling. When I had offered them to the brethren, they felt delicate and declined to accept them, and at midnight came to help themselves. I took the bunch out and distributed its contents among the sailors.

The captain, Hendee, was *very* kind to me. As I was the *only* passenger, and had none to speak to (as the sailors are not allowed to speak to any while on duty), I found Captain Hendee very agreeable. Mr. Dall could not have put me into the care of a better man than Mr. Hendee. He was a friend, teacher, guard, and pastor to me. Every day he would take notice of what I had done, how much I had read, what exercise I had taken, etc. Occasionally he would explain some difficult passages in the New Testament and other books. When less sea-sick, in mild weather, I used to read from the following books: Waverley Novels, the Life of Napoleon, Pope's Poetical Works, The Tower of London, Paul and Virginia (in Bengalee), Dr. Kane's Arctic Explorations, the Bible, and Channing, etc. Besides, Captain H. had American papers, such as Gleason's Pictorial, the Olive Branch, and the New York Ledger. This last paper did not give a good idea of American people. Its stories I found to be fictitious love affairs, sentimental. I felt surprised to think that such stories were put into the hands of the boys and girls, — these will certainly corrupt them, and create romantic, short-lived affections in their hearts. The Hindoo parents do not read nor tell the stories of love affairs to their children, because the influence of such things is very bad upon the young. They fill their hearts with strange passions, which do not belong to them. Hence, in this country I hear so much of elopement, coquetry, strange unions between a boy of eighteen or twenty, and a woman of fifty!

Mr. Hendee undertook to teach me American etiquette, the discipline at the table, in the parlor, etc., but he is such a jolly man that whatever he taught I took for fun. He would ask me every morning, and a great many times during the day, "Philip, how do you feel?" My answers varied according to the true state of my feelings. While sick, I said so, and while cheerful, I said *so*. But this would not satisfy him. So he taught me to answer him as follows: "Philip!" "Sir." "How do you feel?" "All serene." Then he would respond, "*Salubrious.*" He told me, in fun, no doubt, that in Divinity Schools they make such long prayers, that the students find their limbs stiff, having had to kneel down so long. I hoped my friends would not put me in a school like those, that would cause me to go home lame after prayers.

We had a remarkably pleasant voyage. Very few storms were experienced on our way. One day, after a severe squall, Captain Hendee sat on the gangway, tired yet cheerful, and, as usual, cried, "Philip, how do you feel?" He asked me what I thought of the late squall, and hearing me speak indifferently of it, said, "Philip, you are just like a baby that knows not what is going on before him," etc. And then he began to sing, "From all that dwell below the skies," etc. He would not hear any one swear in the cabin, and often would say, "Mr. C., (the second mate,) don't, don't."

Every soul on board was kind to me, and I trust I was not less to them. "Antoon," a Spanish sailor, hearing that I did not eat salt meat, gave me a sharp exhortation. "You are no good Christian! Me, the captain, Mr. B., etc., are good Christians. We eat beef, ham, pork, plenty,—we fat," putting his hand on his stomach.

After a voyage of four months, we reached Boston on the midnight of 24th of May, 1858. Early in the morning, I got up from my bed and waited for some friend, who, as Mr.

Dall had told me, would come to take me into the town; but none came, not knowing, as yet, of my arrival. One by one the sailors left the ship, and I was on board with "Antoon." The whole day passed, yet no Unitarian friend made his appearance to welcome me to the distant land. Not knowing what to eat, hungry and low, I sat on the gangway to gaze upon the harbor. I was delighted to see "Dorchester Heights," which I took for a mountain, as I had not seen any high ground before. Looking at the buildings around the harbor, I believed they were churches, on account of the chimneys which our Calcutta houses do not have. In order to spend the time and forget hunger, I began to draw a sketch of the Navy Yard, East Boston Ferries, etc. As the demands of nature must be met, I took a piece of hard, square cracker and a little brown sugar, and made a supper of them. In the evening I left the ship and ventured to go on shore in East Boston, although "Antoon" feared I should get lost. Going a little way I came to a place where a young couple were sitting near the water. The girl went down to see whether the water tasted salt or fresh. I knew then that, "even in heaven there are moles." Anybody who has even read of or seen the sea and its ways, knows, I am sure, that the water therein is salt.

Next morning Mr. Hendee came on board and inquired if I were crying. I told him that my heart was crying indeed. He sent his boy to escort me to the office of the American Unitarian Association. As I passed through the streets I was struck with the neatness of all around me, except the dirty tobacco-chewers and cigar-smokers. The sidewalks were novel to me. Although there are thousands of foreign or Western women in Calcutta, I never was so near to them as to have any idea of their dress. The dress of the females struck me, and I guessed there must be some framework within, as it could not be that a woman would have such large limbs. I feared to walk too close to a woman, lest by coming in contact I should break her framework. But they walked so fast by me, that I felt thankful that their frameworks did not tear my coat.

By eleven o'clock the boy brought me to the office where a young man, Mr. Fox, spoke to me kindly, and said if I waited a couple of hours I might meet Dr. Miles, the Secretary of the Unitarian Association. There came in an elderly-looking gentleman, who, being informed of my mission, conducted me to the church in Bedford Street, in which the meeting of the Association was in session. I stood in a small room leading into the church, and the gentleman took the letter of "greeting and introduction" from me, and went in and put it in the hand of the Rev. Dr. Lothrop, the President. I heard my friends say that only a half an hour before my appearance, the Secretary had told the congregation that he was expecting me every day. I was led to the platform, the President received me by his right hand in the name of the American Unitarian Association, and gave me a chance to speak a few words, which I did. My appearance was so sudden, that I did not know what to say until I opened my mouth; but he who assured his disciples that they would receive words from above, favored me with the promised gift. The meeting looked so solemn to me, that the impression it made in my mind shall never be forgotten. The Secretary of the American Unitarian Association took me to his house, where I stayed nearly a week. I had dreamed while on the sea that the secretary was a man of light complexion, without a beard,. moustache, or whiskers, that he had a daughter seventeen years old, and I would stay at his house. These proved to be really true in every respect. In the evening of the same day I attended the

Unitarian Festival in the Music Hall, where again I had to speak a few words to the brethren.

I had read about Christian fathers, mothers, and families, while in India, but now at Dr. Miles's I realized all. The gathering of each member of the family at the same table, the exchange of kind greetings between the sexes, their songs and innocent frolics, made me think that these, when perfected and guarded with unfeigned simplicity, and done absolutely for the glory of God and the good of man, are what might be angelic.

After staying a week at Dr. Miles's, I went to board with Mrs. M——, only a few doors below his house. This excellent family did not treat me as a boarder, but adopted me as one of its members. Good Mrs. M—— says she lost her son of my age, who died at sea; so she regards me as her son. Not merely in words did they say so. In their untiring attention to my wants, in their perpetual anxiety about my welfare, they have shown a mother's and sister's hearts. They have done unto me what I could not expect from them. They resorted to every available means to make me comfortable. I owe my health and freedom from sickness mainly to their care. I did not know well the flexibility of the weather here, so could not dress accordingly. I did not learn to dress properly, nor even know the names of many pieces of clothing until now. It would take a long time if I entered into details of their kindness. So I will pass on to notice my other homes and friends in America. The Executive Committee of the Association desired me to spend the summer months in studying with a country clergyman. Accordingly, on the 6th of July, Dr. Miles took me to Rev. James Thurston's, in Lunenburg, Mass. Of course I felt very much confused at the frequent removals from place to place, as such a custom is unknown to the Hindoos. This is a charming place in regard to scenery, and, above all, I liked it for its many hills, which I am fond of. The kindness of the family soon cured my home-sickness for Boston, and I entered into my studies with a cheerful heart. There was one source of pleasure here which I did not have in either of my two Boston homes: that is children, of whom our Blessed Teacher said, "Of such is the kingdom of heaven." The inhabitants of this quiet place, both my Unitarian brethren, as well as other denominations, were very kind to me. The Orthodox and the Methodist clergymen, too, manifested much interest in my mission.

The Methodist brother has more than once cordially invited me to speak to his people. The first time I spoke in the Methodist church I had rather a novel experience. It was while I was speaking that a brother close by shouted "*Amen!*" I thought it was a hint for me to stop, as in Unitarian churches, "Amen" is only uttered by the ministers at the close. As it was a wrong place to stop I made a long pause, thinking that if they really wished me to stop the pastor would rise and offer benediction; but nothing of this kind happened. I proceeded, and to my utter confusion, "Amen! Amen!" from different parts of the church. Immediately I stopped and was going to ask pardon, while "go on, brother, go on," etc., revived my sinking spirits. At the close the good brethren explained to me what they meant by "Amen."

On the second of October I removed to Boston, to Mrs. M——'s, in Allen Street, and there stayed until the twentieth of January. Then my course was toward Medfield, Mass., a place not so charming as Lunenburg, but it has more people in it. My host and teacher here was Rev. S. W. Bush, who is said to be, and I am sure is, an excellent scholar and good Christian. As my stay with him has been longer than with others in this country, I had a good chance to notice his fatherly love for me, and his sanguine interest in the cause of Truth. Every morning and evening, while at home, his prayer has unceasingly risen to the Throne of Mercy for my welfare, and for the success of the Gospel in all countries. His wife, as far as I can judge, is a remarkable woman, social, refined, wise, literary, and good. Both the husband and the wife have contributed much towards my mental and spiritual culture. The people in this town of Medfield were kind to me, a stranger, and nothing has happened during my sojourn among them to pain my feelings. Besides Mr. Bush and wife, there were a good old lady and daughter, — the owner of the house we lived in, who were not in the least slow to confer their blessings and helps whenever I needed them. The other clergymen of the place, one a Baptist and the other Orthodox, were not wanting in the spirit of love in their acquaintance with me. Our good brother, Rev. Mr. Sewell, deserves my regards and notice too. He is a Unitarian clergyman, preaching to the Society in Sharon. Besides his ministerial labors he does a great deal to promote the welfare of his fellows, and is connected with several beneficent institutions. He is an experienced farmer, a judicious manager of the schools, and a good, kind gentleman. I have had the pleasure of spending several happy hours with this Christian man.

In order to spend the "second winter," which is trying to those from warm climates, in Boston, as well as to receive instruction from the clergymen there, I removed to Boston, where I stayed till the day appointed for my start for India, Monday, the 11th of June, 1860. I cannot drop my pen here without recognizing the kindness of my other dear friends to whose care my Father has committed me. I hope the reader will not regard me impertinent if I notice some of my friends by their names. I know there are others in Boston and in other places in the Union, whose hearts beat in Christian sympathy for me, who have shown their interest in various *material* ways. As they do not tell me their names, I cannot enjoy the happiness of thanking them personally. My Father who knoweth all and "seeth in secret shall reward" them openly. Being absent from my dear mother, I first recognized a motherly affection in the heart of Thomas Gaffield, Esq., of Boston. I cannot call his love and interest in me by any other name, as they were not common nor temporary. During my stay in this country, whether in Boston or in other places, he has exhibited an unabated interest in me, has attended to all my personal affairs, and I sincerely hope, while I am gone to work for God, his heart will find its way to India. His Christian wife and sisters have been equally kind and attentive. Mrs. G——, of Concord, Mass., will be remembered ever for one among many other things. After my arrival in this country, Dr. Miles removed me from place to place as a raw chess-player does his Knight. My other friends did not have the opportunity of knowing whether I had all the clothing that I needed. The garments I had already were either too loose or too tight. Uncomfortably as I felt, I knew not to whom to go for relief. But there is one who is not unmindful of even the trivial wants of his children. He whispered to his noble daughter in Concord, and she, with other kind young ladies, made me comfortable clothing. Her interest for me did not drop down with her needle and thimble, but is fresh, and will be, I trust, as long as I stand a worthy recipient. The Christian ladies of Rev. Mr. Muzzey's Society in Newburyport, deserve my hearty thanks for their sympathy shown me in different ways. Besides the contributions given for my benefit, these daughters of God worked fancy articles and held a fair, the proceeds of which were given for my personal comfort.

That noble woman, Mrs. L. M. Child, favored me with her acquaintance lately, and I might name many other kind friends. I deem it a privilege and honor to have become known to such persons. Reluctantly I pass by my excellent friends and earnest Christian helpers, such as Rev. Messrs. Hale, Bartol, Winckley, King, Ellis, Clarke, etc. The last friends that my Father brought to me are Mr. and Mrs. Spring, of Eagleswood, N. J. Since I became acquainted with them I believe that this gentleman is really "*Spring*." His heart knows no winter. Such is his pleasant appearance and such are his Christian graces, that in a few moments I felt myself drawn as closely to him as if I had known him always, and as if his heart was my "OLD HOME."

The little children even have been kind to me and brought me their little presents. The first gift which I received in America, a handsome Bible, was from a little thing, Miss Lucy Sands, whom I called in the language of Bishop Heber, "Golden Sands." A little girl in Newburyport sent me twice some copper and silver pieces, making fifty cents in all. She is the daughter of an Orthodox divine. A little child like this, so full of love and kindness in her heart, does not look like a "totally depraved" creature, although her father's theology would call her such.

If my paper has no room for other kind friends, or my pen has forgotten to chronicle their names, yet I know my heart has room for them all and will never forget them. Their names have been recorded in the Book of God, who will reward them abundantly for their kindness toward one who is a stranger, and an outcast for the sake of the

Truth. The benediction of our Master will certainly be pronounced upon them saying: "Come, ye blessed of my Father, inherit the Kingdom prepared for you from the foundation of the world," for "Inasmuch as ye have done it unto one of the least of my brethren, ye have done it unto me."

FAREWELL!

BROTHERS AND SISTERS IN THE FAITH:—

THE time has come for me to bid you farewell. The circumstances under which I came here just two years ago, and the circumstances under which I return to India, are quite different from each other. I came with fear, weakness, and low spirits. I go with courage, strength, and hope. I came here a runaway from the Hindoos, without scrip, or a second suit of clothes, but go with all the necessary help with which you have provided me.* I came to a strange land, with little hope of finding friends, and I go now with the pleasant memories of many friends, whose hearts, prayers, and sympathies will accompany me in my labor in the harvest of the great King.

I have availed myself of every opportunity to improve, to store my mind with useful information. But I have studied or read very few books during my stay among you. The main subject of my study has been Human Nature in its different editions and volumes. The only possible way of knowing God and his righteousness is through human nature. The image beareth the likeness of the original,— the son inherits his father's nature in a degree; so our

* Of course I had second and third suits of clothes with me when I reached Boston, which were bought for me. I mean when I left *home* I did not bring *any* dress except what I had on. Just as I was I had to come out of it.

common Father manifests himself in his child, man. Corrupted, mistaken, sinful as he is, you will find a great deal in him to remind you of his Father. In us there are only extracts from the sacred subject, God; but in our Elder Brother it is complete. Whatever we are permitted to know of God, and as much as is necessary for our life, comfort, and salvation, we may learn in the great volume of humanity to which Christ gave "the finishing stroke."

My friends had very many fears about my coming. First, I should return to India with the vices and dirty habits of this country, such as drinking wine and spirits, smoking cigars, etc. Second, I should not be able to stand the severe winter of this country. Third, being among the clergymen, who are said to be more sectarian than their people, I should go home a narrow-minded Christian. But I am happy to say, as far as my near-sighted eyes can see, that I stand above these fears. I never was in the habit of drinking wine or using tobacco in any form, and in this country I have carefully avoided these dirty things. Eating much or little meat is another ugly habit in the opinion of the Hindoos, and the native converts are often charged with becoming Christians simply for the purpose of eating "cow and hog." Although I have no prejudice against meat, yet I presume that owing to my peculiar taste, I have not eaten as much meat in two years, as a boy or girl of ten in New England would eat in six weeks, especially if "Thanksgiving" day should fall within them.

Having had no idea what an American winter was, I came unprepared; yet I have not suffered in the least in these two years. The very coldest days you had in the winter before the last, I rode in an open sleigh over the hills of Lunenburg, without anything to cover my ears. In the last winter, on the second of January, I rode in a similar conveyance from Medfield to Boston with no protection for my ears. Thus, I have passed unharmed through real winter days. Again, the good husbandman who brought me a tropical plant from his garden into this part of the world, put me in the green-house of your hearts, whose warmth, I perceive, is as genial as that of the glorious luminary that shines over the land of my fathers. Brothers and sisters, your hearts never stood below zero in my case, never reached the freezing-point, but always were warm, affectionate, kind.

In regard to the narrow, sectarian feelings of a bigot's heart, I think I have very little to fear. I do not condemn nor hate *any* body for his creed; yet, as a firm believer in the undivided Unity of our God, I differ very much from some others. But I pray to God that I may daily learn to love all his children. I like the creed-makers but not their creeds, if they contain anything that is absurd and untrue. I trust I have within this slender frame a heart whose commodious hall can accommodate Unitarians, Trinitarians, Mohammedans, and Hindoos; for He who has given it to me has given it on purpose that it might hold all His children.

My visit, on the whole, has been a satisfactory one. Nothing seriously disagreeable has happened to injure my health, heart, or usefulness. No country has a canopy of clear sky over it always, no heart is beyond the reach of sorrows. The dark clouds have hung over my head, and thunders have rolled noisily, yet my earnest eyes have seen a clear firmament beyond, and I can say with fulness of heart,—

> "In trouble and in grief, O God,
> Thy smile hath cheered my way,
> And joy has budded from each thorn
> That round my footsteps lay."

The practical confidence in God's parental care is a source from which I draw consolation, courage, and strength. May we all truly believe that our Father is good, and that his whole counsel aims for the eternal welfare of his children. My second source of joy, courage, and hope is my "confidence in man." I do not wish to loose my trust in him. If I am deceived by ninety and nine, I would still have confidence in the remaining one. Thus with such views of God as a good, loving parent, and with such feelings toward man as a trustworthy brother, I hope to make my way while a sojourner in this beautiful world of God.

In this connection I would ask pardon if I have in any way pained, offended, or done injustice to any. I know not that I have done so. Yet how many things we do unawares. A kind lady wrote me a letter and gave me some scoldings, saying that I had pained a great many for the seeming coldness of my heart, that when people came to shake hands with me and speak to me, I did not take respectful notice of them. This, however, is a new thing in my nature. Those who know me know well the average temperature of my heart. It might be (as she says) that, in public gatherings, when tender greetings have crowded upon me, from many persons at once, perhaps I have failed to speak to all. But this is excusable, I know. How can one person speak to several at a time? Frequently I have met four, five, or six brethren or sisters round me. I have used both my hands to "shake hands" with them. Besides, in my country, only one person expects to be spoken to in the same moment.

Again, I do not — though I have tried to do so — observe the formalities and use the local phrases as much as they do here. There are some fixed set of words which the people use, such as "How are you?" "Fine day, or weather," etc. These do not show real warmth of the heart, but come out of the national disease of loquacity, I believe. My training has been quite different, so I am liable to make a great many mistakes. Once more, I would say, Christian friends, if I have done any wrong to any of you, take it as unintentional and overlook it charitably.

Let it be known to you once more, that I go to India, but not to my *Home*. You have frequently heard me say that on account of my embracing the Christian religion I cannot live with my Hindoo mother and other dear friends,—or rather, they cannot live with me. I am going as a lamb among wolves; and in days of trials, sorrows, and discouragements, I shall look first to my Father in heaven, and then to you as my brothers and sisters. I go to preach and teach the truth to my beloved countrymen, in your name and under your auspices, and I look to *you* for your help, prayers, and blessing.

The cause of Christ suffers severely from the injudicious preaching of the Missionaries who go out to India from western countries. They think that anything outside the Bible is *humbug*, *untrue*, and *nonsensical*. They tell the Hindoos that their Holy Books contain no truth, and that they themselves are going headlong to everlasting damnation. These errors and follies I will carefully avoid. I would not offend a Hindoo by insulting his gods, or puzzle him with a doctrine of a Triune God and its attendant absurdities. I know the best way for me will be to take a Hindoo saying, and present its truth in a practical way. In order to attract respect, I would rather appeal to the Hindoo Scripture, if it serve my purpose, than to Isaiah, Job, or Solomon. St. Paul, while in Greece, appealed to a poet of the country, and thereby secured the attention of the people. One can preach years from texts taken from Hindoo proverbs, such as, "If you wish to be the greatest, be the humblest," "Feel for the world as you do for yourself." Will you say these are *humbugs* because they belong to the Hindoos? No. Christ uttered these very things. What I most earnestly want to do, is to take Truth wherever I find it, and present it to my brethren in the spirit of Christ, and show its applicability to our lives. If we are faithful and labor patiently and prayerfully, aiming at the glory of God and the good of Man, success will be ours. Our part is to sow and water, and our Father will give the increase.

God bless you, dear, kind Christian friends! God bless you for your kindness toward me! Do not let the interest die out when I go out of your sight. I go to fight against sin, idolatry, and superstition, and you who stay at the camp, or in the magazine rather, send me ammunition and instructions, according to my need. This is the way to carry on work. Trust in God, India's future religion will be Liberal Christianity.

Farewell to you all for a while. If Providence spares my life, I may again, after four or five years of Christian labors, seek rest in your homes, and personally tell you about the work of God. And if it be his will that I shall depart from the world soon, what shall hinder our meeting in our Father's mansions? Farewell! "Lo, I will be with you always" in the spirit. Heaven's smile be upon you all, is the prayer of your friend and brother,

J. C. GANGOOLY.

Cambridge: Stereotyped and Printed by Welch, Bigelow, & Co.